The ACT of MARRIAGE after 40

Books by Tim and Beverly LaHaye

Non-Fiction
Tim and Beverly LaHaye
The Act of Marriage
The Act of Marriage After 40

Tim LaHaye
Anger Is a Choice (with Bob Phillips)
Finding the Will of God in a Crazy, Mixed-Up World
How to Win Over Depression
Revelation Unveiled

Beverly LaHaye
Spirit-Controlled Woman
Understanding Your Child's Temperament

Fiction
Tim LaHaye and Jerry B. Jenkins
Left Behind Series

Beverly LaHaye with Terri Blackstock
Seasons Under Heaven
Showers in Season

TIM & BEVERLY LAHAYE

with *Mike Yorkey*

The ACT of MARRIAGE after 40

MAKING LOVE FOR LIFE

ZondervanPublishingHouse
Grand Rapids, Michigan

A Division of HarperCollinsPublishers

The Act of Marriage After 40
Copyright © 2000 by LaHaye Family Group, LLC

Requests for information should be addressed to:

ZondervanPublishingHouse
Grand Rapids, Michigan 49530

Library of Congress Cataloging-in-Publication Data

LaHaye, Tim F.
    The act of marriage after 40 : making love for life / Tim and Beverly LaHaye,
with Mike Yorkey.
      p. cm.
    ISBN: 0-310-23114-0
      1. Middle aged persons—Sexual behavior. 2. Aged—Sexual behavior.
3. Middle aged persons—Health and hygiene. 4. Aged—Health and hygiene.
I. Title: Act of marriage after forty. II. LaHaye, Beverly. III. Yorkey, Mike.
IV. Title.
HQ21 .L194   2000
306.7'084'4-dc 21   00-032508
                                                       CIP

This edition is printed on acid-free paper.

Published in association with the literary agency of Alive Communications, Inc.,
7680 Goddard St., Suite 200, Colorado Springs, CO 80920.

Interior illustrations by Jon Post
Interior design by Melissa Elenbaas

Printed in the United States of America

---

00 01 02 03 04 05/❖ DC/ 10 9 8 7 6 5 4 3 2 1

*To all those who believe married love really can last for a lifetime,
and for all who may need some encouragement to believe*

CONTENTS

ACKNOWLEDGMENTS

We are indebted to many friends and acquaintances who assisted in the completion of this manuscript. Space does not permit us to list them all, but at the outset we would like to acknowledge the role that Sandy Vander Zicht, our editor at Zondervan Publishing House, for her persistence and vision regarding *The Act of Marriage After 40*.

My appreciation is extended to writer and researcher Mike Yorkey for his able assistance. Our thanks go to two people who gave the manuscript a thorough read and made thoughtful suggestions: Rev. Garth McGrath, pastor of Monadnock Covenant Church in Keene, New Hampshire, and Gregg Albers, M.D., a physician in Lynchburg, Virginia. Fred Stoeker of Johnston, Iowa, and Lynette Winkler of Spiez, Switzerland, also reviewed the manuscript. Thank you for your input and comments.

We must also thank the 800 men and women who invested a considerable amount of time in answering our seventy-one-question sex survey. They furnished insights that we never would have realized otherwise. Our thanks go to Nicole Yorkey, Bobbi Lucas, Robin Chamberlain, Mary Lou Bottino, and Pete and Anne Yorkey for helping compile the surveys.

INTRODUCTION

Not long ago, our television repairman dropped by our condominium after hours. Matt (not his real name) brought his wife, Jennifer, to our front door, where he sheepishly admitted that Jen had read one of my books and wanted to meet my wife, Beverly, and me.

We graciously welcomed our impromptu guests and showed them around, including a visit to the library/office in which I work. As we made small talk that evening, it became apparent that this couple had something else on their minds. Since becoming a pastor forty-five years ago, I have developed a sixth sense about furtive glances and forced smiles from couples. I offered them a beverage and waved them toward a comfortable couch in my office. Within minutes, their story poured forth.

"We are both forty years old, and we're having sexual problems," Jennifer blurted. "I have no interest in doing it at all." I noticed her husband's eyes were cast downward.

There. The problem was out in the open. I flipped on my counselor's hat and urged Matt and Jennifer to tell me their story. A half-hour later, I believe I understood the situation. Jennifer had been promiscuous before she became a Christian, but after getting married, she swung in the opposite direction. She didn't want anything to do with sex. The result: this long-married couple rarely made love, and when intercourse occurred, the sexual act was nothing more than a release for him.

I counseled Jennifer to forgive herself for what had happened years earlier. I reminded her that sexual intercourse is the most beautiful and intimate expression of love that can be shared by a husband and wife—and one well worth the effort. As they nodded their heads in agreement, I thought of the hundreds and hundreds of couples I have counseled regarding their sexual relationships. I could not recall one couple telling me that their sex life was very good but their marriage was really lousy. A couple's sexual relationship is an excellent barometer of the state of the union: if a couple's love life can be described as healthy and good, the same attributes apply outside the marriage bed.

The topic of marital love and its physical dimension has interested Beverly and me ever since it became apparent to us in the early 1970s that there was a lack of credible, Christian sources on the subject. Once I loaned a young married couple—who came to me seeking counseling regarding their physical relationship—seven books out of my own library, each with rubber bands marking the specific chapters I wanted them to read. I was dismayed that I couldn't find a comprehensive, all-in-one volume on sexual love in bookstores.

Dr. Robert K. DeVries, then executive director of Zondervan Publishing House, took us to lunch one day in 1973 to express his contention that a book about sexual adjustment in marriage was sorely needed in Christian bookstores. He asked Beverly and me if we were willing to write a book on the Christian view of sex in a marriage.

"No," I replied in a knee-jerk fashion. "Ministers don't write about sex!"

Dr. DeVries would not be deterred. "Would you pray and talk it over between the two of you?" he asked. "We feel there is a real need for a pastor—well known for biblical reliability—and his wife to team up together on this project."

We thanked Dr. DeVries for his time and promised to pray about his offer. Beverly, bless her heart, was understandably reluctant to take on this endeavor. Yes, we had been married for twenty-nine years, raised four children, and had been blessed with four grandchildren. Furthermore, we had written several best-selling books on interpersonal relationships, including *How to Be Happy Though Married*, which is still in print after three decades.

"Do you think we should do the book?" I asked Bev.

"Absolutely not!" she said energetically. "That would be like people looking into the privacy of our bedroom!" Then something interesting happened. Bev counseled ten wives over the next two

months, and all of them expressed their aversion to sexual intercourse. Their pleas for Beverly's help were genuine, as were their
words of appreciation after Bev's wise words helped them achieve
success in their love lives. Although Bev was gracious and gentle
by nature, the Holy Spirit had transformed her life several years
before, as she described in her first book, *The Spirit-Filled Woman*.

We continued to pray about the matter, and during that time,
the Lord gave us a strong sense that He wanted us to participate in
this book project. Thus, Bev and I agreed to write *The Act of
Marriage*, setting forth a clear presentation of the intimate physical relationship between a husband and wife. Convinced that God
meant lovemaking to be enjoyed by both partners, we felt that too
many Christian books skirted the nitty-gritty details of what happened beneath the bed sheets.

We agreed that a book on this important topic had to be fully
biblical, scientifically accurate, and highly practical. For two-and-
a-half years, Beverly and I interviewed pastors, doctors, and friends
and surveyed over 3,000 Christian couples who attended our Family
Life Seminars, a Friday-night and all-day-Saturday seminar that Bev
and I led back in the 1970s. I consulted with my mentor in Christian counseling, Dr. Harry Brandt, a Christian psychologist. Out of
that research and those interviews we developed several teaching
principles on marital sex that were based on God's Word, most
notably in 1 Corinthians (7:2–5):

> But since there is so much immorality, each man should
> have his own wife, and each woman her own husband. The
> husband should fulfill his marital duty to his wife, and like-
> wise the wife to her husband. The wife's body does not
> belong to her alone but also to her husband. In the same
> way, the husband's body does not belong to him alone but
> also to his wife. Do not deprive each other except by mutu-
> al consent and for a time that you may devote yourselves
> to prayer. Then come together again so that Satan will not
> tempt you because of your lack of self-control.

From this passage of Scripture, Bev and I believe there are four central principles regarding lovemaking. They are:

1. Both husband and wife have sexual needs and drives that should be fulfilled in marriage.
2. When a person marries, he forfeits control of his body to his partner; the same goes for her as well.
3. Both partners are forbidden to refuse the meeting of their mate's sexual needs.
4. The act of marriage is approved by God.

The fact that God has brought you and your spouse together to love and to cherish until death do you part is a feeling that cannot be denied in the warm afterglow of lovemaking. Lovemaking provides for the legitimate release of sexual tension, which is the original purpose of the act of marriage. It's natural for two people of the opposite sex to be attracted to each other, and it's a natural inclination for them to desire to release that tension. Sexual intimacy is so important to a marriage that the only thing that should interfere with it is a time of prayer (1 Cor. 7:5).

Mental attitude is everything in sexual expression. Almost everyone brings the same sexual apparatus to their wedding beds; what makes the difference in couples is their attitude. I've always felt that a vital sex life tends to hone down some of the rough edges of our marital relationships. For instance, it would be nice to think that Christian couples are wonderful, Spirit-filled people who always show "love, joy, peace, and long-suffering" in their behavior, but that is not life in the real world. Sometimes we go to bed with a partner who has been selfish during the day and wants sex at night. What do we do then? If you give of yourself unselfishly because you believe God has brought you and your spouse together for His purposes, then the "issue" that seemed so important earlier in the day pales in significance, and in many cases, even spark an apology when the importance of the long-term relationship is more readily realized.

THE BABY BOOMERS MARRY

The release of *The Act of Marriage* in 1976 was providential; Christian couples, we found, were eager to read a biblically based sex education resource. *The Act of Marriage* reached bookstores just as the greatest concentration of Baby Boomers was marrying and forming families—and beginning what we hoped was a lifetime of fulfilling, marital sex. *The Act of Marriage* and its subsequent revisions were well received, as witnessed by more than 2.5 million copies in print. We never dreamed the book would become a Christian bestseller in this country or in South America, Europe, and Asia, or that its 1998 revision would still be selling at a fast clip in Christian bookstores today. We thank God that He has used *The Act of Marriage* to enrich both the love and the love lives of those who read it.

Thousands of people have written us to express their appreciation for the way we dealt with the meaning of and importance of good sex right up front. *The Act of Marriage* helped readers understand that sex was good, God-ordained, and should be enjoyed without feelings of guilt. In a sense, our book disarmed readers by helping them realize that we were real people and understood their basic desires.

We especially enjoyed hearing from couples who had been given a copy during premarital counseling sessions with their pastor or from some mature Christian they respected. What I didn't realize was that ministers by the thousands were using the book in counseling sessions for couples experiencing sexual dysfunction problems. I was also tickled when young pastors told me that *their* pastor gave them the book just before they got married and how they make *The Act of Marriage* required reading for those who came to them for premarital counseling. Nothing pleased me more than to read those letters.

TIME OF TRANSITION

These days, the Baby Boom generation that benefited from *The Act of Marriage* has grown older; seventy-six million Boomers are passing through the American scene like the proverbial tennis ball through a snake. Boomers have reached the next stage of life: middle age, a time of transition. It's a time when parents die and children leave the home. A time when fit bodies are replaced by sore backs and flabby midsections. A time when sexual desire diminishes and sexual intercourse becomes "old hat."

This time around, Zondervan Publishing House has asked us to write a new book addressed to those forty and over, the result of which you are holding in your hands. Actually, Senior Editor Sandy Vander Zicht had been after us for years to write a sequel to *The Act of Marriage*. Her first suggestion was a book called *The Act of Marriage After Fifty*, to which Bev replied once more, "Absolutely not! That would be like letting everyone know about the intimate secrets of our married life!"

History repeated itself, however, as Bev and I prayed for direction. When Sandy suggested bringing the age down to when many troubles begin to surface for married couples, we warmed to the topic. We have become more aware of the increase in the breakdown of marriage and the increase in infidelity in both Christian men and women as they pass the forty-year mark. Many couples whose sex lives have never been satisfactory could endure it until the children were raised. But once the kids left home and there was nothing but spiritual ties to bind them together, they often fell into the sin of adultery. In my forty-five years of counseling, I have discovered that nothing causes more pain in a relationship than infidelity.

We are convinced that adultery never needs to happen! We are also convinced that sexual problems or inadequacies should never be ignored either! We are further convinced that with God's help, and by using biblical principles, all inadequate sexual responses can be resolved and that adultery or divorce is never the answer for Christians because there are no problems that God cannot solve. We can "do all things through Christ who strengthens us," as Paul said. To every reader of this book, we can say, "You do not have a problem that your Heavenly Father is not interested in and willing to solve, if you let Him."

We are further convinced that God intended the act of marriage, which is what we call the sexual act of married lovemaking, to be the most thrilling experience two people of the opposite sex can experience on this earth. Not once, but thousands of times over the course of their lives. And not just in their twenties and thirties, but into the troublous forties, the tempting fifties, the maturing sixties, the mellowing seventies, the slowing eighties, and even beyond. Remember Abraham and Sarah? With God's help, they fathered and mothered the Hebrew race when they were in their nineties!

GOING OVERBOARD

Some pundits may scoff at the need for a book like *The Act of Marriage After 40*, but I don't doubt the need. We are seeing a spate of *Sex After 40* and *Sex After 50* books in the mall bookstores—aimed at the aging Boomer crowd—but these secular books go overboard in their description of various sexual acts that couples can employ. Their crude language is a turnoff, not a turn-on. In addition, these books advocate practices considered improper by biblical standards.

My biggest beef with these secular sex books, however, is their worldview that the only people having fun in bed after the age of forty are unmarried couples. Rarely is the advice directed to a husband and wife. Such books talk about being "bold and assertive" with your "partner," "overcoming the five obstacles to a new sexual relationship," or "four steps to building erotic trust with your lover." You won't find such language on these pages because this book is written squarely for *married* couples between the ages of forty and eighty, even older.

One of the great aspects about being happily married is that you don't have to hassle with the world's advice on "safe sex." In researching this book, I read one expert counsel women who had hysterectomies on the importance of using "nonoxymol 9 latex condoms during genital, anal, and oral sex if you are not in a monogamous relationship or you are unsure of your partner's sexual history."

Doesn't that "nonjudgmental" advice sound romantic? I don't think so. Bev and I are in our early seventies, happily married for more than fifty years, confident that the true beauty of sexual love is best found in a Christian marriage. We can assuredly state that the sexual relationship has enriched us in ways that we never thought possible, which is why those of you in your forties need to know that today's sexual relationship is an investment for the rest of your married lives.

From now until you pass from this scene, two of the things that have given you your greatest joy—children and careers—will no longer be as important as they once were. This means the personal relationship you make with your loved one is much more important. I've known many couples in their late sixties, seventies, and even eighties whose happiness and devotedness to each other can be seen on their faces. They are the ones still walking arm in arm with a gleam in their eyes that announces to the whole world that their love is intimate and lifelong. They are the ones who, with maturity, recognized that sex expresses joy and affirms life.

I met one such couple during a yearlong sabbatical that our wonderful church in San Diego gave Bev and me back in 1978 after twenty years as their pastor. (I don't recommend that long for most ministers; three to six months away from the pulpit is usually enough.) We gave ourselves to holding three days of Family Life Seminars (two days lecturing and one day for counseling) to the missionaries of the world. In ten months, we visited forty-six countries and spoke to thousands of missionary couples.

One night after my lecture on the beauty of sexual love, in a packed auditorium of over eight hundred, a veteran missionary lady came up and introduced herself. As soon as I heard her name I recognized her, for she was a legend in that area of world missions. My first thought was that I would be given a dressing down for being so frank. Instead, she commended me for speaking so boldly to these young missionaries.

"This is just what many of them needed," she said. Then she volunteered with a big smile, "My husband and I have enjoyed a wonderful love life for over sixty years!"

As I looked into her well-wrinkled face, I found myself asking, "Do you mind if I ask you how old you are?"

"Eighty-three," she responded.

"How old is your husband?"

Her smile broadened, for she knew exactly what I was implying. "He is eighty-seven," she replied. I left the conference that evening thinking, *That is the way God wants us all to be at eighty-seven.*

But the time to start building that kind of rewarding love life is in the forties and fifties, which is why *The Act of Marriage After 40* will prepare you for the changes that occur in the sexual relationship in the midlife years. You will find our presentation upbeat, interesting, informative—and deliberately frank; to be any less would be a disservice to you. Since the expression of married love was created by our loving heavenly Father and was intended for our mutual enjoyment, it's our position that the best sex is guilt-free sex between a married couple. One study by UCLA psychologists Stuart Perlman and Paul Abramson confirms that view; it found that married couples were more satisfied with their sex lives than sexually active singles, partly because sexual satisfaction was enhanced by "the absence of sexual anxiety."[1]

Make sense? Of course! Just like the original *Act of Marriage*, we conducted a comprehensive, seventy-one question survey of 800 Christian couples on our mailing list. We asked them all sorts of forthright questions regarding topics relevant to this book: sexual frequency, orgasms, impotency issues, and so on. The results of the "Act of Marriage After 40 Survey" are summarized in the Appendix, but we've included some of the relevant findings throughout this book.

Our research indicates that while the frequency of sex is reduced by advancing age, the meaning of the act of marriage can be an enriching, more satisfying event with the passage of years. That is why we hope *The Act of Marriage After 40* will help you experience all that God meant your love to be for as long as you live.

Chapter One

Love for a Long, Long Lifetime

Many people as they grow older—notice I didn't say old—poke fun at their diminishing ability to perform sexually. For instance, one of my favorite jokes goes like this:

The following are the three stages of a couple's love life—

1. Couples in their twenties have sex *triweekly*.
2. Couples in their thirties *try weekly* to have sex.
3. Couples in their forties, fifties, and sixties *try weakly* to have sexual relations.

Those of you crossing the threshold into the middle-age years may hear that there's "a lot of will but no way." But don't you believe it. Sex begins upstairs in the mind God gave you, so if you think you're too old for sex, you'll act accordingly. This would be a shame because we believe couples can—and should—enjoy a vibrant sex life until they are well into their seventies, even their eighties. Psalm 90:10 reminds us, "The length of our days is seventy years— or eighty, if we have the strength." To "have the strength," we must take care of our bodies by exercising moderately, eating the right foods, and taking nutritional supplements. (I'll have more to say about this later.)

One of our major themes in this book is that you can continue to love your spouse in physical and amorous ways that will be even *better* than during those first few sexually adventurous years of marriage. It is possible to enjoy an active, satisfying sex life well into your seventies and eighties. Affection, warmth, and sensuality do not have to deteriorate with age and can actually increase in the midlife years.

Sex in later life is sex for its own sake since our childbearing years are in our rearview mirrors. We make love for pleasure, release, communication, and intimacy. Since the midlife years are marked with fewer responsibilities on the home front (the kids are grown and gone or about to leave the nest), many find this era a time of exhilaration. We lose a step physically, but we more than gain that back with experience. Playwright George Bernard Shaw had it right when he correctly stated, "Youth is wasted on the young."

Sex can remain interesting, fulfilling, and exciting in the forties, fifties, sixties, and beyond. Older women rarely lose their physical ability to reach an orgasm, and many older men exhibit a capability for erections and ejaculations. We can expect the body to slow down gradually in sexual response, however, and for sexual desire to lessen, especially for women.

The fact that you have chosen to read about this topic suggests that your sexual relationship is important to you and your spouse. Based on that interest, we will attempt to answer several fundamental questions in *The Act of Marriage After 40*:

- What are satisfying love relationships like in the midlife years?
- In what ways does the act of marriage change as spouses grow older together?
- How can the sexual relationship improve in the second half of marriage?

To begin our discussion, let's debunk these common myths about sex in the midlife years.

Myth #1:
Couples should expect to lose their ability to make love after they reach a certain age

We all know that males reach their sexual peak in late adolescence—between the ages of eighteen and twenty. A young male can ejaculate three to six times a day. We also know that after this sexual peak, males show a steady decline in their sexual ability to climax throughout the rest of their lives.[1] A male's ability to make love will not drop off a cliff when he hits forty, fifty, sixty, or seventy; instead, it's a steady descent. Picture a Boeing 757 following a "glide path" into Chicago's O'Hare Airport, and you get the idea.

On the flip side, women reach their sexual peak ten, twenty years *after* men when they are in their late thirties and remain on that plateau through their sixties, after which they may show a slight decline in sexual response capability.[2] Fred Stoeker, coauthor of *Every Man's Battle: Winning the War of Sexual Temptation One Victory at a Time*, once looked forward to the time in his marriage when he and his wife, Brenda, would experience a "sexual nirvana" when his wife's peaking line of desire crossed his descending path. If only physical relationships were that simple, Fred says. "In the end, it wasn't the match of ability or desire that mattered so much, but accepting the fact that there would likely be no match. Men and women are different, and understanding those differences was the key to sensitivity and tenderness for us," he said.

One of those differences is that, biologically speaking, women experience little sexual impairment as they age. Many women feel that sex is more enjoyable after menopause since there is no risk of becoming pregnant. Others feel their sexual assertiveness increase because they feel comfortable in a stable marriage. Since men and women achieve emotional maturity in the midlife years, they can pave the way toward a superior intimate relationship.

Myth #2:
The quality of sex declines for men and women in the midlife years

Your body certainly changes with age. A twenty-year-old man can be erect in five seconds, while it takes a fifty-year-old male half a minute. Maybe a septuagenarian needs several minutes of manual stimulation to become aroused. While an older man may take longer to achieve an erection, he often gains *more* control over ejaculation because he can sustain his erection longer. With more control, he can take his time to bring his wife to orgasm before intercourse.

The biggest difference is the "rebound," or the refractory time, before sex is again possible. At a male's sexual peak (in his late teens or early twenties), he could orgasm as many as three to six times in one night. Older men need twelve to twenty-four hours before they are capable of ejaculation—sometimes several days. We need to keep our eyes focused on *how good* the sexual experience can be, not *how many* sexual experiences one can have.

Myth #3:
Couples in their midlife years are lucky if they make love once or twice a month

In our comprehensive "Act of Marriage After 40 Survey" of 800 people, 59 percent of men and women, aged forty to seventy and up, said they were having sexual relations once a week *or more*. A whopping 10 percent overall said they were making love three, four, or *five* times a week! This compares favorably to a major survey conducted by the National Opinion Research Center at the University of Chicago in the mid-1990s in which the average number of times that men and women (aged forty to seventy and up) made love was thirty-six times a year, or three times a month.

Let's take a closer look at sexual frequency and satisfaction from our "Act of Marriage After 40 Survey" by breaking down the results by gender and age group:

16. Over the last few months, what was the average number of times you had sexual relations?

Females	40–49	50–59	60–69	70 and over
Five or more times per week	4%	0%	0%	1%
Three to four times a week	13	13	7	4
Twice a week	19	18	17	10
Once a week	29	34	29	19
Once every two weeks	25	13	17	19
Once a month	6	12	13	16
Once every few months	4	6	7	10
Once in the last year	0	1	0	1
Our sex life is nonexistent	0	3	10	20

20. To what extent have you been satisfied with intercourse?

	40–49	50–59	60–69	70 and over
Very satisfied	52%	47%	37%	44%
Satisfied	27	29	45	35
Somewhat satisfied	16	18	16	18
Not satisfied	5	6	2	3

16. Over the last few months, what was the average number of times you had sexual relations?

Males	40–49	50–59	60–69	70 and over
Five or more times per week	5%	0%	1%	2%
Three to four times a week	15	12	5	5
Twice a week	16	11	15	10
Once a week	30	43	39	20
Once every two weeks	17	19	18	17
Once a month	11	9	10	15
Once every few months	5	4	4	11
Once in the last year	1	0	0	2
Our sex life is nonexistent	0	2	8	18

20. To what extent have you been satisfied with intercourse?

	40–49	50–59	60–69	70 and over
Very satisfied	62%	54%	62%	45%
Satisfied	27	31	31	35
Somewhat satisfied	8	12	7	18
Not satisfied	3	3	0	2

Of course, sexual frequency will be much less at fifty-five than it was at twenty-five, and our survey audience agrees with that statement. Overall, 72 percent said their sexual frequency is less or a "lot less" than the first half of marriage. While sexual drives and capabilities decrease with age, many people who live longer are staying sexually active even beyond the age of eighty. What is a given is that sexual activity among older adults may be less frequent and less intense, but it still can prove to be a more meaningful experience. Most of our intimate friends are ministers and missionaries who have served the Lord for over fifty years. When I talk to men about the frequency of their experiences, the message I hear repeatedly is that their lovemaking may not be as frequent as their younger days, but the event has become more meaningful to them because it's an expression of the depth of their lifetime relationship.

Myth #4:
Women don't want to make love after menopause

Sexual desire often lessens during menopause, but this is caused by the gradual reduction of estrogen hormones released by the ovaries. Less estrogen results in decreased libido and insufficient lubrication of the vaginal wall. These issues can be solved by estrogen replacement therapy or using lubricants.

Myth #5:
Youthful orgasms are better

Men admit that the force of their ejaculation is not as intense in the midlife years, but they also report feeling a more diffuse orgasm throughout the rest of the body. Women often say that their orgasms are just as intense after the age of forty.[3]

Myth #6:
Older men keel over and die of a heart attack during orgasm

You've seen one too many Hollywood movies, although you may remember the celebrated case of Nelson Rockefeller, the U.S. vice president when President Ford was in office in the mid-1970s. Mr. Rockefeller divorced his wife and married the doctor's wife next door (they lived in side-by-side mansions in New York). Several years later he left his second wife at a basketball game to have sex with his "kept" paramour, and he died in the act.

At any rate, a study of 1,600 patients conducted at Boston's New England Deaconess Hospital found that the risk of heart attack during sex was roughly equivalent to the risk of heart attack from getting out of bed in the morning. Heart attacks during intercourse account for less than 1 percent of all coronary deaths—but 70 percent of those occur during extramarital liaisons.[4]

Which reminds me of an interesting event. We once attended a church in which the forty-year-old choir director, married with a family, flirted with the pretty female choir members. He began an affectionate relationship with a married choir member. One evening, when he knew the husband was out of town, he called the woman and asked to come over to her house. One thing led to another and they began have sex in her bed, but he suffered a heart attack right on top of her. In her shame, she figured she had to get some clothes on him before she dialed 911, so she spent precious minutes dressing him before calling for paramedics. We always wondered if his life could have been saved, but I have a hunch that guilt contributed to his sudden death. Since you're making love with the spouse God gave you, you won't have that anxiety.

Myth #7:
Sex is the cross women must bear

The key to a lifetime of good sex is attitude! A man must offer approval and a craving to touch, kiss, and caress his wife. Criticism and finding faults are turnoffs to women. Likewise, a woman must understand that her sexual desire is affected by many factors, including menopause, health and fitness, and the love that she feels for her husband. The latter factor is often based on whether a husband continues to romance his wife and treat her special.

WHAT SCRIPTURE SAYS ABOUT SEX

Genesis 1 and 2 remind us that marriage and sex are of divine origin. God thought this all up, and like all God's gifts, they are good and perfect. Scripture teaches a threefold purpose of why God designed sex. The first purpose is for parenthood, to bring forth the next generation. As the father of four children, I have no greater joy than knowing that my adult children walk in God's truth. Apart from becoming a Christian and then falling in love with Bev, knowing that my children (and their families) believe in Jesus Christ as their Lord and Savior gives me the greatest satisfaction, and I will die with complete fulfillment.

God's second purpose for sex is to prevent fornication and adultery, giving us a legitimate outlet for our sex drives within the sphere of marriage. The fifth chapter of Proverbs warns against the dangers of adultery ("Keep to a path far from her, do not go near the door of her house"). Proverbs 6:32–34 is more direct: "But a man who commits adultery lacks judgment; whoever does so destroys himself. Blows and disgrace are his lot, and his shame will never be wiped away; for jealousy arouses a husband's fury, and he will show no mercy when he takes revenge."

The third purpose of sex is to promote mutual love and pleasure. When God says, "Marriage should be honored by all, and the marriage bed kept pure" (Heb. 13:4), He has said nothing here about the conception of children. When God says, "For this reason a man will leave his father and mother and be united to his wife, and they will become one flesh" (Genesis 2:24), nothing is mentioned about the conception of children. One flesh symbolizes the closeness and intimacy of the marriage relationship.

My good friend Howard Hendricks says nothing tears him up more than seeing a long-married couple, who built their entire lives around their children, lose their reason for existence when the kids leave home. For all practical purposes, they are psychologically divorced. They may live in the same home but not in the same room. They may put on a front for themselves and others, including their social contacts and their church friends, but they have absolutely nothing in common.

They can't even carry on a discussion when they go out to eat together. That happened because they did nothing to develop the companionship feature of their marriage. Even if a couple like that failed to become fast friends and develop a good sexual relationship during their younger child-raising years, it's never too late to begin with God's help. They will have to work hard at establishing a physical and spiritual foundation for their marriage, but if they have love toward God, they can have love toward each other.

Speaker Charlie "Tremendous" Jones once made an interesting point. He said, "What you are today is the result of the books you've read and the people you've met in the last five years." I would add to that the television programs and the movies you've witnessed in recent years. What has your mind been digesting? Who is influencing you or your spouse?

One thing that Bev and I have learned to do is share our reading time together. We like nothing better than to curl up on the couch after dinner and discuss books and magazines and newspaper articles that we're reading. Said Eleanor Roosevelt: "Great minds discuss ideas; average minds discuss events; and small minds discuss people." We talk and talk, and being close to each other at the end of the day has helped our physical relationship.

Have you noticed how much time young people spend building a friendship relationship before marriage? Love takes time to develop. It can't be hurried. Sex is not love. Anyone can have sex. Real sex is an expression of love, and love takes time. If, after the kids are grown, sex is the only thing a couple has in common, they are in trouble. Sex in marriage without love is something that can't last. Bev and I have seen many couples with lackluster sex lives use that recognition as a basis for rebuilding their friendship.

ON GROWING OLD

The irrefutable fact that we are living longer and longer underscores the need for a resource such as *The Act of Marriage After 40*. As someone who's reached his early seventies, I'm aware of how fortunate I am to live this long. Many of our forefathers weren't so fortuitous; up until the twentieth century, life expectancy hovered around the mid-forties. Consider this chart:

Years of Life Expected at Birth, 1900–1995

Year	Male	Female	Both sexes
1900	46.3	48.3	47.3
1910	48.4	51.8	50.0
1920	53.6	54.6	54.1
1930	58.1	61.6	59.7
1940	60.8	65.2	62.9
1950	65.6	71.1	68.2
1960	66.6	73.1	69.7
1970	67.1	74.7	70.8
1980	70.0	77.5	73.7
1990	71.8	78.8	75.4
1995	72.5	78.9	75.8

Source: National Center for Health Statistics (1999).

With such a significant increase in the average life span, a healthy person in his or her midlife years today can savor the fullness of life and the act of marriage for many years to come. To illustrate how quickly our society has changed because of longer life expectancy, you need to know that in 1900 only 3 million of 76 million Americans were sixty-five years of age and older. These days, thanks to the "aging of America," nearly 30 million Americans are sixty-five and older—a little more than 12 percent of our population.

Today's average life span has increased nearly thirty years since 1900, which correlates into longer marriages—a new sociological development. A century ago, both partners rarely lived to see their last child marry and leave home. Since today's married couples live longer, raise smaller families, and finish child rearing sooner, they can reasonably expect to remain married for twenty or twenty-five years *after* their children leave home. (Men are around fifty-four and women are around fifty-one when their last child is married.[5]) Since married couples are living longer, it stands to reason that they could be in a sexual relationship for thirty, forty, or fifty years.

Wait a minute, you might be thinking. *Fifty years with the same spouse?* Let's listen to a fictional couple from Texas describe their "state of the union":

Billy Bob: "We're in our mid-fifties, and our sex lives are old hat. I was doing the math the other day—some mental calculations. Figuring that we make love twice a week, that's around one hundred times a year. Multiply that by thirty, add a few hundred times for those exciting first years of marriage, and I come away with a figure of 3,300 times that Agnes and I made love. If you do anything 3,300 times over the course of a lifetime, even something as physically intense and exciting as sexual intercourse, there's a tendency to go through the motions. Lovemaking is always the same; at least it's been that way since our first child was born twenty-five years ago."

Agnes: "You mean my husband has made love with me *only* 3,300 times? He has to be joking. If we had sexual relations every time he *wanted* sex, that number would be 33,000 times! Frankly, I'm tired of sex. Been there and done that. A half-dozen times a year would suit me just fine. I could even handle once a month if he ever got off his duff and wined me and dined me for a change. He hasn't gotten it through his thick head that I feel romantic when we're happily ensconced in a country inn with the wind billowing the drapes on a hot summer's night. When the feeling of romance washes over me, the years rush away. On those occasions, I look forward to surrendering myself like yesteryear. That's when I feel like making love."

Time out.

I don't want to sound like a sexual Pied Piper, merrily blowing my flute with a siren song that urges middle-age Christian couples to drop everything and rush to the master bedroom. Based on my many years in counseling ministry and from personal experience, though, I know that what happens behind closed doors unites couples in unfathomable ways. The act of marriage binds a couple together and serves as a constant means of expressing their commitment to one another. Through sexual intimacy, a couple communicates their love to each other in a manner not shared with any other person on earth. Such a relationship is not achievable on any other level. As actor Charleton Heston once told an interviewer, "Doing it 3,000 times with the same woman has been wonderful."

Moses, I mean Mr. Heston, has the right attitude. Aside from gaining intimacy that we share with no one else, lovemaking has many physical and psychological benefits, ranging from reducing stress to preventing depression. Orgasm floods the body with endorphins, a group of hormones with pain-killing and tranquilizing abilities that are secreted by the brain. Remember the "endorphin rush" you experienced during the jogging craze in the late 1970s? Regular and consistent sexual climaxes give you a similar "runner's high" as your brain pours endorphins into your bloodstream.

Endorphins are not the only hormones released upon orgasm says author Dr. David Reuben:

> Almost by accident, researchers discovered that when a person has an orgasm, the concentration of a hormone called "oxytocin" suddenly zooms up to 362 percent of its normal value! The implication of that finding is the best news anyone over the age of sixty could have. Oxytocin is a type of chemical called a "neuropeptide" because it acts directly on the nervous system. Oxytocin increases a person's interest in sex, it makes them much more affectionate, and it is a powerful antidepressant. That's one of the reasons that almost everyone feels warm and tender after sex. And that warmness and tenderness tend to persist long after orgasm has passed. Even more important, the more orgasms a person has, the longer and deeper the affectionate phase is. So the more orgasms they have together, the closer and more devoted they tend to become. That's why oxytocin can help a husband and wife get along better in every area of their personal lives—in areas far beyond sex.[6]

In a revealing study published in the *British Medical Journal*, scientists discovered that men who have frequent orgasms live longer and that men who have sex at least twice a week have a 50 percent lower risk of death than men who have sex less than once a month, based on a ten-year study in Wales. Another study of cardiovascular risk in women found that the more they had sex, the less likely they were to die of heart problems.[7]

Not only that, sex can boost the immune system. Researchers at Wilkes University in Pennsylvania found that moderate sexual activity stimulates a natural compound called immunoglobulin A (IgA). In turn, IgA triggers the immune system to destroy bacteria that causes colds and flu. A British neuropsychologist, David Weeks, interviewed 3,500 people in Britain, Europe, and the United States and noticed those who had sex more often looked younger. Dr. Weeks theorized the "fountain-of-youth" effect to the hormones released during sex. Other factors seen in those with healthy sex lives included a nutritional diet and regular exercise.

The meaning of oneness resulting from the act of marriage is far more important than endorphins or boosting the immune system or looking younger. If your once-a-week lovemaking sessions last thirty minutes, that is just three-tenths of 1 percent of your week, yet no other repeatable experience is more important to you. I've found that couples who relate enjoyably to each other spend many hours in emotional and mental harmony in anticipation of the lovemaking experience and follow it with more hours of mutual contentment and expressions of affection. Probably no powerful human encounter cements your relationship more firmly than the act of marriage. In your quest for love and protection, for a sense of well-being that can't be duplicated in any type of relationship, sex is a win-win situation that benefits both spouses.

HIGHER SATISFACTION

Scientific research these days is backing up what common sense has told us for generations: mainly, that churchgoers live longer, stay married, report higher sexual satisfaction, and feel happier than those who say they don't believe in God.[8]

Psychiatrist and medical researcher Dr. David Larson said,

> Most studies of marital adjustment are based on measurements of satisfaction, perceived cohesion (how close and unified one feels with the other), and how free one feels to express and exchange feelings. A woman who goes to church regularly and who takes her religion seriously will report generally higher marital satisfaction, regardless of whether sex is satisfying or not. But the *most* religious women were *most* satisfied with the frequency of intercourse and felt free to discuss sex openly with their husbands, and were *more* orgasmic than the nonreligious.[9]

That last bit of information turns conventional wisdom on its head. One of my beefs with the Woodstock generation is that when they came of age in the 1960s, millions of young people acted as though they *invented* sex. The sixties chants of "free love," "make love, not war," and "love the one you're with" spawned a cultural landscape that has left us—more than thirty years later—with millions of busted relationships, broken families, and children who never knew both parents. We are reaping what we sowed. Free love didn't turn out to be free after all, and this philosophy has been the main cause for huge numbers of emotionally disturbed, physically damaged, and brokenhearted people today.

The cultural elite (firmly ensconced in higher education), most of the political infrastructure, and nearly all the mainstream media, waged a campaign to paint married churchgoers as prudes who think sex is dirty. They still must be thinking about St. Augustine, who said 1,600 years ago that sex was a necessary evil for the propagation of the human race. That's preposterous, but attitudes die hard. Susie Bright, the resident "sexpert" columnist for *Salon*, the Internet magazine, says that she always presumed that the evangelical churches denied and repressed every kind of sexual expression.

"But I was wrong," she states. "There *is* a sophisticated discussion on the Christian way to conduct one's sex life, and its most articulate form can be found in the pages of some very popular Christian sex manuals." Ms. Bright gave a thumb's up to *A Celebration of Sex* by Dr. Douglas Rosenau, *The Gift of Sex* by Clifford and Joyce Penner, and Ed and Gaye Wheat's *Intended for Pleasure* as resources that give couples "an explicit and compassionate guide to going absolutely hog-wild in your sacred marriage bed."

Adds Ms. Bright:

> All the Christian authors I've read went on to further their medical training, particularly in psychology and sex research, which they found immeasurably helpful in spreading a simultaneously pro-sexual and pro-Christian message. They find nothing standing in the way, biblically speaking, of advocating joy in the body, orgasms galore, and experimentation with different positions and foreplay. They are downright feminist in their insistence that in order for a man to respect his wife, he must respect her sexual needs and become "Christlike" in his approach to her pleasure. In other words, slow down, Mr. Premature Ejaculation.

I'm not sure I would use those same words, but I enjoyed seeing someone from the other side of the cultural fence recognize what Bev and I, the Penners, Dr. Rosenau, and the Wheats have been talking about for years: that sex is good, sex is right, and sex is a wonderful gift from God. You show me two healthy people who are filled with the Holy Spirit and living in the close crucible of marriage, a couple who has a wedding license so that there's no guilt in the relationship, and I'll show you a husband and wife who's going to spark more passions that contribute to a sexual relationship than a non-Christian couple.

Spirit-filled Christians don't have an obsession about sex. We don't read dirty books about it. We don't rent erotic videos to "spice up" our sex lives. We don't use crude terms to describe various sex acts. Because of the spirit of God, we enjoy the sexual relationship more than other people. When Jesus said, "I have come that you may have life, and have it to the full," I believe He gives abundance to everything in our lives, and that includes the act of marriage.

Final thought: While we may be living longer and exploring love for a longer time than the previous generation, may I remind you that in Adam and Eve's day, couples remained married for over nine hundred years. So it can be done!

Chapter Two

THE CHANGE OF LIFE

Twenty years ago, when Stephanie DeGraff Bender founded the Full Circle Women's Health Center in Boulder, Colorado, many women sought out her expertise to help them negotiate the difficult passages of premenstrual syndrome and postpartum depression. Grateful husbands didn't mind writing the checks.

Today, our aging female population—21 million Baby Boom women will reach menopause in the next ten years—has the M-word on their minds. Their husbands are poised with checkbooks in hand.

"Let me describe a woman who comes to my clinic," Stephanie says. "She arrives with a list of health concerns—some little, some big—that are beginning to interfere with her daily life. She's in her early forties and has always had extremely regular periods, but lately she's missed a period or two. When she does menstruate, her flow is notably different than before. Also, she's never had trouble sleeping before, but now she suffers through two or three nights of insomnia every month. Oh, and there's one more thing: her sex life is different. It's harder to make love because her vagina doesn't lubricate like before.

"Her appearance is changing in subtle ways. She's not exactly getting fat, but her shape seems to be . . . shifting. She's more upset about these developments than she cares to admit. And then she wonders: *Am I menopausal?*"

Stephanie is in great demand as a speaker on the transitional decade of the forties. Each time she stands up before an audience, she is invariably swamped by women afterward, all saying the same thing: *I can't believe it! You're talking about me. Have you been secretly living in my house?*

A WORKING DEFINITION

Menopause has been called the "change of life" for generations because it marks the end of a woman's ability to bear children. In starker terms, menopause is the slow death of the ovaries and its ability to produce ova, or eggs. Since menopause has been called the greatest physical change a woman faces in middle age, it's not an event that should be discounted by eye-rolling husbands who wonder why their wives are behaving so *irrationally.*

Women react differently to the fact that their biological clock has finally gonged with the stroke of midnight. Some are ecstatic that they will never have to experience monthly cramps or purchase another tampon in their lives. Others click their high heels knowing that they will never have to worry about becoming pregnant again.

On the other hand, menopause causes some women to turn wistful since they will never be able to bring another child into the world (the old-fashioned way, of course), even if their last birth happened three decades earlier. What troubles other women about menopause is their awareness that we live in a youth-oriented culture that identifies menopause with old age, and old age with uselessness and mental deterioration. For them, menopause signals the end of their days as attractive, desirable, and sexual women. Like the first set of "crow's feet" around the eyes, menopause is perceived as an irreversible sign of aging and the start of the slow, inevitable march toward the end of life.

We need a little perspective. As you shall see, menopause is not the end of the world, and when you stop and think about it, menopausal symptoms should be a sober reminder that you're fortunate to have lived this long. Billions of sisters who lived before you did not experience menopause simply because they were no longer alive to do so. For centuries, life expectancy hovered around forty years, meaning that women died long before their ovaries stopped producing eggs. Dr. Judith Reichman, author of *I'm Not in the Mood*, offers this observation: "We're outliving our ovaries by thirty to thirty-five years," she says. "The question is, what do we want to do during that period of time?"

Great point. God is affording us years, even decades, that were not available before the advances of modern medicine. As we continue this discussion of menopause, however, I'm going to assume that you are in your forties, still having periods, still fertile. Menopause awaits you, but the inevitable "change of life" can't be put on a timekeeper because women don't go from fertility to infertility at the throw of a switch.

Instead, women enter a transitional time called perimenopause, a recently coined word that pairs up the Latin prefix *peri*—meaning "that which surrounds"—with the noun *menopause*. The perimenopausal years usually begin in the early forties (even the late thirties) and last an average of seven to ten years as the ovaries wax and wan before sputtering to a stop. The blood supply to these small egg-shaped glands begins decreasing during perimenopause, which causes the ovaries to slowly wither away.

Looked at another way, perimenopause is the tapering-off of a woman's fertility—a fertility that began in the early teen years with *menarche*, the beginning of menstruation. Picture your fertility as a thirty-five-year-long arc that began gradually when you were twelve or thirteen, functioned strongly for the next three decades, and then began tapering off during perimenopause.

When the ovaries awakened during puberty, something amazing happened. The ovaries began releasing up to 300 micrograms of a hormone called estrogen, the female counterpart to testosterone. Estrogen secretions wend their way through the blood system, affecting nearly every organ in the body. Among other things, estrogen causes the breasts to develop, the hips, thighs, and buttocks to swell, and keeps a women's complexion soft and relatively hairless.[1]

Estrogen also plays a large role during a woman's monthly cycle. Estrogen levels rise and fall every twenty-eight days. During the first two weeks of the menstrual cycle, between 4 and 60 micrograms of estrogen are released, but up to 100 micrograms enter the bloodstream during the *last* two weeks of the menstrual cycle. When estrogen levels are up, women experience sexual desire because they are content and more confident. When estrogen levels bottom out, women feel tense and unsure—and not very interested in sex. In a nutshell, estrogen influences everything from a woman's physical well-being to her mental outlook. "Women complain about premenstrual syndrome," says comedienne Roseanne, "but I think of it as the only time of the month that I can be myself."

All these hormonal dynamics are going on during your fully fertile, reproductive years when the ovaries produce eggs capable of being fertilized by the male sperm. By the time you reach your forties, however, your ovaries are winding down their production of your primary hormones, estrogen and progesterone. This slow, gradual process is replete with fluctuations that cause noticeable physical and mood-swinging changes.

For instance, you may have experienced highly regular periods that began every twenty-eighth day. During perimenopause, however, it's not unusual for three or four days to be clipped off that four-week cycle or for your menstrual flow to be reduced from four or five days to just a day or two. Predictably, this can be explained by the hormonal shifts rumbling through your body. During your fertile years, estrogen caused the uterine lining (the endometrium) to thicken, and that material was later sloughed off as menstrual flow. But when estrogen production declines, less lining builds up, which means there is less tissue to be sloughed off.[2]

When Stephanie Bender meets with women at her Boulder clinic, she walks them through a questionnaire called "Your Place in the Perimenopausal Process." If you are in your forties and yet to experience menopausal symptoms, take a few minutes to review these questions. The answers will give you a clearer sense of where you are in the perimenopausal years:

1. Have your menstrual cycles changed?
2. If yes, how? Are they longer? Shorter?
3. Is your flow heavier, lighter, or the same as it has been in the past?
4. Are your periods regular, or have they become more unpredictable recently?
5. When did the changes in your cycle begin? Last month? Several months ago? Last year? Several years ago?
6. Is sexual intercourse more difficult because of vaginal dryness?
7. Does your sex drive seem to be changing?
8. Do you notice that you are very interested in sex at certain times and totally uninterested at other times?
9. Does your lack of interest in sex seem unexplainable?
10. Do you feel that your memory is less sharp than it used to be?
11. Have you walked into a room and wondered what you were doing there?
12. Have you forgotten someone's name even if it is someone you know well or see often?
13. Do you have less overall stamina than you once had?
14. Do you urinate more frequently?
15. Do you have frequent bladder infections?
16. Is your skin drier than it used to be?
17. Is your body changing shape?
18. Is it more difficult to stay at your ideal weight?
19. Do you know how old your mother was when she went through menopause?
20. Are your moods more changeable than you would like?
21. Do you become tearful, irritable, or anxious more often?

22. Are you waking up at night soaking wet with perspiration?
23. Have you turned beet red in the face from a hot flash?
24. Do you have heart palpitations?
25. Do you find yourself lying wide awake at night, only to drift off to sleep an hour before your alarm is set to go off?

You should discuss the results of this questionnaire on your next visit with your ob-gyn, or call the Full Circle Women's Health clinic (800-418-4040) to learn more about your options.

Now that you are aware of perimenopause, I'm going to switch gears to discuss menopause and how that event has a distinct bearing on your sexual relationship. The way you and your husband deal with menopause can pave the way to a successful transition from your child-bearing time to the middle-age years.

CLASSIC SYMPTOMS

The sudden or gradual cessation of menstruation can occur any time in the early forties to early fifties, but the average age for menopause is 51.4. If you're wondering when menopause will visit you, consider this corollary: the younger you began menstruating, the *older* you will be when you stop your monthly bleeding. It's not the other way around.[3]

Ask women to play a word association game with menopause, and many grimace and reply with phrases such as: "hot flashes," "depression," "dizziness," "weight gain," "headaches," "sweating," and "excitability." No wonder why the onslaught of these menopausal symptoms doesn't cause women to rub their hands with glee. The fact is many women will experience hot flashes or patchy skin flushes, along with drenching perspiration in varying degrees of discomfort. Some women suffer from backache, nausea, loss of appetite, dizziness, or a sudden rise in blood pressure. Others experience fatigue, nervous irritability, or an irritation of the bladder that causes them to urinate frequently.[4] Such disturbances, however, are prevalent when cessation of ovarian function is relatively rapid. When menstruation ceases gradually, menopausal symptoms are mild or nonexistent.

Unfortunately, most women will see major changes in their bodies, which range from sagging of the breasts, coarsening of the skin, weakening of the bones (osteoporosis), to redistribution of body fat. But wait, that's not all. Let's have a closer look at these menopausal symptoms:

Hot flashes. Because "hot flashes" is a colorful phrase and a popular punch line, many people have preconceived notions of what a hot flash is. Medically speaking, a hot flash is a feeling of intense heat, usually beginning in the chest or scalp area. The skin reddens and produces a heavy sweat. The heart races and the hands tingle. Rarely lasting longer than five minutes, hot flashes are sometimes followed by a sudden chill. Some women experience very mild hot flashes, describing them as "feeling mildly warmer."

Hot flashes occur more often at night, which is why some refer to them as night sweats. Hot flashes may happen periodically for a year or two, although some women report having to deal with hot flashes for up to five years. Only about 15 percent of women experience real trouble with hot flashes.

Irregular menstruation. Periods may occur further apart or closer. They may be heavier, lighter, more painful, less painful. Women who never experienced PMS may start having it; those who had PMS report having worse symptoms.

Urinary problems. Menopausal women often become susceptible to urinary tract infections and bouts of incontinence or frequent urination.

Skin and hair. The skin may become thinner and drier—more itchy. Hair loss and hair thinning is possible, and some women report losing pubic hair. On the other hand, other women notice an increase in facial hair.

Memory. Women have trouble concentrating, resulting in short-term memory loss.

Insomnia. With hot flashes and night sweats, who wouldn't have difficulty sleeping and receiving enough rest?

Emotions. Mood swings, increased irritability, anxiety and apprehension, even periods of depression, are classic menopausal symp-

toms. If this list isn't enough to send premenopausal women scream-
ing into the next county, then you can add even more symptoms to
the pile: headaches (sometimes migraines), constipation, leg cramps,
joint pains, bloating, breast tenderness, upset stomach, dizziness,
faintness, and decreased libido.

The vaginal tract. You were probably not aware of this, but natural childbirth stretched and changed the barrel-shaped vagina for
the better. "After vaginal childbirth the folds in the vaginal wall form
a rich and undulating surface, somewhat like the interior of a many-
petaled carnation," writes Dr. Winnifred B. Cutler. "A vagina that
has sufficient underlying muscle tone can provide an exquisite series
of multiple sensations for the penis, much different and potentially
richer than the smooth, albeit narrower, barrel of the woman who
has not given birth.[5]

As women age and estrogen levels decline, however, the vaginal
canal shrinks, a condition called vaginal atrophy, and tends to lose its
thickness. Most importantly, as it relates to the sexual relationship,
women are not able to lubricate very well during foreplay. This condition leaves the vaginal lining thin, dry, and less supple, and penetration can cause itching, tenderness, inflammation, and even bleeding.

If you and your husband have been enjoying an active and vigorous sex life during your marriage, however, vaginal atrophy and
inelasticity is mitigated. These symptoms are generally prominent in
women who have had relatively inactive sex lives prior to menopause.
If vaginal dryness has made intercourse painful, however, you must
inform your husband and undertake measures to counteract it by using
over-the-counter lubricants such as Vagisil, Astroglide, Replens,
Lubrin, Moist Again, Aqua Lube, or K-Y Jelly. Some women break
open a vitamin E capsule and rub the oil directly in their vagina. Those
not wanting to deal with a messy interruption can ask their husbands
to wear a lubricated condom during intercourse.

For some couples, the shrinkage in the size of the vagina may
mean that more direct stimulation can take place, providing more
enjoyable lovemaking. A smaller vagina results in more friction and

closer contact with the nerves that produce sexual pleasure for both partners. It is these nerve endings, called proprioceptive endings (a type sensitive to pressure, movement, and stretching) that are found in the muscles around the vagina. When stimulated during intercourse, the muscles will respond with an automatic contraction which increases the contact, thus helping to build the tension that leads to feminine climax.

Dr. Arnold H. Kegel, a specialist in female disorders in the 1940s and 1950s, once treated a patient named Doris Wilson for an embarrassing problem called "urinary stress incontinence." A laugh, a cough, or a sudden movement prompted Mrs. Wilson to involuntarily let go of a few drops of urine. In humiliation, she was forced to wear an adult diaper.

Dr. Kegel believed her problem stemmed from weak muscles in the pelvic area, but before resorting to surgery, he urged her to try a new exercise he had developed. She was told to tighten her pelvic muscles as if she was trying to keep from urinating, and to hold that feeling for ten seconds. Mrs. Wilson accepted the direction to begin these special exercises, and within two months, her distress and embarrassment ended.

But now the rest of the story must be told. Mrs. Wilson bravely confided to Dr. Kegel that for the first time in fifteen years of marriage, she had reached orgasm during intercourse. "Does this have anything to do with the exercises you gave me?" she asked.

Bingo. Dr. Kegel was skeptical at first, but he launched a full-scale research effort that resulted in the development of a six-to-eight-week pelvic exercise program. Your gynecologist should be able to provide you with a PC muscle exercise chart (PC standing for the puboccygeus muscle). The PC muscles form a muscular band around the bladder, vagina, and anal region. The stronger these muscles are, the easier women can achieve sexual climax through clitoral or vaginal stimulation.

A good test to discover whether your PC muscles are strong (and this works for a man, as well) is to see if you can perfectly stop and start, stop and start your urinary stream. If not, your PC muscles have weakened and started to sag, which means you need to see a doc-tor. A gynecologist can explain the position and existence of the PC muscle and show you how to properly exercise it. In addition, many doctors, gynecologists, and marriage counselors recommend a unique gynetic exerciser called "Femogen" that was designed to enhance and simplify the performance of the Kegel exercises. This inexpensive approach is said to shorten the time of the exercises and has proven extremely successful with women. Results are guaranteed. (For a complimentary descriptive brochure, write to Family Services, P.O. Box 9363, Fresno, CA 93792.)

I devoted an entire chapter to the Kegel exercises in *The Act of Marriage* because I firmly believed in their efficacy on the sexual relationship; many couples I counseled informed me that the wife was now able to orgasm. I am still quite enthusiastic about the Kegel exercises as a means of enriching the love life by improving the mus-cle tone of many women and increasing the sensitivity of the gen-italia. This is especially true for women later in life following menopause. Otherwise many of her muscles in the pelvic area begin to relax just a little with age, making sexual feeling for both her and her husband less stimulating.

That's why this is the time to implement those Kegel exercises you learned during your childbirth classes. Bev and I are convinced that a woman should not quit this exercise regime after she achieves her desired results. We think it wise to plan to do them at least three times a week for the rest of her life. This makes sense since physi-cal fitness experts tell us that even the most conditioned athletes lose their muscular buildup if they stop exercising altogether. All it takes is sticking to a three-time-a-week exercise program.

In researching this chapter, I've learned that Kegel exercises can be adopted by men fifty and older. Their muscles also begin to relax with age as well, especially those muscles that help them maintain an erection and control urinary drip. In both cases, researchers have discovered that faithful exercise of the sphincter muscles is a tremen-dous help for men. Again, it is persistence that pays off.

TO TAKE OR NOT TO TAKE ESTROGEN

Until the 1950s, women had no option but to go through menopause naturally and cope as best they could with the aforementioned symptoms. Thanks to significant strides in medicine, doctors and researchers have begun to understand how estrogen-replacement therapy can reduce hot flashes, night sweats, and chills, and stop bone loss in its tracks. Estrogen can also do wonders for your sexual relationship. Here's how Dr. David Reuben describes it:

> The vagina is a fascinating structure in many ways. It has a very special lining made up of squamous cells, the same kinds of cells that line the mouth. But in the normal adult vagina, there are many layers of those cells and the lining is thick and durable. As the estrogens dwindle, the vaginal lining gets thinner and thinner until it is only a few layers thick. That's bad news, because when the penis gets going, it makes a lot of commotion inside the vagina. If the layer is thin, it gets scraped away, and that can hurt![6]

The introduction of estrogen can lengthen the vagina, moisten the vaginal lining, and make everything feel "right" in the genital area. This is done through the use of estrogen cream, which can be applied to the vaginal area. Take a dollop of cream and insert a finger or two into the vagina, massaging the cream directly into the vaginal lining. Rub the cream over the clitoris as well.

Your husband can also administer the estrogen cream during your sexual foreplay, which may also serve as a reminder that he needs to take it easy on you. He should wear a condom, however, since estrogen on the penis is not a good idea. If estrogen cream is used faithfully for a month or two, the vaginal lining should regain its normal thickness. If you don't like applying messy creams, insert an estrogen ring, which releases estrogen over a three-month period. If you prefer a lubricating cream without estrogen, you can also choose to use over-the-counter intimate moisturizers. A popular brand name is Vagisil.

Besides creams and uterine rings, estrogen replacement thera-py comes in several other forms: pills, patches, and implants. An estrogen patch is similar to those nicotine patches you see advertised in national magazines. Plug a new patch on your upper arm (once or twice a week), and estrogen enters your body continuously, solv-ing the problem of hormone fluctuations or forgetting to take a pill every day. Patches work well for women who experience hot flashes or headaches after taking estrogen in a pill form.

Tablets remain the preferred form for estrogen replacement, however. Back in the early 1960s, research scientists developed a "wonder drug" called Premarin, which is a mix of estrogen com-pounds extracted from the urine of pregnant mares. Premarin has become so successful that is has been the most-prescribed drug in the United States since 1992. Premarin and its hormonal cousins account for $1.8 billion in sales. Estrogen does more than increase the thickness of the vaginal lining or end hot flashes. The hormone has demonstrated an increase in life expectancy. Women who took estrogen for ten years showed a 37 percent decrease in all causes of mortality. An American Cancer Society study of 400,000 women revealed that 16 percent lived longer their expected life expectancy.

Estrogen reduces heart disease. When you were in your child-bearing years, you probably were not aware that the estrogen swirling throughout your body protected you from cardiovascular disease, ath-erosclerosis, high blood pressure, angina, and stroke. When menopause begins, however, the risk increases. How much? For women over fifty, cardiovascular disease is a much greater threat than cancer.[7] Although women are not known to have heart attacks like men, estrogen reduces the risk of heart attack by 50 percent.

A $40 million Heart and Estrogen Replacement Study in 1998, however, released findings that pointed to a 50 percent increase in heart attacks of women who started taking estrogen. The study of 2,700 women, averaging sixty-six years of age, noted that in the first year, women on hormones had fifty-seven fatal and nonfatal heart attacks, compared to thirty-eight women who took a placebo. Since the first year, the rate of heart attacks and deaths has leveled for both groups. Researchers are now waiting the results of a major test of 27,000 women, called the Women's Health Initiative, to be released in 2005.

Estrogen has been demonstrated to lower bad cholesterol counts and raise good cholesterol. It reduces the risk of Alzheimer's disease and helps with memory loss. Even more significant, estrogen reduces bone loss, or osteoporosis, a condition in which bones become thin and fragile. (When you watch an elderly woman hunch over as she walks, you can be sure that osteoporosis has taken its toll.)[8]

The Postmenopausal Estrogen/Progestin Interventions Trial (PEPI), sponsored by the National Institutes of Health, showed that without hormones, women lost 2 percent of bone density in three years; on hormones, they gained 2 percent to 5 percent in that time. Other studies have shown that women who take estrogen for the rest of their life reduce the risk of fractures up to 70 percent. Preventing osteoporosis was the number-one reason that *Consumer Reports* readers gave for starting estrogen replacement therapy.[9]

The downside to estrogen replacement therapy is the risk of developing breast cancer. British researchers, who studied 160,000 women who had participated in fifty-one separate estrogen replacement studies, found that taking hormones increased the lifetime risk of breast cancer by 2 percent to 3 percent. The British doctors also made an interesting observation: women who took hormones and later developed breast cancer found that the cancer was more localized in their breasts, which made the breast cancer much more treatable. The upshot: women who take hormones get breast cancer slightly more often but die from breast cancer in fewer numbers.[10] Studies that *do* show an increase in breast cancer speculate that women who take estrogen and drink alcohol increase their chances of developing breast cancer.

So, returning to our fundamental question: Should you take estrogen replacement therapy or not?

My qualified answer is yes, but not before prayer and consultation with your gynecologist. In my mind, the proven benefits of taking estrogen outweigh the slight risks. No medicine is perfect, but drugs such as Premarin can help couples through menopause.

Since there are two sides to the estrogen replacement therapy coin, you should follow this five-point set of guides developed under the sponsorship of the National Institutes of Health. According to the guidelines, a menopausal woman should:

1. Talk to her physician in detail about the pros and cons of estrogen therapy in her case.
2. Take estrogen only by prescription, following all instructions carefully and remaining under the doctor's care.
3. Be alert for signs of side effects caused by estrogen therapy.
4. Stay informed about estrogens, seeking out the latest information.
5. Find out about alternatives to estrogen, including improved nutrition, regular exercise, improved lifestyle, food supplements, and other, less-hazardous symptoms, such as lubricants to ease vaginal dryness.[11]

Regarding the latter advice, there are "all natural" plant-based estrogens on the market. Called "phytoestrogens," these products are not regulated by the Food and Drug Administration, and thus their claims of "maintaining healthy estrogen levels" should be eyed warily. Various herbal remedies such as the intake of dong quai, black cohosh, licorice (in pill form), and red clover may or may not work, although Stephanie Bender has noted that the herb black cohosh can help alleviate uncomfortable vaginal dryness and hot flashes. Consult with your physician.

While the jury is still out on herbal supplements, I can recommend soy-based foods, which are rich in isoflavones, a class of phytoestrogens. Japanese women, whose diet is rich in soy-based food, eat tofu, tempeh, and other soy products in amounts a hundred times more than American women. Fewer than 25 percent of Japanese women report hot flashes, compared to 80 percent of American women experiencing menopause.

Author and speaker Sandra Aldrich says her doctor suggested adding tofu to her diet during menopause. "I made several disparaging remarks, but then I checked the ingredients," she said. "Tofu is soybean curd, which is a fancy way of saying that tofu is nothing but bean curd. Hey, I like beans, so I started adding tofu to any dish I was cooking. I added it to my scrambled eggs or cooked it with beef. I dropped a heaping teaspoon into my casseroles. And you know what? Tofu takes on the taste of whatever it's cooked with.

"The results were just amazing," continued Sandra. "I just felt better. I had a general feeling of well-being. When I heard that Japanese women don't have a word for menopause, I understood why. Now I tell my younger friends that we modern women don't have hot flashes—we have power surges!"

Besides estrogen replacement therapy and adding tofu to your diet, exercise can be beneficial to menopausal women. Regular exercise builds muscle tone, increases strength and stamina, and reduces anxiety since you can be assured that you are reducing the risk of osteoporosis and heart disease.

If menopause arrives at the same time as the empty nest, you should have more free hours each day to pursue an exercise regime. Three days a week in a nearby gym or pursuing a sport you haven't had time to enjoy (tennis, bicycling, long walks) can stem the aging process. Menopause is *not* the time to embark on a crash diet. A combination of eating right and exercising well will be the best approach.

A FINAL THOUGHT

One other characteristic of menopause is a woman's loss of interest in sex. First of all, most women *do* experience a decreased libido in later life. This can be accounted to the natural aging process and the decreased estrogen production in women, which is another reason why I recommend the taking of hormones.

I also recommend educating yourself on what menopause is all about. Check out a book or two in the library. Use the Internet. Ask older friends for advice. Talk to your doctor about a book that he could recommend. The more you understand what's going to happen to your body during menopause, the more prepared you will be.

Stephanie Bender raised an interesting point earlier in this chapter. What she hears women saying today is that they want to know what is happening to their bodies. She uses an analogy with childbirth. Back in the 1960s and 1970s, in order to have childbirth and a satisfying experience, women were saying, "Teach me. Teach me what happens when I am carrying this baby and what happens during labor." This same generation is now saying, "Teach me what happens with menopause. Tell me how my body will change."

The key is being proactive, whether it be the commencement of estrogen replacement therapy, taking vitamin supplements, eating tofu, or any other nutritional aids that you've come upon. A good place to start is with a gynecologist who takes menopause seriously.

Menopause, as it relates to your sex life, shouldn't be a good excuse to let your sexual garden be overrun with weeds. A good attitude is key. If you fear that menopause will lower your interest in sex, I can assure you that will happen. (In fact, your attitude about sex *before* menopause is a strong predicator of what your attitude will be *after* menopause.)

But if you approach menopause with a mind ready for the physical changes ahead, your sex life can be maintained or even sizzle as never before. Because pregnancy is no longer possible, many women feel this decreases their anxiety level during sex. (Since reproductive hormonal levels decline slowly, women are warned that they could still get pregnant up to one year following their last period.)

Women who have made the successful transition say that not having to worry about getting pregnant is probably the biggest reason they enjoy sex more. They find themselves more relaxed, which increases enjoyment. Couples who have abstained from sex during menstruation no longer have to deal with the one-week-a-month "out of commission" period. Look at that as a blessing.

Chapter Three

THE MALE MENOPAUSE

From my perch in life, looking back over seven decades, I find it amusing—and understandable—that some men regard their forties as the time everything starts to go downhill. I've never subscribed to that view, however, since I believe God planned a series of mountaintops and valleys for us to experience; I remain optimistic that the best is yet to come. These days, however, fortieth birthday parties are festooned with black balloons, black party hats, and miles of black crepe. The "over the hill" motif spills over onto silly birthday cards for guys. Some examples:

- "At our age, heavy breathing may be a sign of unbridled desire, sexy feelings, and wild, animal passion . . . on the other hand, it may be Mother Nature's way of telling us to wear looser underwear."
- "Don't let another birthday frustrate you . . . we have women for that."

And finally my favorite, which shows a close-up of a doctor slipping a latex glove on his hand:

- "You're forty. Take a deep breath and try to enjoy it."

I will grant you that the male body slowly but surely displays signs of physical decline in the years and decades following any "over the hill" party. The forties are the time when the guys are making one last stab for glory on the church softball team, but they can read the handwriting on the outfield wall. They know their bodies cannot match their playing abilities from the glory days of youth. If they swing for the fences, they are more likely to pull a muscle than pull a ball into the bleachers. If they play a doubleheader, they can't play for a week. If they take a closer look at themselves in a full-length mirror, they behold bellies hanging over belt buckles and hair that stopped growing on top but sprouts like springtime weeds in their noses and ears.

Sex? Men in their forties can't help but notice that they are having difficulty getting erections as effortlessly as in the past and that the urge—and need—to ejaculate just isn't what it used to be. They've even noticed that their penises are starting to shrink—a stark and visible sign of the hormonal, physiological, and chemical changes occurring in men between the ages of forty and fifty-five. Some pop psychologists even have a name for it: male menopause.

Dr. Tu Nguyen, an endocrinologist at the Mayo Clinic in Rochester, Minnesota, scoffs at the words "male menopause," believing that it is not a valid medical term. He says that menopause describes a natural event in women—the cessation of menstrual periods. After all, the male sex glands do not sputter to a halt like the ovaries; the testes keep on manufacturing sperm that are waiting to be expelled for many more years.

However, with 25 million men between the ages of forty and fifty-five—some employed as influential members of the mainstream media—I predict that we'll be hearing and reading a lot about "male menopause" in years to come. Why? Because men can't help but notice the physical changes sapping their energy level and sexual performance. Father Time stops for no one. Andy Fletcher, a fortysomething humorist and Young Life International deputy director based in Colorado Springs, Colorado, wryly noted these changes in this manner:

You think I'm kidding. Here I sit with my new bifocals, trying to read the Sunday newspaper, hunched over like I've been working in a rice paddy from sunup to sundown. Despite my discomfort, I'm *overjoyed*. I can finally see again.

Except when I drive. Then the entire instrument panel sits in the wrong half of the glasses. It's like I'm under water from the middle of my eyeballs down. Now I can't see how fast I'm going or whether or not I'm out of gas. If I want to check my speed, I have to lean my head way down, and then I tend to hit the odd cow because when I lean my head way down, the actual world outside the car is off the top of the glasses altogether and I drive into pastures.

That's why we old geezers—I'm forty-six years old—drive so slow. Suddenly, life has become very clear to me. Well, at least as clear as things get when half of the entire visible world is under water at any given point in time. We also have to look for places with bathrooms all the time. You know how they always say that when you get older, time passes more quickly. Well, the time between bathroom stops is really zipping along these days. Sometimes we have to make a "pit stop" at both ends of town. And these are not big towns. Time is not the only thing that passes quickly, if you get my drift.

Besides getting my first bifocals in the last year, I had my first root canal and my first crown. I had my first skin cancers cut off my head. I grew a bunion. I sprained my ankle at a soccer game. No, not playing. Being a linesman. I stepped in a hole. When I told the coach, he looked at me like I was an old geezer.

Driving down the road, now, with my kids, we get a lot of attention. The guys are checking out my fifteen-year-old daughter, Maren, and the girls are checking out my seventeen-year-old son, Dylan. I'm like a hubcap.

Used to be the kids would keep us awake at night, crying, needing a diaper changed, whatever. Now they are nice enough to wake us up when they come in. We've been asleep since maybe mid-afternoon.

You know what they use as a nostalgia theme for high school dances? The *eighties!* That's not nostalgia. That's my life! You know what they play for Golden Oldies? The *seventies!* Golden Oldies are supposed to be the fifties. Nostalgia is the sixties.

My best friend Doug and I used to sit around in his bedroom during my senior year of high school singing Beatles songs like "When I'm Sixty-Four" off the *Sgt. Pepper's Lonely Hearts Club Band* album. *When I get older, losing my hair, many years from now.* Ha. Watch me laugh now. It wasn't supposed to actually happen. Not to us, anyway.

And this sex thing. Yes, I know all about making love since I've been married twenty years to Kam. We have a wonderful marriage, but we make love about as often as the kids offer to fill up the gas tank. Our idea of foreplay is, "Wanna?" Last time she said, "Wake me up when you're finished." And check this out: I actually read those "Improve Your Sex Life" ads you see three times a week on the sports pages. You know, the ones asking if you have erection problems and promising "separate waiting rooms to ensure your privacy" and a "98 percent success rate." *All it takes is a toll-free call. . . .*

Then I read something in my "Style" section about guys going through the male menopause.

"Kam, do you think I'm going through male menopause?" I asked my wife, who has yet to experience the "change of life."

"Maybe so," she said. "You've got a bald spot the size of a Frisbee."

"Thanks, I needed that."

"Don't mention it. Besides, all that male menopause stuff is in your head. That's what you used to say to me about my PMS."

Ouch.

I grunt and ruffle my sports pages. It's going to be a long rest of my life.

COMPROMISING SEXUAL FUNCTION

One male menopause proponent is Dr. Theresa Crenshaw, who states in a book called *The Male Menopause* by Jed Diamond,

Men experience a "lite" version of menopause—physically, that is. Their hormones and neuropeptides diminish, albeit less abruptly. Their bodies sag and change shape. Characteristic medical conditions like enlarged prostate develop. Sexual functioning is often compromised by hormonal imbalance, disease, medications, mind, or mood. Emotionally, like their female counterparts, men can have repercussions of catastrophic magnitude, including severe depression and suicide.

The period between forty and fifty-five is certainly littered with stress-filled landmines: the looming empty-nest years as the children leave for college and adulthood; narrowing career horizons; friends and acquaintances succumbing to disease and death; and the inevitable rocky patches in the marital relationship.

If men in the midlife years are experiencing some degree of lethargy, bouts of depression, fluctuating mood swings, and difficulties in making love, they are exhibiting symptoms of the male menopause, also known as viropause or andropause.

The rationale behind the male menopause is the steady decline of testosterone production in middle-age and older men. The drop is gradual—about 1 percent a year. From its height in young adulthood, a man's testosterone levels drop to about a third to a half of its peak by age eighty.[1] Testosterone at puberty was responsible for developing such male characteristics as beard and body hair, a muscular physique, as well as the male genitalia. Testosterone fuels the sex drive and gives men the ability to sexually perform, from arousal to erection to ejaculation.

Lower levels of other hormones (dopamine, oxytocin, vasopressin, growth hormone, melatonin, DHEA, pregnenolone, and thyroid hormone) also affect the sex drive, but the good news for men is that testosterone decline doesn't impact their sexuality as much as estrogen loss does for women. For most men in good health, testosterone levels remain adequate for lovemaking.

The steady loss in hormonal production, however, often results in six sexual changes that occur in healthy, normal males:

1. Sexual desire shows signs of abating.
2. Erections take longer to happen.
3. Men often need direct physical stimulation to become erect. The sight of a spouse undressing doesn't arouse him as before.
4. The full erection is not as firm or as long as in the past.
5. Ejaculations are not as forceful, not as intense. Sometimes men may not feel the urge to ejaculate at all.
6. The testicles shrink and the scrotal sac droops.

Listen up, guys: these are good news/bad news situations. Sure, you're going to have more difficulty becoming erect and climaxing as often, but you also have more sexual experience and knowledge that can be put to good use.

"Sex does change as we age; and that's the good news," says Joel Block, psychotherapist and author of *Sex Over 50*. "Around fifty, men tend to become more emotional about lovemaking, and they start seeking the closeness and intimacy they may have disdained in their callow youth."

Erections today are your best defense against impotence tomorrow. It's an old saying, but true: "If you don't use it, you'll lose it." That advice is especially relevant to men as they reach the middle-age years. An erect penis is similar to a hydraulic pump, and if the organ is not "oiled" every now and then through sexual use, veins contract and sacs collapse.

If you have not experienced erectile difficulties (which will be covered in detail in chapter 7), count your blessings. As your marriage enters the middle-age years, however, you need to understand how to counteract the physical changes in the male genitalia wrought by aging:

1. You will need more and more of a hand to make love. The days of your penis springing to attention at the sight of your wife's naked body—and staying hard until ejaculation—may be a misty memory for you. You will undoubtedly take longer to become erect, and the anticipation of making love won't be enough to keep you hard, even as you undress and begin hugging and kissing.

Sometimes, ladies, all guys need is a hand—your hand. Maybe you didn't caress his penis during foreplay in your early years of marriage; he was probably plenty hard anyway, or it didn't seem "ladylike" to touch his genitals. Now, because erections take longer to achieve (or rarely happen on their own), you're going to have to help out. Reach over and take his penis into your hand. Use the thumb and first finger to stroke the middle of his shaft. Lightly stroke the perineum—the area between the scrotum and anus—with your fingertips. The testicles must be fondled tenderly since this is still a man's most vulnerable area. You can run a fingertip along the underside of the penis, and as he gets harder, accentuate the male organ by using your fingertips to outline the ridge surrounding the base of the penile head. Continue to stroke the hardening shaft while spending extra time caressing the head, a most sensitive area.

Playful stimulation for several minutes is often all a man needs to trigger the start of blood flow into the corpus cavernosum and a full-blown erection to ensue. You can also use your breasts and other parts of your body to stimulate him. Bringing him to an erection could become part of your new foreplay.

Men, if she has not readily touched your penis previously, you can guide her hand to where it counts. If she still doesn't get the hint, you should explain why you need physical stimulation; that as you get older, spontaneous erections become a thing of the past. It's entirely possible that you can become hard in your foreplay but lose your erection during the twenty or thirty minutes spent in pleasuring her. If so, again communicate your need for physical stimulation so you can complete the act of marriage.

2. Don't worry if things don't firm up. Men can't help but notice changes in their sexual apparatus as they grow older, and that includes firmness. Not only does the penis take longer to become erect, but once the reproductive organ is filled with blood, it's not as firm as in years past—and the penis is not as long.

Length is not an issue. No matter how tall or short a man, his erect penis is almost always six to eight inches long. If you lose an inch with age, not to worry. Three inches is more than adequate for wifely satisfaction, and your erections don't need to be as firm as those "rock-hard" days of yore. In fact, a less-firm erection may be a blessing in disguise since post-menopausal women often experience difficulties with vaginal lubrication. A less-than-hard penis is still capable of entering the vagina and providing sexual satisfaction for both of you.

3. Erections will come and go. Twenty years ago, you had no problem remaining erect during an hour-long lovemaking marathon. Now, your penis goes limp during lulls or when you are attending to her pleasure with your fingers during clitoral stimulation. Is your erection lost for the evening?

Of course not! As you become older, you will find yourself becoming erect and going limp three, four, five times during your lovemaking. There is nothing wrong with you when this happens, nor can it be helped. Usually when it comes time for penetration, most men do not have difficulty becoming erect again, if they have been erect off and on during foreplay. If you are not becoming erect "on demand," keep your cool. Ask your wife to help you along until your erection returns.

A wife can help in other ways. She can ask for manual stimulation of her clitoris, which will take his mind of his issues and encourage him to be a good lover. Men are often deeply aroused when their wives become deeply aroused. A certain no-no for women is making fun of her husband's inability to stay hard. A man's penis is linked very heavily to his self-esteem and his view of his manhood.

4. You will climax less often. In the early years of marriage, men get antsy if they have not had a sexual release in seventy-two hours. That period stretches out as we are older, but even when we do make love with a good erection, sometimes we are not able to "get over the top" and ejaculate.

During the thrusting stage, the feeling that an ejaculation is about to happen may be shorter. And when ejaculation finally occurs, it pales in comparison to those long, intense ejaculations back in our twenties. The loss of erection after orgasm is not only more rapid, but it takes hours or even a day or two before we can become fully firm again—and that's only if there has been more manual stimulation than in the past.

Trying to *force* a climax may cause more harm than good, since climactic failure is rather frustrating and likely not to be forgotten soon. If the body doesn't want to climax, let it go. This is not the time to get all stressed out about it, which only brings on more problems later. It's not written in stone that you *have* to have an orgasm before you can call it a night. You can continue thrusting and working to bring your spouse to orgasm. Perhaps this is a rare opportunity for her to "double dip" if she reached a climax earlier through the manual manipulation of her clitoris. Women, unlike men, are capable of multiple orgasms.

5. *If all else fails, you can employ a technique called "stuffing."* Ladies, this is when you straddle your husband and take his limp or half-aroused penis and "stuff" it into your warm, moist vagina. Your hip movements should be sufficient to trigger a full erection, and from there you can both proceed with intercourse. If you're not well lubricated, then use K-Y Jelly or some other lubricant to help insert the penis into your vagina.

A partially erect penis is still capable of giving the woman sexual pleasure, as you can use it to paintbrush her clitoris with the head of the penis, bringing her to orgasm that way. Stroking other erogenous zones (inner thighs, breasts) with your partially erect penis could be enough to bring you to a complete erection. Don't be afraid to experiment with different ways of penile stimulation. You may have fallen into a rut.

6. *If you lose your erection upon entering the vagina, that's a signal*

something else is wrong. It's called anxiety performance, which may indicate a psychological conflict. If so, a urological exam is called for since a doctor can eliminate physical causes before you pursue personal issues. Losing an erection after several minutes of intercourse is not a cause for concern, however. This could come from just being tired. You just need a good night's rest and a respite from work.

NOTHING TO WORRY ABOUT

After reading all this laundry list of how the male reproductive organs change as you grow older, you may not be feeling upbeat about your future lovemaking abilities. Let me put those worries to rest. Yes, it can be disconcerting that our penises are not capable of performing in the manner we were once accustomed. But are we really talking about "performance" when it comes to making love? Of course not. Sex in the later years is a way for affirm the love of your life— the wife God gave you for this time and place.

You can adjust your mental outlook and understanding that your ability to make love has naturally diminished with age. You can regard this development in a positive sense; I know I have. Look at the bright side at the passage of time: you are more experienced sexually, and you can use this knowledge to please your wife in ways you never thought possible in your early years of marriage. The changes in the penis do not represent a decline in your physical prowess, just a difference. The process of aging is as unpredictable as the people involved. Consequently, some experience malfunctions, some don't. When vital energies run down in our maturity, many youthful activities are pursued less energetically and frequently. Life doesn't have to be that way when you reach your middle-age years. Remember, we're talking about middle age, not old age.

We'll talk more about you can use your maturity and experience in the realm of sexual love in chapter 5, "A Refresher Course." But for now, I urge you to feel upbeat about your sexual future. Your expressions of sexuality in these years can—and will—be more refined and enhance your love relationship.

Chapter Four

A Streetcar
Named Desire

Sandy was initially overjoyed with the news that her husband, Brian, had won a hard-earned promotion to senior management at the TransAmerica insurance firm. His new position, however, necessitated a move to the San Francisco Bay Area, where an office awaited Brian on the forty-seventh floor of TransAmerica's distinctive "pyramid" tower in the heart of San Francisco's skyline.

Brian and Sandy suffered sticker shock during a house-hunting trip in Sausilito, a trendy peninsula community north of the Golden Gate Bridge. They gulped and approved an offer to purchase a three-bedroom, 1,800-square-foot Victorian home without a bay view—a "steal," said their real estate agent, for $665,000. "I can't believe it," said Sandy. "We're paying twice as much as our house in San Antonio and getting half the square-footage."

"I know," replied Brian, "but you said you wanted to be closer to your parents in Santa Rosa."

"I suppose so," said Sandy. "Yes, this has been a dream come true to live closer to home." Something about the renovated house bothered her, and Sandy figured it out the first Saturday night that Brian initiated love-making. All three bedrooms were situated on the second floor, and adjoining their closet wall was Carrie's room, her sixteen-year-old high school junior. Across the hall was Brent's room; he was a high school senior who liked to dabble in painting while listening to Stephen Curtis Chapman. Fortunately Amberlin, their oldest child, was happily ensconced three hundred miles south at Westmont College in Santa Barbara.

Sandy couldn't imagine sex being any more unpleasant. Sure, she was tired from a week of unpacking and running errands, but the knowledge that her children could hear something through the wafer-thin walls stifled any of the joy that usually accompanied the experience.

Over the next six months, she rebuffed nearly all of Brian's attempts to make love. The act of marriage became perfunctory on the rare occasions she acquiesced; start to finish rarely took longer than a three-minute egg. One time, however, both kids joined the church youth group for a Lake Tahoe ski weekend. For once all alone for the weekend, the couple enjoyed a candlelit dinner at Chez Michel's, a romantic French restaurant overlooking San Francisco Harbor. That night, Sandy gave herself to Brian, who was more attentive than usual in pleasuring her.

"If only we could do it like that every time," whispered Brian in the afterglow.

"We could, if we didn't have a bedroom right next to Carrie's."

Then the light came on in Brian's mind.

It's a physical fact that women (and men) change sexually when they reach their forties, but many overlook how life's circumstances change as well. The sexual equilibrium that women settle into over ten, twenty years of marriage can change overnight. Moving into a new house, deciding to enter the workforce full time, suffering a herniated lumbar disk, worrying about wayward children—these are just a handful of the external reasons why women suddenly, or gradually for that matter, lose their sexual desire. Then there are the internal (or physical) reasons that decrease sexual libido, which stem mainly from menopause.

Over the span of a marriage, many women find their sexual arousal undermined by distracting thoughts that prevent them from (1) getting into the mood and (2) staying in the mood. When women finally reach for the bed stand light, a zillion thoughts race through their heads. Men might call them distractions, but more often than not, she harbors these thoughts:

- *It's cold tonight.*
- *My back hurts.*
- *Did Melissa finish her science project?*
- *What time does Nordstrom's big sale start tomorrow?*

Then if hubby reaches for her, her thoughts turn inward:

- *I look fat.*
- *I didn't shave today.*
- *He finds me unappealing.*
- *I'm too tired.*

Sexual desire can be compared to lightning in a bottle: a nebulous happenstance that can't be diagrammed or explained in a chalk talk. Desire can come on like gangbusters or evaporate like an August thundershower, and no one really knows why. If truth be known, lovemaking has never ranked very high on a list of a woman's needs. Affection is the number-one need of women, says Willard F. Harley Jr., author of *Her Needs, His Needs*, adding that men's number-one need is a fulfilling sex life. No surprise there. Women, on the other hand, score sex way down the list at number six. As comedian Billy Crystal observed, "Women need a reason to have sex. Men just need a place."

Women exhibit enormous differences among themselves regarding sexual appetites, which experts can't explain either, which is just as well. Men like to joke that when women are ironing, they think about sex, and when they are having sex, they think about ironing;

that shows just how little men know about how women view the act of marriage. What we do know is that a chart of female sexual desire looks like the classic Bell Curve, where the greatest numbers of women are represented by the center region of the curve, reflecting an average desire.

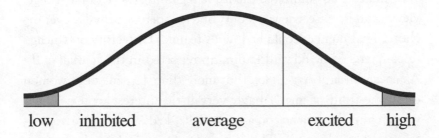

low   inhibited   average   excited   high

Note that the shaded area at the left represents 2 percent of the adult female population judged to have low sexual interest, or what we would call sexually frigid women. May God bless those husbands matched up with women who exhibit little, if any, interest in love-making. The latter view intercourse with a cold eye and would rather break rocks in a land quarry than make pillow time with their husbands. For couples such as these, counseling is recommended so at least both sides can understand what they're up at against.

At the other end of the spectrum are women with high sexual interest, again with a representation of around 2 percent of the female population. I'm sure more than a few men approached their wedding day secretly wishing their bride-to-be turned out to be a Christian nymphomaniac. I once heard a story about Jay, who said his goal in life was to marry a godly Marilyn Monroe. He learned in due time that he did not marry a sexpot; his attractive wife, Donna, let it be known that she did not seek a pin-up role after Jay bought her a sexy negligee—one of those see-through jobs you'd see in a Frederick's of Hollywood display window. When Donna opened the box and held up the skimpy teddy, she thought he was playing some kind of joke. When she realized he was serious, she beat him over the head with the box. That event prompted their first major crisis in their marriage because Jay had purchased something in black lace for someone who was used to pink flannel.

Donna exhibited an average interest in sex, which is where a majority of the female population resides. A significant amount of the female population (estimated between 20 to 25 percent), however, indicate an "inhibited" attitude regarding the act of marriage, viewing intercourse as a wifely duty and an onerous Saturday evening chore. That number could be low. A team of University of Chicago researchers led by Edward Laumann reported in the *Journal of the American Medical Association* that more than 40 percent of women (and one-third of men!) have very little interest in sex. These women rarely experience orgasms and, if asked, would express a negative attitude about sex. This is how Dr. James Dobson, host of the popular "Focus on the Family" radio program, described the feelings of a sexually unresponsive woman:

> It is certain that she is keenly aware of the erotic explosion which burns throughout her society. While her grandmother could have hidden her private inhibitions behind the protection of verbal taboo, today's woman is reminded of her inadequacy almost hourly. Radio, television, books, magazines, and movies make her think that the entire human race plunges into orgies of sexual ecstasy every night of the year. An inhibited wife can easily get the notion that the rest of America lives on Libido Lane in beautiful downtown Passion Park, while she resides on the lonely side of Blizzard Boulevard. This unparalleled emphasis on genital gymnastics creates emotional pressure in enormous proportions. How frightening to feel sexless in a day of universal sensuality!
>
> Sexual misfire—those icy bedroom encounters which leave both partners unsatisfied and frustrated—tend to be self-perpetuating. Unless each orgasm is accompanied by Roman candles, skyrockets, and "Stars and Stripes Forever," the fear of failure begins to gnaw on body and soul. Every disappointing experience is likely to interfere with the abil-

ity to relax and enjoy the next episode, which puts double stress on all those which follow. It is easy to see how this chain reaction of anxieties can assassinate whatever minimal desire was there in the first place. Then when sex finally loses its appeal, great emotions sweep down on the unresponsive lover. A woman who finds no pleasure in intercourse usually feels like a failure as a wife.[1]

Couples are extremely reticent to talk to each other when things are going badly in the bedroom, and the thought of seeking outside counsel is shameful to him and incomprehensible to her. Why would he want to tell someone else (especially a man) that his wife doesn't want to come on to him? Why would she want to divulge her most intimate thoughts and personal activities to a total stranger?

Nor would she be desirous of sitting down with a counselor she *does* know, which is usually her minister. If truth be known, however, counselors would agree that loss of sexual desire is the most common form of sexual dysfunction today. In many cases, sexual problems aren't about sex at all but rather stem from conflict in other areas of their marriage. Couples with money problems, errant teens, demanding bosses, and yes, spiritual differences (one's a believer, and one isn't) can slam the brakes on desire. Reestablishing a mutually satisfying sex life will take time and work.

Some pastors are reluctant to counsel for two reasons: (1) they could become "too close" to a woman who shares her intimate needs and fall into temptation; or (2) the men and women who bare their souls think that they will have to leave the congregation. Counseling was such a vital part of my pastoral ministry that I never hesitated to counsel our church members. God protected me from temptation, and when nervous types spilled forth their most intimate secrets, I assured them by saying, "What's said here stays here." I found people appreciative of the help they received, even when the subject was sexual dysfunction.

One day a very unfulfilled woman (I'll call her Mrs. Blue) came to see me with desperation written all over her face. Her youngest child had left for college, and although she and her husband were faithful in church attendance, they were not getting along well in their marriage.

"Pastor, ever since our last son went off to college, my husband has been sleeping in the boys' room," she began. "We have not made love in two months."

As she continued talking, I judged Mrs. Blue to be a woman highly undesirous of sex, and I further assumed that her husband was highly frustrated with her.

"What brings you here today?" I asked.

"Do you know Mrs. Cunningham? She lives down the street from me. I heard that her husband ran off with a young woman half his age! I don't want that to happen to me."

A thin smile creased my lips. Here was a wife willing to do whatever it takes to hold her marriage together. I love that motivation!

"Before I can help you, Mrs. Blue, I need to ask you a few questions about your sexual relationship. How do you feel about sex?" I probed.

She shifted uncomfortably in her seat. I can read body language, and her disgust with sex was an open book.

"I find sex to be somewhat an onerous chore I do for my husband whenever he wants it."

Her husband had obviously caught the same message. Most women don't realize how their husband can read their spirit, nor do they realize just how important good sexual relations are to both of them and their marriage. I have found that a good and frequent sex life can help any man through the pressures of being passed over for promotions, realizing that his vocational dreams will never come true, losing his job, or getting older. These are such devastating experiences that it often takes a strong and vital spiritual life and the unselfish love of an aggressive wife to keep from developing the "roving eye" that can ruin a marriage forever.

Most couples don't realize that lovemaking is not something we do when we are both "in the mood." It is something we do out of love when we realize our partner is in the mood. When her husband approaches her for love and she says, "I'm not interested tonight" or the perennial "I've got a headache," she may turn down his motor for the moment, but I can assure you, if done frequently, putting him off will ruin their relationship.

It is far better for her to respond to his expression of affection, and if she does, it won't be long until her mood begins to match his and both of them are swept up by the God-invented means of pleasuring each other. In addition to the exotic orgasmic event she experiences as he explodes in ejaculation, she shares in the warmth of the afterglow. I find that people don't "wake up on the wrong side of the bed." They wake up on the side they got in on. The man or woman who goes to sleep sexually frustrated doesn't wake up in a good mood the next morning.

Back to Mrs. Blue. I listened as she described not liking sex after giving birth to her first child and how she told her husband that it would be fine with her if they never made love again. Then a friend's husband ran off with a woman young enough to be his daughter. Now it mattered!

For the next twenty minutes, I launched into my oft-repeated song and dance about the beauty of sexual love and how essential it was to a long-lasting marriage. I then handed her a copy of *The Act of Marriage* and asked her to read it.

"What do I do now?" she asked.

"Read it!" I grinned.

"No. I mean about my husband. How can I get him to move back into our bedroom?"

"You seduce him!"

"Seduce him?"

It was obvious that she had never "come on" to him during the life of their marriage.

"Yes, seduce him by wearing something sexy and letting him know you would like to make love to him. That will get him back in your bedroom!"

She nodded and began to gather up her things.

"Mrs. Blue, before you go, let me pray for you," I said. I then asked that God would give her creativity in her love life and that her husband would be desirous of her. Looking back, I'm shocked at my frankness, but it worked.

The next Sunday after the service was over, she lagged behind him a bit and tugged on my sleeve. "We're back in the same bedroom," she whispered like a schoolgirl.

I patted her on the shoulder and wished her the best. Over the next few months I kept an eye out for them. Two weeks later, they were holding hands during the service; I had never seen that before. I noticed that they walked closer together, that he took her arm to guide her through the crowded exit doors. Within months, Mr. Blue became Mr. Sunny for the thoughtful way he treated his wife. Today they are considered one of the most loving couples in the church. Through the years, she's stopped me for a brief moment to say, "Thank you, Pastor, for the advice you gave us. It has changed our home." The look of tearful gratitude was worth it all.

MORE DESIRE

Christian psychologist Dr. Archibald Hart, author of *The Sexual Man*, wondered what influenced the cycle of sexual desire in a book he co-authored called *Secrets of Eve: Understanding the Mystery of Female Sexuality*. After noting that almost one in three women in his study confided that low sexual desire was a difficulty to them and wished they possessed more, Dr. Hart makes this statement regarding women:

> Sexual desire is set in the brain, which, in turn, is influenced also by both internal and external factors. Internal factors include your menstrual cycle, how you view your physical body, your energy level, and your health. External factors include the habits of your partner (many women complained how unpleasant it was when their husband didn't bathe before sex), the number of children running around in the room next door, whether the setting was romantic, and how you've been treated lately.

Your brain is smart, and it knows how to compute all of these together before it says "go" or "no go." The sum total of all these factors sets your level of sexual desire. It can range from none to high, or anywhere in between.[2]

Accelerators that can push up a woman's sexual desire, according to Dr. Hart, are:

- Love
- Romance
- Physical and/or emotional closeness
- Imagination (daydreaming or fantasy; see ironing board story)
- Attractive partner
- Testosterone
- Erotic stimulation
- Husband's praise of wife's body

The following can put the brakes on lovemaking faster than a New York minute:

- Fatigue
- Depression
- Stress and anger
- Body image
- Negative thoughts
- Unattractive partner
- Criticism
- Medications with sexual side effects
- Illness or pain
- Previous sexual trauma

"In contrast to those with low sexual desire," says Dr. Hart,

women with a normal sexual drive naturally focus on their partners' positives, selectively seeing their good points, as well as overlooking their partners' negative features. Women who are in love "prime the pump" by thinking about spending time with their partner and imagining (daydreaming, fantasizing) about time spent together, sharing affection, and physical pleasure. There is an ongoing high expectation for pleasure with their partners.[3]

Increasing sexual desire in the midlife years can't happen at the wave of a wand. Furthermore, I realize that sexual desire is often a two-way street that leads right to the bedroom. Women aren't primed to pump anything if their husbands make no attempt to talk to them, fail to shower before bedtime, or don't have a romantic bone in their body. If lack of sexual desire reigns in your boudoir, consider what you and your husband can do in the following scenarios:

Dilemma: You aren't in the mood for lovemaking very often— maybe once every couple of months.

Answer: I mentioned earlier that in 1 Corinthians God calls us to meet one another's physical, sexual needs. Making love once every couple of months doesn't cut it for most guys. It's very easy for me to say, "Well, just make love a lot more often," but I understand how convoluted and complicated the sexual dynamics can become in a marriage, especially if you've been together for several decades.

Can I offer some scientific evidence that making love—at least once a week—is physically good for you? Dr. Winnifred B. Cutler devoted an entire book to her thesis statement that the frequency of woman's sexual behavior influences a woman's hormonal patterns and her general health, especially during the premenopausal years. "My research with more than seven hundred women confirms the value of weekly sexual contact, a weekly love cycle," Dr. Cutler writes. "Regular weekly sex is still good for women, helping to ensure hormonal levels that promote good health, retard aging, and increase fertility. With a period of abstention when the menstrual blood is flowing, regular sex is ideal."

Dr. Cutler stated that women in their late forties who had regular weekly sex showed almost twice as much estrogen circulating in their blood than those who were celibate or sporadically active. "Women who had regular weekly sex showed other benefits as well," said Dr. Cutler:

They reported less symptom distress. Hot flashes were rare, and if they did occur, tended to be milder than in women who had sporadic exposure to a sex life. I closed my scientific paper on perimenopausal sexuality with the conclusion that women in their late forties are fully sexual, showing high levels of sexual desire, sexual response, and sexual satisfaction when they have intimate partners. These women who were using it were not losing it.[4]

If you *can't* bring yourself to make love more often, perhaps you will have to take that difficult step and seek Christian counseling, either with a therapist or minister you can trust. Most couples, from my experience, can work things out in the bedroom, if they take to heart Paul's reminder to mutually submit to each other. *Mutuality* is the key word here, and by that I mean doing things for each other.

For men, this means meeting the number-one need for women, which is the desire for affection. I'm not talking about once-a-year forays to her favorite French restaurant; I'm talking about creating an environment of affection in your home. Bringing her flowers on Friday nights. Holding her hand on a walk around the neighborhood. Giving her a back rub. Surprising her with a little gift. Kissing her in the morning. Hugging her during the day. Letting her orgasm first on the marriage bed.

Men, let me paint a word picture regarding your wife's sexual desire. Let's say you have two cars parked in the garage. One is a two-tone, red-and-white '56 Corvette that you purchased in your courtship days and drove to park and well, you know, do that lovey-dovey stuff. Early in your marriage, the two of you eagerly cruised in that 'Vette several times a week, but as the years passed by, she made it clear that she wasn't interested in "parking" with you on Saturday nights. Her sexual desire had lessened, and your sports car gathered dust in the garage.

Meanwhile the both of you began driving the other vehicle, a family minivan. The minivan represents the more mundane aspects of marriage and child rearing. That seven-passenger vehicle racked up a lot of miles over twenty-five years, but few trips to Lover's Lane.

How can you get your wife to join you in your '56 Corvette? She is waiting for you to romance her all over again. Speaker Zig Ziglar, who's been married to "The Redhead" (his affectionate name for his wife, Jean) for more than fifty years, doesn't believe his wife has opened her car door more than a dozen times over the course of their marriage. Sure, she's physically capable, but Zig insists that he perform this favor because a simple thing like opening the car door reminds the both of them that she is still important.

If you take similar action steps to remind your wife that you love her, your odds increase greatly that she'll accept your invitation to go for a spin in your red sports car next Saturday night.

And ladies, if he's holding the car door open for you, accept his solicitous attitude. He's making an effort to treat you special and make your marriage happier. Even if you are not particularly desirous of the act of marriage, you will see sex as important to you because it is important to him.

Dilemma: You've put on too much weight.

Answer: Very, very few women can become pregnant, bring several children into this world, age gracefully into their forties and fifties, and still fit into their wedding dresses. It's just not going to happen. Physical decline is inevitable, although some women are born with fabulous genes and a small frame. Others are blessed with bodies that respond well to a rigorous physical exercise program and eating sensibly. For too many women, however, all they have to do is look at food and they gain weight.

May I offer an observation? Your husband probably does not care that much. After all, he has grown older as well, and one of the joys of marriage is the experience of growing older together. Let me relate a startling statistic from a 1999 major survey by *Modern Maturity* magazine. If the survey is to be believed, 60 percent of men ages forty-five to fifty-nine gave their wives a "10"—the highest possible rating—for being "physically attractive." Beauty *really* is in the eye of the beholder.

No one is more physically alluring than you, and that's the way it should be. Unless your husband has washboard abs and buns of steel while you have the firmness of a Stay Puft marshmallow, you're probably in the same weight-and-fitness class anyway. If so, I recommend that you begin some type of exercise program and make a serious attempt to eat the right foods and lay off desserts. Trimming pounds now will help you live longer.

Dilemma: The kids are still awake when you go to bed.

Answer: You may feel like your teens' bedrooms come equipped with arousal alarms any time you're feeling amorous. Or they are constantly knocking on your bedroom door to talk about what dress to wear to Homecoming or if they can borrow the car next weekend.

Or maybe your teens exchange knowing looks when your husband is being especially courteous, has brought home flowers for no reason, or resurrected your "Date Night." Kids have a way of picking up on that sexual energy, although they prefer to act cool and not say anything.

You can still remember how you made love with reckless abandon when the preschoolers were soundly sleeping in their bunk beds down the hall. But now you can't make any noise and can't move forcefully enough to orgasm. You're becoming sexually frustrated.

The best answer I have is that you need to become *very* creative when it comes to the act of marriage. Take advantage of the times when the kids are not home. If your teens are at youth group on Wednesday night for two hours, make love while they're gone, not when they come home. If they're gone some Saturday afternoon at a high school football game, take a bubble bath together as a prelude to a sexual encounter. If the kids are sound asleep at 7:00 A.M. Saturday morning, but you're both awake, go to the bathroom, brush your teeth, and hop back in bed.

Dilemma: Always feeling pressure to have sex.

Answer: If you don't have the energy for romantic, passionate love like the B.C. (Before Children) days, that's okay. There will be times when you'll just be meeting his sexual needs. Try not to lay a guilt trip on him for asking, begging, or whatever (men's egos bruise easily here). But once in a while, you can shock his nervous system by initiating sex.

Don't forget that God has made you a responder by nature. He has placed within your feminine heart an amazing ability to respond to your husband. Most women admit to having exciting experiences they would have never had otherwise after responding to something initiated by their husbands. This can be said for your sexual relationship, as well.

Yes, it is the husband who initiates lovemaking most of the time, and yes, his fumbling attempts will often come when lovemaking is farthest from your mind. How you respond determines the outcome, of course. If you react with a "No, Honey, not tonight," as you may often do, it will probably end right there. On the other hand, if you cuddle close to him for a few minutes and accept his advances, however passively at first, you will gradually find your mood beginning to match his. Many a wife has cheated herself and her husband out of numerous lovemaking experiences because she did not understand the unique responding ability of a woman. Who knows? You may touch off a sexual renaissance and trade in those pink flannel pajamas for a black satin teddy.

Dilemma: Constant fatigue dogging your steps.

Answer: Some evenings you're so tired that sleep arrives moments after your tender head hits the pillow. It's hard to get yourself mentally up for sexual intercourse if you can't even keep your eyes open.

The answer is getting on that aforementioned exercise program. You may be thinking that stair-stepping three times a week or joining a tennis league will make you even *more* tired, but the opposite is true. Consistent exercise will stimulate the release of endorphins and other helpful enzymes into your muscles and cardiovascular system, giving you more energy to attack the day and still have something left in the tank at bedtime.

Women in the midlife years often have a great opportunity to initiate an exercise program for the first time in years. The child-rearing season is nearly over—or finished for empty-nest mothers. Fitness clubs can be found just about anywhere, and they come complete with Hoist machines, treadmills, StairMasters, stationary bicycles, and teacher-led aerobics classes. Three times a week for thirty to sixty minutes will be enough to rejuvenate the body and soul, giving you more pep. A cheaper alternative is to check out exercise videos at the local library and hot-step your way into shape in front of the TV.

Don't let a full-time career lessen your resolve to get into shape. If your office building has shower facilities, jog around the neighborhood or run the stairs at noontime. Eat a light lunch afterward. If you can't change out of your work clothes, bring soft shoes and go for a brisk walk. Take stairs instead of elevators. Keep moving during the work day and don't be desk bound.

By getting in shape and increasing your odds of living longer on this earth, you should have plenty of time to get to know your grandchildren. Who knows? The time you spend with your children's children could make the difference in whether they come to know Christ.

Dilemma: You exercise, and you're still tired.

Answer: Turn off the TV! It seems like there's always one more program to watch, one more "20/20" segment to see, one more news segment to view, and before you know it, it's past 11:00 P.M. Can you reserve television viewing for weekend nights? Isn't the TV one more time-grabber that can be easily excised from your busy schedule? If it's 9:00 before you have the dinner dishes cleaned, the mail sorted, and the newspapers put away, wouldn't you feel better by relaxing and reading for a half-hour or hour before bed? Better yet, why don't you read in bed with your lover?

The television set is a thief of love, and when TV becomes an ingrained habit each evening, at least one of the partners is just too exhausted to make love enthusiastically. We suggest that shutting off the TV or at least cutting down on its use and developing the habit of going to bed regularly at or before 10:00 P.M. would increase the frequency of lovemaking for almost any couple. It would probably increase the quality of the experience also.

WHEN ALL ELSE FAILS, PRAY

Yes, it may sound like the strangest thing on earth to pray that your sexual desire increases, but I am convinced that God never intended any Christian couple to spend decade after decade in a sexless marriage. I believe that He has placed within every women the sexual capabilities to enjoy sex as He created it. His only prohibition relates to their use outside of marriage. When kept within the confines of that sacred institution, these capabilities should be a pleasurable experience, not one to be dreaded. If sexual desire continues to be an issue, pray about it and expect Him to direct you to an adequate solution. "Until now you have not asked for anything in my name. Ask and you will receive, and your joy will be complete" (John 16:24).

I like that word, "joy." If there is one thing that the act of marriage brings to a couple, it's joy.

THE TOP TEN REASONS WHY
SEX IS BETTER IN MIDLIFE

10. With the kids out of the house more often, you can see what she looks like during daylight.

9. Your bodies have more "give."

8. The late-night electric shave has become a habit.

7. You're not too proud to admit to being exhausted three-quarters of the way through.

6. Before he turned fifty, hubby learned that there are better ways to set the mood for intimacy than begging, pouting, or negotiating.

5. Beginner's luck is no longer a factor.

4. You can afford a weekend getaway at a downtown hotel.

3. She finally knows what you want.

2. He finally learned what you want.

1. You got used to her no longer taking her socks off.

Chapter Five

A REFRESHER COURSE

Tommy Nelson, a dynamic pastor of a large Dallas-area church, tells the story of a woman who asked her husband one morning to zip up the back of her dress. He began to play around with the zipper in a flirtatious way—zipping it up and down, up and down—and in the process, the zipper broke. The dress had just been dry-cleaned, and she was late for a meeting; now she was standing there with a broken dress. She was furious.

That evening, after a day's work, she stepped through the front door. "Yoo-hoo, honey, I'm home," she called out. Hearing no response, she rummaged through the house. She opened the door to the garage and spotted her husband working on his car. He was lying underneath a four-door sedan with his legs sticking out.

Here's my chance to get even, she thought. She bent over and grabbed the zipper to the front of his jeans and began zipping it furiously, up and down, up and down, just like that rascal had done that morning. She congratulated herself, patted her hands, and strode into the house.

To her astonishment, she found her husband standing in the kitchen. There was no way he got from underneath the car to the kitchen so fast.

"What are you doing here?" she asked, blood draining from her face.

"What do you mean here?" replied her husband. "It's our kitchen."

"You were under the car just two seconds ago."

"No, that wasn't me. That's Bill, our next-door neighbor. He volunteered to fix my muffler."

His wife turned pale as a white sheet.

"Oh, no! I was zipping his fly up and down because I wanted to give you a little bit of your own medicine."

"Oh, no!"

"Oh, yes!"

The couple laughed as they ran out to the garage.

When they arrived, they found Bill lying totally still.

"Bill, Bill, you okay?"

Their neighbor was out cold. After dragging him out and letting him come to, they discovered that Bill had done what any man would have done if someone suddenly grabbed the zipper to his pants. He jerked straight up, and bam, he hit his head on the underside of the car with such force that he knocked himself out![1]

A SEXUAL PRIMER

Although Tommy Nelson's story ends there, let's assume this couple continued to giggle about their day as they retired to bed that evening. Their mirth and laughter led to hugging and kissing, which led to fondling and undressing, which led to sexual intercourse. During their long, warm embrace following intercourse, they agreed that their impromptu Tuesday night tryst put a little zip into their marriage.

Did they make love, or did they have sex?

There's a difference, as you're well aware. Making love is a two-way street with generous dollops of patience, unselfishness, concentration, and persistence. Having sex, on the other hand, is a one-sided "you meet my sexual needs now" experience.

The ideal, of course, is that the husband is cognizant that his wife should climax before he receives his release. Sometimes we wake up one morning, however, and discover that we've been caught in a twenty-year-long wagon rut in the way we make love; if so, perhaps a refresher course is in order. First of all, men and women experience four distinct phases of sexual arousal:

1. the excitement phase
2. the plateau phase
3. the orgasmic phase
4. the resolution phase

Men can almost be universally categorized in figure 1. The penis becomes erect, and from there, it's a steady line upward until ejaculation

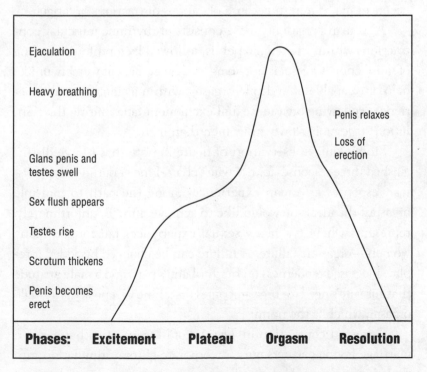

Fig. 1. Sexual response of the husband

occurs, but this changes when a man reaches his middle-age years. During lovemaking, he may need direct stimulation of his penis to get an erection and steady stimulation afterward to *remain* erect.

For women, the excitement phase generally begins with excitement in the mind. She has to be *mentally* ready to make love, so initiation may be stymied by household worries or distractions. Physical stimulation increases psychological excitement, with erectile events occurring in the clitoris, the labia, and the lower third of the vagina. This is when lubrication of the vaginal walls should begin, unless reduced estrogen levels accompanying menopause prevent natural lubrication. Couples may want to add lubricant in order to continue the sexual encounter.

During the plateau phase, the upper two-thirds of the vagina expand, the cervix is elevated, and the breasts may change with nipple erection. This state of heightened arousal may persist until orgasm occurs or may diminish because of various distractions or fatigue.

A woman's orgasmic phase consists of rhythmic muscular contractions within the female pelvis, followed by a profound feeling of satisfaction. Orgasm is not an assured outcome, but women, unlike men, are capable of multiple orgasms within a single sexual experience. Following orgasm, sexual excitement fades during the resolution stage more slowly in women than men.

From a quick observation of figure 2, note that I have distinguished three responses for the wife's chart. Line A outlines the physical responses a woman experiences along the path to multiple orgasms, the ideal she would like to achieve. Line B, unfortunately, represents where too many sexual experiences fall for too many women—orgasmic failure. A failure can be changed by added foreplay, increased tenderness on her husband's part, and a male attitude that his wife's need for orgasm comes first. Line C represents a single orgasm, which is the norm.

Our great contention in *The Act of Marriage* was that early in marriage loving partners must incorporate clitoral stimulation into their lovemaking. Without this necessary and meaningful part of foreplay, women often feel cheated out of the exciting experience of orgasmic fulfillment since the majority of women do not orgasm during intercourse. The French have an old saying: "There is no such thing as frigid women, only inept men." That's overstating the problem of course, but it can't be denied that most women respond orgasmically to manual clitoral stimulation. This is why I've long advised the husband to bring his wife to orgasm first because after his climax, he has great difficulty remaining vitally interested in lovemaking.

Rachel Maines, author of *The Technology of Orgasm*, directed her attention to how men and women arrive at Mount Orgasm via different routes. While men are brought to climax through arousal and penile penetration, women are aroused by clitoral rather than vaginal stimulation. What's good for the goose is unsatisfying for the gander, however, since intercourse almost always leads to a male orgasm. Simultaneous orgasm between partners is closer to Hollywood fiction

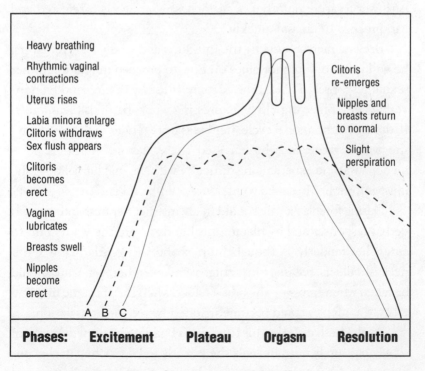

Fig. 2. Sexual response of the wife

than reality. Because of the physiological differences of men and women, a real man (as they say out West) learns how to please a woman first.

In our "Act of Marriage After 40" Survey, women said they orgasm before the husband in these percentages:

- All the time: 13 percent
- Most of the time: 30 percent
- Sometimes: 39 percent
- Never: 18 percent

Where do you fit in?

The act of marriage begins with foreplay, and every man should know by now that foreplay makes or breaks their wives' enjoyment of lovemaking. How long the couple engages in arousing each other depends on their sexual history and her mood. Sometimes a woman is slower to arise; on other occasions, she is eagerly interested and can proceed to orgasm quickly.

Because men are usually the initiators and women the receivers, he will have to watch for clues on how to proceed in relation to her sexual responses. This can be accomplished by talking and by non-verbal cues. She can help by expressing what she finds pleasurable. If, during her hormonal cycle, her breasts are tender to the touch and she would rather not be caressed there, say so. If she is post-menopausal and experiencing difficulty with vaginal lubrication, she must inform her husband so measures can be taken.

During foreplay a wife should freely instruct her husband through verbal responses and by placing his hands where she wants him to caress her tenderly. A thoughtful husband will gently massage her neck, shoulders, breasts, inner thighs, and even her feet. Care should be taken when caressing the breasts since when they become firm and erect, the nipples could become irritated by too vigorous action.

As the husband takes his time, he is building up his wife's arousal slowly but surely until he feels she is ready to be touched in the vul-val region. (A man must be mindful to keep his fingernails trimmed to avoid producing any discomfort.) When she voluntarily spreads her legs, she is making her most sensitive area available for fondling. She is ready for the next step to the gateway of orgasm: manual clitoral stimulation.

Gently and Rhythmically

A primer for clitoral stimulation begins with the husband lying next to and slightly above his wife. Begin by hugging and kissing. After an appropriate amount of time, begin to tenderly caress her clitoris and vaginal area with your fingers. A light, teasing touch is most satisfying. When the labia minora (inner lips) are sufficiently swollen, indicating that she is responding well to his ministrations and her vagina is well lubricated, he will feel that the protective hood has covered the clitoral area, and he can create friction in both places at once. The husband can gently insert one finger, usually the middle one, and begin to make slow rhythmic movements inside while his other fingers continue contact with the outer vulval area. This will give her a delightful sensation and help increase her excitement. She should feel free to guide her husband's hand and fingers to the most responsive areas. Her breathing will become more rapid, and she may groan audibly. Husbands find this all very exhilarating.

Most women prefer stimulating motions around the clitoris rather than directly on the head. Women respond better when their arousal is allowed to build rather than receive continuous stimulation. She should concentrate with abandon on those vital areas of friction and let herself go. If she wishes to groan, cry, wiggle, rotate, or thrust, that's fine.

If clitoral manipulation has not been part of your lovemaking repertoire—or a once-in-a-blue-moon event—it's never too late to incorporate it. Women must signal if their husband is going too fast or needs to speed things up, or if she is feeling pain. Rubbing directly on the clitoris is usually more irritating that arousing, so guide his hand on either side of the clitoris and allow him to stroke the shaft rather than the tip of the clitoris. Men must try to create an atmosphere where their wives want more and more as they vary the speed and intensity of the stimulation.

Men, if you want to increase the frequency of sexual intercourse, then start by increasing the frequency of orgasm for your wife. The most exciting sensation any women can experience in the act of marriage is orgasm. If you ensure that your wife experiences the real thing, you'll be amazed how her appetite for lovemaking will increase.

Readers of this book will be curious on how I stand regarding oral stimulation. One thing I can attest to is how much the Christian community is divided over this issue. I have received a lot of mail—pro and con—regarding oral sex ever since I addressed the topic in *The Act of Marriage* nearly twenty-five years ago.

As I noted in the original book, husbands tend to desire this experience more than wives, but with so many sex books on the market and sex advice found on the Internet, there seems to be an increasing curiosity on the part of women in this form of sexual excitement. For sure, the practice of cunnilingus and fellatio is on the upswing, which many couples find pleasurable. Others feel guilty about it and wonder if oral sex is proper Christian conduct.

In our "Act of Marriage After 40" Survey, we asked three questions regarding oral stimulation.

25. Does the husband manipulate the wife's clitoris orally?

	Women	Men
All the time	4%	2%
Most of the time	8	9
Sometimes	44	47
Never	44	42

26. For the wife: How do you feel about being orally manipulated?

	Women	Men
Enjoy it	48%	40%
Neutral	22	22
Dislike it	30	38

30. How often does the wife use oral stimulation?

	Women	Men
All the time	2%	1%
Most of the time	10	8
Sometimes	41	41
Never	47	51

Generally speaking, a little more than half of the couples engage in oral sex regularly or periodically—predominantly the latter. You won't find a "thou shalt" or "thou shalt not" in Scripture; the Bible is completely silent on this subject. When we wrote *The Act of Marriage*, we surveyed Christian doctors regarding their opinions; 73 percent felt it was acceptable for a Christian couple as long as both partners enjoyed it. To our utter amazement, 77 percent of the ministers felt oral sex was acceptable, which was more astonishing because many couples who approached us for counseling over the years said their pastor expressed their opposition to the practice. Privately, we wondered if ministers adopted this position because they thought they were *expected to*.

Nonetheless, some object to the practice for hygienic or spiritual reasons, but doctors discount the former and, as noted previously, the Bible remains mute on the latter. Therefore, we do not personally recommend or advocate oral sex, but we see no biblical grounds to preclude two married people from enjoying the practice, if they mutually agree that this is something they want to incorporate into their lovemaking, with the *proviso* that it not be used as a substitute for coitus. We suggest that it be limited to foreplay and that one partner (and I'm addressing this to the males in the audience) never demand the experience since the request can create a rift in the sexual relationship. Many women simply do not enjoy performing oral sex and would prefer not to do so. If so, let it be.

While we're on the subject, there is one sexual act that we do not favor: anal intercourse. We don't believe God made our bodies for that practice, and the anus doesn't serve a sexual purpose for the body. That act (known as sodomy) is highly dangerous for both partners. Once inside the anus, the penis can become contaminated with disease-producing organisms, thus causing danger to the man's reproductive and urinary structures.

"Anal intercourse should be avoided for physical reasons," write Clifford and Joyce Penner.

> It's just not wise! If the man enters the woman's anus and then her vagina, he then contaminates her reproductive tracts and sometimes her urinary tract since it is so close to her vagina. When the man's penis enters the woman's anus, the stretching often causes the blood vessels in her rectum to burst, which makes both her and her husband vulnerable to infection.[2]

Obviously God did not design the anus for sexual intercourse.

LOVEMAKING TECHNIQUES

When men are in their twenties, the dominant urge during sex is the need to ejaculate. Young men become erect as soon as the lights switch off and could proceed to intercourse with little or no direct physical stimulation. The pressure for rapid intercourse and rapid ejaculation doesn't mesh with the sexual needs of women, who need a considerable amount of unhurried time (twenty to thirty minutes, as opposed to two or three minutes) to become sexually aroused and ready for orgasm. As author Gary Smalley once remarked, men heat up like microwave ovens but women simmer like Crock-Pots.

Perhaps in your early years of marriage, men, you were too impatient or self-centered to view lovemaking as a prolonged, sensual experience that met *her* needs as well as yours. You have the fortunate opportunity to turn things around in your middle-age years because older men gain the capacity to hold off their ejaculations for a longer time.

If your sexual experiences fall into a certain pattern (kissing, foreplay, manual clitoral stimulation, intercourse with male orgasm), you may want to add vaginal orgasm to your playbook. Although certainly clitoral stimulation is the natural way that most women climax to orgasm, the vagina is endowed with the necessary nerve endings to cause an orgasmic response.

Adventurous couples can embark on a mission to give her a vaginal orgasm by stimulating different walls of her vagina while stimulating the clitoris at the same time. The so-called "missionary position" of lovemaking—the woman on her back, knees raised, legs apart, with the man lying on top of her—makes it tough to do both. Women often feel that when they are on top they can control how the clitoris rubs on the male's pubic bone; they can bring themselves to climax this way. If couples adopt a lovemaking position in which the woman lies on her side and the man lies behind her, he can insert his erect penis and begin gentle thrusting, using the head of the penis to rub the front wall of the vagina while gently stroking her clitoris with his finger.

You can experiment with other positions. Women on top can often locate the right coital alignment, especially since they have great control of where the penis rubs inside the vagina and their clitorises on the pubic bones. In a rear-entry approach, she can press her legs together, which can increase the friction to just the right amount. A woman lying on her stomach with a pillow underneath her to raise her hips may find that the penis hits the right spot.

A variation of this technique involves the man entering the woman from a higher angle to ensure that his pubic bone presses against her clitoris. Instead of the male thrusting in and out, they work together by rocking up and down. This allows for increased stimulation of the woman's clitoris and less stimulation for him so he can keep from ejaculating.

When trying for a vaginal orgasm (or clitoral, for that matter) during intercourse, this means that the husband must hold off his climax until his wife attains her orgasm. The knowledge that a man could ejaculate at any time while he is thrusting is enough for many women to "block" and not allow an orgasm to happen.

Nowhere is it written that a woman has to orgasm every time. Some do, some don't. There is no right or wrong. The woman's enjoyment of the sexual experience may have nothing to do with having an orgasm. For her it may be the closeness and connection that is most satisfying. This varies greatly from woman to woman. A successful sexual experience is not dependent upon arousal, orgasm, ejaculation, or intercourse.[3]

If you are a couple who has mastered the ability to reach orgasm together (or allow the woman to climax first), I salute you. But many couples are not as skilled, or lucky, which means that clitoral stimulation is the main thoroughfare for female orgasms.

Various Positions

Which brings us to lovemaking positions. All the sex-book-advice to the contrary, lovemaking positions boil down to what I call the Basic Four:

Man on top, woman lying on her back. I have no way to prove it, but I'm sure this is the number-one position in bedrooms of America. Men like it (come to think of it, men like *any* position) because they are relatively free to thrust to their heart's content. While women do not appreciate men who are rough, they prefer the face-to-face contact and holding their man close while his body tauts during sexual climax. Couples looking for a new twist on this position could have the woman bring her knees all the way up to her chest, or wrap them around her husband's waist, or, for those former members of the U.S. Gymnastic Team, bring her legs over his shoulders. These movements tilt the pelvis in different ways and offer a new kind of vaginal stimulation.

Woman on top, man lying on his back. This is probably the second-favored position. Women enjoy it because they can control how much and how fast the erect penis slides up and down the vaginal canal. Other women find orgasmic delight in rubbing their clitoris against the male pubic bone; they can bring themselves to climax in this manner. Women with bad backs or other ailments may find this position painful, too uncomfortable, or not worth the effort. Women who have gained weight or who are skittish about their husbands seeing "everything" may not like this position since it's hard to stay under the covers, although the view could be one of the reasons why your husband *really* enjoys the woman-on-top position. If you are conscious about your weight or wish to be more modest, you can adorn your body with a sexy bustier or negligee.

Man entering her vagina from the rear. This position has several variations: the man laying on top of his wife, whose is lying on her stomach, and penetrating her vagina from the rear; the "spoons" position in which the woman lies on her side and her husband lies behind her; and the "doggy style" in which the woman hunches on her knees, presses her chest against a pillow, and allows the man to mount her. Many women feel degraded adopting a sexual intercourse position that they associate with the animal kingdom, plus it can be hard on aging knees. A nice compromise is the woman lying on her side with the man behind her, who slides his penis in from behind. From there, both of you can decide if there is extra sensation when using this position.

Man sitting on the edge of the bed, in a chair, or on a couch, and having his wife draw herself onto his erect penis á la discretion. Postmenopausal women who experience great difficulty in lubricating may find this position to be good since she can control the entrance of the penis into the vaginal tract and minimize any pain. Generous amounts of lubricant should be used.

LET HER GO FIRST

No matter what position you use, no matter how "good" a lover you are, the art of lovemaking is characterized by an attitude that seeks to render emotional and physical satisfaction to their mate. If that attitude has been part and parcel of your marriage bed since your honeymoon days, it will be difficult to change. My good friend, Dr. Ed Wheat, once said, "Every physical union should be a contest to see which partner can outplease the other."

Men should keep in mind that lovemaking is an experience where you want your wife to cross the finish line of orgasm before you do. With a little practice, you can be right behind her!

Chapter Six

GREAT SEX AT ANY AGE

While Bev and I were in Washington, D.C., during the writing of this book, one inside-the-Beltway event caught our attention. The Association of American Retired People, better known as AARP (and the number-one lobby group in our nation's capitol, I might add), invited us to a luncheon to discuss the organization's findings after surveying 1,300 people forty-five years and older about their intimate sexual lives. The event was billed "Great Sex: What's Age Got to Do With It?" Being the curious sort, we sauntered down to AARP's impressive downtown headquarters to be flies on the wall.

We listened to their panel of experts discuss sex, love, and intimacy. Typical of the secular mind, little effort was given to discussing *marital* sex. One thing I agreed with that day, however, was their assertion that the older we get, "intimacy" plays a more important role in good sex.

What the panelists failed to note is something that I have asserted for years: Christians have the best sex lives on earth because the spiritual foundation we share creates the greatest and deepest intimacy. I still think we Christians enjoy sex more than anyone in society. We have more frequency, more pleasurability, more satisfaction, and more intimacy. We have love that we cannot wait to give.

When we were writing the original *Act of Marriage*, Bev and I ate lunch with two very close friends of many years. At that time, he was seventy-six years old; his bride of fifty years was three or four years younger. We treasured their friendship and the sight of the beautiful relationship they shared.

Over salads, they asked what Bev and I what we were up to. We casually mentioned that we were working on *The Act of Marriage*. When informed of our subject, he jokingly said, "I could tell you a lot to put in that book."

Bev and I exchanged knowing glances.

"That's wonderful," I said. I gathered up some courage and asked him how often he and his wife made love at their age.

"At least three times a week!" he interjected.

Bev and I exchanged knowing glances again.

Our friend wasn't finished talking about the subject. "Now that I'm retired, we have more time for that sort of thing."

We shared a good laugh, but afterward I was struck by the fact that he didn't know that he was supposed to slow down, so he didn't! And that's the way it should be. Two healthy people should be able to make love into their eighties. Yes, eighty years old. We know plenty of couples who claim they celebrated their golden wedding anniversary by making love.

We will concede that as people grow older, various parts of the body begin to wear out. But the process is as unpredictable as the people involved. When vital energies begin to run down, many activities of our youth are pursued less energetically and frequently. It is not uncommon for senior citizens, particularly men, to experience occasional malfunctions in lovemaking. It's going to happen. Unfortunately they jump to the conclusion that "it's all over" after a few nonorgasmic experiences. If they were to analyze the situation more carefully, they would notice something that gives them hope and inspiration to try again.

Contrary to masculine obsession, a man does not have to ejaculate to enjoy coitus. Upon arousal, he can have a substantial erection, experience many minutes of exciting stimulation, bring her to orgasm, and gradually lose his ejaculatory drive. Instead of the usual high peak, his feelings just seem to pass without the customary explosion. Although this type of lovemaking is not as satisfying as the ejaculatory climax he so enjoys, it does satisfy both his sex drive and his wife's. If he learns to settle for this lessened experience, he will still occasionally ejaculate. As his confidence returns, so will the frequency of his success. Many, however, erroneously short-circuit their long-range capabilities by *thinking* that it is all over when actual experience would dictate otherwise.

Love and sex are twin arts requiring effort and knowledge. Those who find sex exciting and fascinating search for ways to enhance the experience. Years of maturation teach us what sexual intimacy is all about—a soft tenderness, a gentle touch, an affectionate embrace, a tingly orgasm, and the afterglow of each other's physical presence. You will probably make love less often as you mature in life, but you will experience more affection for each other. Your endearing love has ripened and now finds its rich expression when cuddling under the sheets on cold, wintry nights, enjoying the warm embrace of someone who has shared a long life of trials and triumphs with you. Not to mention a lifetime of shared memories.

Exploring sexual expressions of love should begin with slow-and-easy foreplay since midlife men and women need longer times for arousal to build. To short-circuit the prelude to intercourse usually cheats the woman out of orgasm—particularly if she is like many women who are not orgasmic during vaginal intercourse. A playful touch means much here. For confirmation, ask an older widow or widower what they miss most about not making love, and they would reply that they long to be touched, held, and caressed. They miss the pleasure of those vital experiences and *giving* pleasure during the act of marriage. If they had a message for you, it would be: *Enjoy it while you can*.

The following are some reminders regarding romance and ideas regarding sexual techniques that mature couples can incorporate into their lovemaking. If these are already part of your bedroom repertoire, you're well on the way to enjoying seasoned love.

THE PRELUDE

Let's back way up for a minute—no, make that several days. What has your relationship been like recently? Not much time together due to work commitments? Lots of grunts and mumbled sentences and little eye contact? If so, do you remember in chapter 4 how a man's number-one marital need is sexual fulfillment, while affection tops the list for women? If so, good. Dr. Willard Harley furthermore states that the number-two need of men is recreational companionship and the number-two need of women is conversation. These basic marital needs must be maintained in the midlife years. Dr. Harley points out that prior to marriage, the both of you probably spent ten to fifteen hours a week doing things and talking together—going out to dinner, bowling, attending ball games, driving somewhere. You used those times to map out your future and dream big dreams. You bonded by doing just about everything together, including recreational pursuits.

These days, recreational companionship means different things to the sexes. Men envision taking their wives fishing for rainbow trout, attending a Saturday afternoon football game at State U, or snowmobiling through the frozen tundra together. These activities may not prove exciting for her. Her idea of recreation is *going out to dinner*. A close second would be a daylong shopping spree, taking in a "chick flick" movie, or attending a cultural event.

Some compromise will have to be struck since the best recreational activities are ones that couples can pursue together. In our "Act of Marriage After 40 Survey," walking beat out the competition by a country mile when we asked couples what sports they participated in. Why not walk together in the early morning or early evening hours? Bicycling and gym workouts are other possibilities. Finally, I would be remiss if I didn't put in a plug in for golf, a great social game that couples can play and enjoy well into their seventies. Walking a verdant, well-manicured course and chasing Titleist balls down a freshly mowed fairway is a beautiful way to enjoy the outdoors.

Remember how I said that a woman's second-greatest need is conversation? Well, you can kill two birds with one stone by taking her out to dinner and conversing. Restaurant meals can be a respite from the "busyness" that gulps our waking hours. Howard Hendricks once said,

> We're living in such a rat race that we really don't have time to enjoy life, particularly the things that God has created in life to be enjoyed. You know, years ago when the people out West missed the stagecoach they said, "That's okay, we'll catch the next one next month." Today if a guy misses a section of a revolving door he's in a tizzy. God knew, my friend, that marital relationships take time. They must be cultivated and nurtured.

Cultivate your relationship in a bistro or eatery with loads of atmosphere.

While we're on the subject, gentlemen, can you treat her like you did during your courting days? Can you open the car door for her and pull out her chair when she is seated in a restaurant? No matter what their age women like to be treated special, as if they are the only one who matters.

What do women find inspiring? Words. Women are blessed with an auditory system that won't quit. That's why women are always saying, "He doesn't talk to me." Men, talk to her! Don't worry about what to say, just say something. She'll keep the conversation ball in the air for the both of you, believe me. Discuss what's on your mind, without sounding belligerent. Tell her that you love her. She should never question whether or not you love her. I have never counseled a couple in which the man spoke lovingly, kindly, and graciously to his wife, only to have her leave him. Only angels and humans are able to communicate verbally—use that gift to positively influence her. Think of her auditory system like the thermostat on the wall: you can turn it up, or you can turn it down. Say nasty, sarcastic kinds of things, and you'll get a frigid woman. Speak kind, positive words with tender touch, and she'll warm up to you and love you.

Good communication bodes well for the sexual relationship. Couples that have a good love relationship find it relatively easy to talk about sex. Couples that have a bad relationship find it almost impossible to talk about their sexual relationship unless they're mad at each other, and that's the wrong time to talk about it.

Of all God's living creatures, we human beings are the only ones with the skill to communicate in words the thoughts in our heads. That gift of speech has brought much pleasure to millions through the centuries. Unfortunately, that same gift has sparked disagreements, fights, and even wars. The difference is the spirit with which the communication is made.

Communication over the long haul of life between two people is an art that can be learned. Some, of course, do it naturally; others can learn if they value their marriage and want to enrich the golden years of life. All it takes is an unselfish spirit and willingness to try to reach into the heart and mind of your mate by talking about things that are of interest to him or her.

CLEANING UP

If the husband hasn't showered recently (by that I mean in the last couple of hours), he might as well not bother making a sexual advance. Women love clean and fragrant men. Splash liberal amounts of cologne on the face and neck.

The power of smell is one of our primary senses. Unfortunately some people experience more difficulty in this area than others, but today there is little excuse for body odor, bad breath, and other offensive smells. A thoughtful lover prepares for lovemaking by taking a bath or shower, using effective deodorant, and practicing good oral hygiene.

Men should also regard their nails. Since they use their fingers to manually stimulate her clitoris and vagina, long nails (especially with any dirt underneath) are unhygienic and a gross turnoff to women. Cut and file your nails to the right length. This is also the time to brush your teeth, swish some Listerine in the mouth, and perhaps even shave, depending on the length of your stubble.

On the subject of odors, I've met perfectionist men in my counseling office who admitted to me that they were "turned-off" by their wife's natural vaginal odors. Women have a problem unshared by men, for the strong odor of a man's seminal fluid is usually not detected because it remains inside of him until he ejaculates it into his wife's vagina, where it is not easily detected. But for the wife to permit penile entrance, she must secrete a vaginal lubricant that usually gives off an odor. A husband should simply learn to disregard that odor.

One husband complained to me that he couldn't maintain an erection because her odor was so strong. Taking note of his limited sex education, I took the time to explain the function of his wife's vagina during sexual arousal. After convincing him this was a normal procedure over which his wife had no control, I concluded, "You should recognize that odor is the smell of love. Your wife's response to your love causes the lubricant to flow in anticipation of coitus with you; therefore you are the one causing the odor." With a sheepish grin, he conceded, "I never thought of it that way." He later indicated that the "smell of love" concept had transformed their lovemaking.

THE SETTING

Years can flash by, and the setting is always the same. It's late at night, the bedroom is dark, and he's on her side of the bed, trying to get her to agree to sex. But late evening might be the *worst* time to make love, especially after a filling dinner. Tired bodies make for tired sex. Erectile problems can be exacerbated by fatigue.

If your children are grown and gone, can you make love in the morning? You will certainly be rested and raring to go. Mid-afternoon on a weekend can be a great stress-buster from the pressures of the work week. Many women, however, prefer darkness. If this is true in your household, then invest in heavy curtains or blinds that can make the bedroom very dark when the sun is up.

Men, don't forget that you are stimulated by sight, but women are not stimulated passionately by seeing a nude male body. I remember when a thirty-six-year-old Polish weightlifter won the body-building title of Mr. America. I was reading a *Sports Illustrated* story about the event, which was accompanied by a color photo of Mr. America posing in his skivvies, bursting with oiled muscles that glistened under the hot lights. Bev looked over my shoulder and said, "Yuck! How grotesque!" Frankly, I was relieved that she thought his bulging muscles were a turnoff. My point is this: women are not sexually stimulated by the sight of a male body, so don't expect a welcome-home reception when you parade around the bedroom in the nude or your old cotton briefs.

Grab a fluffy bathrobe. Can you play some soft, melodic music to set the mood? Other items that stir a woman's senses are a bouquet of flowers, a bowl of fresh fruit, or 100-gram bars of Swiss chocolate (chocolate has been known for its aphrodisiac qualities for centuries). Candles and scented potpourri create atmosphere in a heart beat.

FOREPLAY

Fellows, when is the last time you offered to rub her back without harboring expectations that it would lead to intercourse? Some evening give her a full-body massage, but done in a manner in which you make it clear that you are not expecting intercourse afterward. Touching for touching's sake is often neglected in the race for arousal. Keep this thought from English poetess Kathleen Raine in mind: "Here, where I trace your body with my hand, love's presence has no end."

Perhaps you could start by coming to bed in your bathing suits, which can be an erotic event of its own, or you can certainly slip into bed naked or with your usual nightclothes. The best idea is to come to bed dressed differently—or not dressed at all! Lie on your belly and close your eyes. Let all your worries and daily stresses evaporate as your spouse sits behind you and begins massaging your back.

Some couples employ lightly scented oil for massage, although you have to be careful about soiling the sheets. If you incorporate oil into your massage, have your spouse lie on a large beach towel to keep the offending product off the sheets.

The spouse performing the massage should start by making short, round circles on the back. Use your imagination to vary your hand position, type of stroke, and speed. Alternate between short, choppy strokes and long, smooth caresses. Glide those hands up and down the back, and then let those long strokes go to the buttocks and continue down the legs. Your fingers can make like a crab as you "walk" the fingers up and down the torso; keep the touch light and teasing. Don't massage the genital area just yet. When your hands return to the shoulder area, be sure to massage the neck; many people vastly enjoy their hair and scalp being rubbed. The ears are surprisingly delicate.

As you're lying there, concentrate on what the hands are doing, and don't be bashful about asking for a kink in your back to be rubbed down or for certain shoulder muscles to be worked. Your spouse can knead your muscles like dough, but he or she shouldn't be too vigorous. This is the time to feel treated like a king or queen. Besides, people pay $50 an hour for a good back rub these days.

Skin is certainly an erogenous zone, which is why most massages pave the way to a wonderful sexual encounter. After a while, allow the hands to playfully massage the buttocks, with occasional caresses of the genital area. After your spouse turns over, you can massage the front of the torso.

Women, if you are using oil (corn oil or safflower oil from the kitchen cabinet will do), now is the time to apply it to his penis. The oil will help him become erect as your hands slide up and down without irritating his manhood. Neither of you should worry if his erection goes away during foreplay lapses of manual stimulation. Just resume using your hands until he becomes hard again.

INTERCOURSE

I've mentioned that the most common way to have intercourse is the man lying on top of the woman—the missionary position. Few couples ever try anything else, which I don't have a problem with, but several of the other positions described in the previous chapter could be tried out prior to orgasm, which is accomplished when couples return to the missionary position. If you are physically up to it, put a little adventure into your lovemaking.

"With any relationship, the sexual relationship is something we have to work at," say authors Robert G. Wells, M.D., and his wife Mary C. Wells, in their book *Menopause and Midlife*.

Wise couples will not allow their sexual intercourse to become humdrum, conventional, and void of creativity. So when either husband or wife wishes to try something sexually different, then he or she should just say so. It's that simple. In the marriage bed, creativity should reign unless it causes pain, embarrassment, or disrespect.

Sometimes a different type of pain and embarrassment becomes part of the marriage bed. We'll discuss "erectile dysfunction" in the next chapter.

Chapter Seven

WHEN YOU'RE DEALING WITH ED

I could usually see the look in their eyes whenever they came in to take a seat in my counselor's office.

With eyes searching the room, the muffled voice says, "Dr. LaHaye, I have this problem."

I usually hear a clearing of the throat at this junction, another telltale sign of nervousness.

I nod, making sure my nonverbal language states that I am not in any rush.

"You see, Dr. LaHaye, Cindy and I were making love last week, and when it came time for me to, ah, do it, there was nothing there."

"Nothing?"

"Nothing. I couldn't make myself erect."

"Is there anything unusual happening in your life?"

"My new start-up company is having troubles. Maybe I shouldn't say troubles, but I worry if we're going to run out of money before we can get it off the ground. Then I was on a red-eye flight the night before, and the plane was full, so I didn't get any sleep."

"Anything else?"

"No, not that I can think of, but what happened last week has been bugging me. I haven't tried to make love to her for fear that I couldn't do it. Do I have a problem?"

Erection Problems

My friend sure did. Men have difficulty uttering the word "impotence" because we all tend to view ourselves as virile and effective as the day we got married. But all it takes is one wrong episode under the bed sheets, one "failure" to consummate sexual intercourse, and we begin casting self-doubt on our ability to sexually perform. Once erection problems surface, men deem themselves inadequate, and their love lives head rapidly toward the trash heap.

I have counseled too many men over the years not to realize that an evening of impotency is the stuff of nightmares. Middle-age males fear that it's *hasta la vista* to good-time Saturday nights and weekend getaways. Male pride is punctured as well; feelings of self-worth, self-esteem, and sexual prowess are wrapped together in how men feel about themselves sexually. Whereas we could tell our best friends about hypertension or even hemorrhoids, we could never tell them about our inability to make love.

Many, many men will not discuss impotence with their wives either, nor would they disclose their malady to their family doctors. They are afraid that a series of probing questions could unearth some unseen "psychological problem" or result in a doctor's knee-jerk diagnosis that "it's all in your head."

New research has completely disproved this theory. Most impotency stems from physical problems or a failure to understand that as men age, it just takes *longer* to become erect. All it takes is one bad incident in bed—a tired, distracted husband going through the motions—and suddenly there is a "problem."

Emotional problems can render men unable to sexually perform as well. Overtired husbands, teetering with tension from the workplace, contesting an illness, or abusing alcohol, will have problems in bed. Sometimes even *worrying* that he could become impotent is enough to make his penis flaccid.

Then there are those who flat-out lose their sexual desire, either by being turned-off to their spouse or by taking up golf (sorry, bad joke). Seriously, the forties are a difficult time for many marriages. This is peak career season for most men, the final surge for the brass ring. This is also the peak season for the demands of children, many of whom morphed from angelic grade-schoolers to fire-breathing adolescents, seemingly overnight. With fires burning hot on the home and work front, some men wake up in the middle of the night saying, "I'm sick of this pressure and postponing gratification. I'm going to do something about it while I still can."

This is a description of the classic midlife crisis. Some deal with it by purchasing a two-door, shadow blue Mazda Miata and a three-month supply of Rogaine; others go overboard and jettison their marriage and career, thinking a new honey and work surroundings will be the meal ticket to happiness. Most of us, however, soldier on with a nagging suspicion that something is not right.

Men, if impotence or the fear of not being able to sexually perform or any other reason is keeping you from making love, then consider what your wife may be thinking: *He no longer loves me. He doesn't find me attractive anymore. I'm no longer desirable.* Before too long, she is in the lowest frame of mind imaginable, and those thoughts become a self-fulfilling prophecy.

GOBS OF TESTOSTERONE

Many men are unaware that their bodies and reproductive organs are undergoing subtle but unmistakable changes in their forties, fifties, and sixties. The reason is related to lessening amounts of testosterone, the male hormone largely responsible for sexual desire. When gobs of testosterone were flowing through your teenage veins, you could get an erection by the sight of a pretty cheerleader bending over and displaying her décolletage. When you married in your early twenties, you probably couldn't get enough sex in the first few years of marriage; you were always raring to go.

As age and declining hormones set in, gradual changes occurred that may have caught you off guard. If truth be known, potency until the day you die is a fantasy. At the age of fifty, 10 percent of the American male population are already impotent; at sixty, that number climbs to nearly 20 percent. Thirty percent of males seventy and older cannot become erect, which escalates to 75 percent by age eighty. From my reading, the most-quoted figure is that impotence affects some 30 million American men, but only 10 percent seek medical help, further underscoring the shame felt by males.[1]

Erectile trouble is not something to be discounted by spouses. Consider this view by Dr. Bernie Zilbergeld:

> While any problem in the critical area of sex is very upsetting to a man, nothing generates as much concern, anxiety, shame, and even terror as an inability to get or maintain erections. Only the loss of his job can make a man feel less of a man. The primary meaning of impotence, the term traditionally applied to erection difficulties, is a lack of power, strength, vigor, the negation of all that we consider masculine. Men have been taught to tie their self-respect to the upward mobility of their penises and, when their penises no longer rise to the occasion, they no longer feel like men.
>
> Women are often baffled by the agony a man goes through when he fails to get or keep an erection, but they have no parallel experience with which to compare it. A woman can participate in intercourse or any other sexual act without being aroused or even interested. A man is in a more

---

SNAPSHOT FROM THE
"ACT OF MARRIAGE AFTER 40 SURVEY"

49. Have you experienced impotency?
- Yes, frequently: 16 percent
- A few times: 28 percent
- No: 56 percent

difficult situation. Because of the incorrect belief that sex demands a rigid penis, his "failure" is obvious, dangling in full view. There is no way to fake an erection and, though not impossible, it is difficult to have intercourse without at least a partial erection. So he feels that he cannot have sex; and in his eyes, a man who can't have sex is not really a man.[2]

The psychological effects of impotence are devastating. Men are afraid to kiss their wives because kissing could lead to sex, and they know sex can't happen. I've known many men who think they have no hope. My reply is that hope springs eternal because help is available on several medical and psychological fronts. If that fails, there's always a blue pill called Viagra.

POSTER BOY

I always thought Kotex tampon advertisements on prime-time television were inappropriate until I saw Bob Dole's earnest face look straight into the camera and say, "It may take a little courage to ask your doctor about 'ED,' or erectile dysfunction, but everything worthwhile does." I can't wait for one of my younger grandchildren to ask, "Grandpa, what's ED?"

Dole's image campaign for Pfizer, a pharmaceutical company, has been buttressed by Viagra commercials (often aired during PGA golf tournaments) showing middle-aged couples slow-dancing cheek-to-cheek in the glowing twilight. *Getting that love back.*

In case you haven't noticed, "erectile dysfunction" is the new, improved, politically correct word for impotence that we'll be hearing in the third millennium, so ED it will be. Courageously, Mr. Dole, the former U.S. senator from Kansas, has become one of the first nationally known figures to discuss ED openly. After submitting to prostate cancer in 1991, one of the excitatory nerves that go from the penis up to the brain—signaling that now would be a good time for an erection—was apparently snipped and rendered Dole impotent. Since losing the U.S. presidential election in 1996, Mr. Dole has become the poster boy for erectile dysfunction in print and TV ads for Pfizer, the pharmaceutical company that produces Viagra. When word got out that Bob was taking Viagra, the azure-blue pill that causes erections, stand-up comedians had a heyday. *Tonight Show* host Jay Leno ribbed, "No wonder his wife, Libby, is always traveling."

We can all laugh, but for those experiencing erectile dysfunction and impotency, the chuckles are fairly muted. Before we discuss what can be done, however, men and women need to be aware of the erection physiology.

Contrary to what some women may think, male sexual arousal doesn't begin in the groin but rather in the brain. For any huge number of reasons (the sight of her naked body, the thought of making love with her), the brain sends a signal to release nitric oxide in the penis. Nitric oxide activates an enzyme that produces cyclic guanosine monophosphate, a chemical that causes the penile arteries to dilate and the muscles that control the spongy chamber in the penis, the corpus cavernosum, to relax and fill with blood. As the penis becomes engorged with blood, it hardens and compresses the veins that drain blood from the penis, preventing outflow. The more blood and the less outflow, the larger and harder the erection. Erectile dysfunction occurs when blood flows out of the penis as fast it flows in.[3]

It was once believed that ED was all in your head or just an inevitable result of getting older. Actually the majority of ED can be explained by physical conditions or events, some of which are age-related. The most common risk factors for ED include:

- Diabetes, high blood pressure, hardening of the arteries, or high cholesterol
- Injury or illness, such as spinal cord injury, multiple sclerosis, depression, stroke, or surgery of the prostate or colon
- Medications that may bring about ED as an unwanted side effect
- Cigarette smoking or alcohol and drug abuse
- Psychological conditions, such as anxiety and stress

Physically caused impotence is more widespread and can be easier to treat. Urologists believe that physical factors underlie perhaps 90 percent of cases of persistent impotence in men over age fifty. Because erection is primarily a vascular event, we shouldn't be surprised that the most common physical causes of impotence are conditions that block the blood flow to the penis, such as atherosclerosis or diabetes.

Certain prescription drugs can interfere with the necessary nerve signals. Among the culprits are a variety of sedatives, diuretics, antihistamines, and drugs that combat high blood pressure, cancer, or depression. Heart medications such as Lopressor, Inderal, Norpace, Congentin, and Artane have been known to suppress erections or reduce libido. Antidepressants (Elavil), muscle relaxants (Norflex), Tagament (for ulcers), and Prozac exhibit the same side effects. If that wasn't all, alcohol, tobacco, and illegal drugs such as marijuana also directly contribute to impotence.[4]

Smoking tobacco is perhaps the most overlooked. I realize that Christians smoke in fewer numbers than the general population: in our survey, 6 percent of the male respondents said they smoke. For any smokers reading this book, new studies are showing that puffing cigarettes can be a drag on your sex life. A 60 Minutes report on CBS television said a host of researchers and studies have found that male smokers have about twice as much chance to become impotent as nonsmokers. Dr. Randolph Smoak, the aptly named chairman of the American Medical Association, stated unequivocally, "Smoking does and can cause impotence." Dr. Smoak's statement rings true. Since smoking has long been linked to coronary artery blockage, it stands to reason that the arteries in the penis are damaged by smoking as well.

The reason why smoking is hazardous to your erection (now that's a new warning label that would get read!) is that toxins in cigarette smoke damage blood vessels, reducing arterial blood flow. Just as smoking men are more at risk for heart attacks and circulatory problems with their legs, damaged arteries restrict blood flow to the penis. Women smokers are also playing with fire when they light up: dysfunction can occur in the female genitalia because of restricted blood flow.

SEVEN STEPS TO TAKE

As you age, this is not a time to take your ability to have an erection for granted. If you're looking for one more reason to keep your body in good shape, then keep your manhood in tip-top condition by following these seven steps to preventing impotence by author Joel D. Block.

1. Eat a low-fat diet and exercise regularly. Remember, a strong heart increases blood flow and circulation, and much of what causes an erection happens through blood flow. Got a pot belly? Is your idea of working out getting off the couch to see what's in the fridge? Time for a lifestyle change; I'm talking about starting up an exercise program at a nearby fitness center and eating less junk food.

2. If you smoke, stop. The image that cigarette advertising has been selling us for generations—light up a smoke, be cool, and let the babes come on to you—is a cruel joke. Smoking causes much of the vascular damage in the penis that results in impotence.

3. Expand your definition of "sex." If you haven't learned that there is more to making love than intercourse, now's a great time to change your view on lovemaking. Dr. Block counsels that a man is more likely to have erectile difficulties if his lovemaking style is intercourse driven. Why? Because the pressure to perform will be greater for him than a man who enjoys satisfying his wife in a variety of ways.

4. Have frequent sexual contact with your spouse. Like the body's muscles, the veins inside the penis become less supple with age. Simply stated, the more you make love the longer you will be able to make love. Put this under the category of "use it or lose it." Men who go without an erection for months at a time could very well lose that ability for the rest of their lives.

5. Don't make ejaculation a goal of lovemaking. Men who don't focus on ejaculating inside the vagina say they have more frequent erections, can sustain them longer, and have more fun. Sounds good to me.

6. *Share information with your spouse.* It doesn't do either spouse any good to shy away from discussing the way your bodies are changing in the midlife years. If you're having problems staying erect, let her know that you need her help.

7. *Don't take medications you don't need.* Some medicines, such as ones for high blood pressure, have nasty side effects, such as not being able to become erect and stay erect. Be sure to ask your doctor what the side effects are when you receive your next prescription.[5]

ASKING QUESTIONS

If you have an ongoing or chronic failure to get or sustain an erection, you need to take an assessment. For openers, ask yourself: *Did I wake up with an erection in the last week?* The way you answer this question profoundly influences whether your ED is psychological or physical. Tests conducted at the University of Chicago Sexual Dysfunction Clinic revealed that 86 percent of the men diagnosed with psychogenic impotence had morning erections, but 100 percent of men with erectile dysfunction for physical reasons did not have morning or nocturnal erections.

The next question to ask yourself is: *Are there any emotional upheavals in my life?* Some men report ED after being laid off, starting a new job, moving to a new city, losing a loved one, or retiring. Stress is a prime component of erectile dysfunction, and one failure can lead to another failure.

Another question is: *Am I losing a firm erection when I attempt intercourse?* A urologist may be able to point to exhaustion as a reason, but a loss of firmness could be the first manifestation of a physical problem, often due to a poor diet, being out of shape, or heavy smoking and drinking. At the same time, a stiff penis suddenly going limp could be the harbinger of psychological problems.

The fact that you are even asking these questions means that you should consult a urologist. They say the road to the doctor's office is paved with good intentions, but picking up a telephone to make an appointment for an initial visit is an act you won't regret. In our

"Act of Marriage After 40 Survey," 15 percent said they had sought medical attention for erectile dysfunction. Before you see a urologist, however, you should be aware of the various treatment options for ED. They range from "tried-and-true" to "could-be-interesting" to "that's-invasive" to "I've-got-nothing-to-lose."

The medical community, under guidelines developed by the American Urological Association, recommend three options:

1. A vacuum pump device
2. Injections of drugs into the penis
3. Penile implants

Vacuum devices are often the treatment of first choice for men and work for approximately two-thirds of those suffering from ED. A vacuum chamber is placed over the unerect penis. A small pump removes air from the cylinder around the penis, increasing blood flow into the penile arteries. The blood is trapped by rolling a special rubber ring down to the base of the penis. The constriction ring shouldn't stay on longer than thirty minutes; longer durations can result in permanent tissue damage due to lack of blood circulation.

Although vacuum devices sound like they were discovered in a castle dungeon, for those who can no longer enjoy the warmth and closeness of the one they love due to ED, it may be a lifesaver. Pumps are safe and simple to operate and can be used as often as desired. The downside is that you need to interrupt your foreplay to slip the vacuum chamber over the penis and start pumping away. Husbands and wives used to spontaneous, unself-conscious sex find this can be intrusive and awkward. Couples who adopt a good attitude and incorporate the pump into their foreplay say it works for them.

Injecting drugs into the penis is another way to jump-start an erection. Although the thought of sticking a needle into your manhood sounds painful, doctors promise it's nothing more than pinching your earlobe. One-third of men who use injection therapy do experience mild to moderate pain, but that's more related to the medicine than the needle. The drug, alprostadil, rushes into the bloodstream and triggers the same reaction that occurs in a spontaneous erection.

Men find injection therapy less intrusive to lovemaking since they can inject themselves five to ten minutes before the commencement of sexual activity. Injection-induced erections last for a half hour or longer, and they come with practically a 100 percent guarantee that they'll work. In 1983, British impotency researcher Dr. Giles Brindley, standing before hundreds of his colleagues at a Las Vegas medical conference, dropped his trousers to reveal the dramatic maximizing effect of an injection that he had given himself.

Drug injection is not recommended more than two or three times a week, but since midlife couples don't usually make love that often, this should not be a barrier. Figuring out *how* to inject yourself takes a little getting used to; proper technique must be employed. One interesting side effect is that one out of every hundred users of injection therapy face a bout of priapism—an erection that shows no sign of letting down. Priapism erections can often last for four hours or more, and such episodes require medical attention. I don't know about you, but showing up in a nearby emergency room at 11:00 P.M. with a fully erect penis, and then having to explain my malady ...

The other favored medical option is the use of implants. These days, two types of implants are commonly used. One is a bendable rod that gives the penis enough rigidity for sexual activity at night but is flexible enough to be tucked away in boxer shorts by day. You can say goodbye to wearing Speedo trunks at the beach, however.

The other penile implant is a cylinder that extends and stiffens the penis with fluid transferred from a reservoir tucked under the abdominal muscle. These implants must be surgically implanted by a urologist, which means more cost unless penile implants are covered by your health plan. Surgery means anesthesia, painful recovery time, and possible risk of infection.

Medical advancements are being made in this area as Baby Boomers confront impotency problems. Therapies on the horizon include erection-inducing creams or ointments rubbed onto the penis before sexual activity. An impotence cream called Topiglan is being tested—a little dab will do ya.

It's doubtful, however, that any new therapy will capture the public's attention like Viagra, which exploded into American consciousness in the spring of 1998 and became a cultural phenomenon. Viagra, a drug taken orally, boosts levels of artery-relaxing agents inside the penis. Instead of creating an erection, however, Viagra (and other erection-producing oral medications on the horizon) amplifies the reaction to sexual signals and allows many heretofore impotent men to resume sexual relations. Viagra doesn't create sexual desire or produce an erection on its own; men must become sexually aroused before Viagra will work. Let's have a closer look at this amazing drug.

THE VIAGRA SENSATION

How Viagra came into being was an accident. Pfizer originally developed the drug to treat high blood pressure and angina, but test studies didn't pan out. When men participating in the study refused to give back their samples, researchers suspected they were on to something else.

They were right. In just a few years, this diamond-shaped blue pill has been hailed as a miracle drug, a restorer of hope to the hopeless, a magic bullet, and the ultimate growth stock. Viagra, the erection-inducing pill, has become such a phenomenon that there are even Web sites devoted to Viagra jokes. Here are a few of my favorites:

- "Did you know that you can find Viagra in chocolate bars? You eat it and she says, 'Oh, Henry!'"
- "Viagra can be compared to Disneyland—a one-hour wait for a two-minute ride."
- "Did you hear about the first death from an overdose of Viagra? A man took twelve pills and his wife died."

Besides providing fodder for stand-up comedians, the biggest thing about Viagra is that it's brought millions of impotent men out of the woodwork and into urologists' offices seeking prescriptions—and a new lease on sexual life to people whose physical drives were slowing down. Viagra is easy to use (just swallow a pill an hour before you want to make love), and there's nothing to vacuum, inject, or apply. Around 50,000 of these pills are being taken *daily* at $10 a shot, except when a price war breaks out between Wal-Mart and K-Mart. Viagra comes in 25, 50, and 100 milligram tablets; most men find 50 milligrams do the trick.

Interestingly, all doses cost the same, so some price-conscious seniors have been requesting 100 milligram pills and cutting them in half. Dr. E. James Seidman, a urologist at Temple University School of Medicine, issued a caution regarding that practice. "Be careful about splitting pills," he said. "There is no way to make certain that the drug is equally concentrated throughout the pill."

An eighty-two-year-old retired garment worker who experienced erectile malfunctioning following prostate surgery, told writer Douglas Martin, "I think it's a revolution. The women should be very happy with Viagra because now men can be much more sexually active for a longer period of time." Now he'll be able to keep up with his eighty-seven-year-old wife, he said.

Viagra doesn't work for everyone, however; efficacy rates are said to be between 64 percent and 72 percent. In our survey, one-fourth of men called themselves "very happy" with Viagra, and 47 percent said they rated their satisfaction as "okay." My respondents are not pill-popping Viagra users: 2 percent said they use Viagra frequently; 7 percent "a few times," while 91 percent have not availed themselves of the drug.

When men seek a Viagra prescription, they are counseled not to bypass a rigorous physical exam, blood tests, and an extensive sexual history with a doctor. In others words, don't purchase Viagra over the Internet. An online "consultation" costs between $50 and $100, but who knows if a real doctor is reading your answers regarding your medical history. A *Consumer Reports* reporter ordered Viagra through a Web site and determined that the pills came from a Miami drugstore, having been prescribed by a doctor licensed to practice in Mexico but not in New York, where the reporter placed the order.

As with just about any potent drug, Viagra does have side effects, which are usually characterized as mild and temporary. The pill can cause blinding headaches, heartburn, upset stomachs, runny noses, diarrhea, urinary tract infections, and, because the eyes contain an enzyme similar to the one on which Viagra works in the penis, blurred vision with a green or blue effect, particularly when taking the 100 milligram size.

The nastiest side effect, however, is death, but that happens in rare cases where the men are taking medicines that contain nitrates. Anti-hypertension drugs, which contain nitroglycerin, lower blood pressure too much when mixed with a Viagra cocktail. New research is being released all the time, so be sure to consult your doctor on the safe and appropriate uses of the drug.

ON THE HORIZON

Very soon, if not by now, women will be able to take a pill that increases sexual desire—a female counterpart to Viagra. A global race is being waged by multinational pharmaceutical companies to develop a treatment that will prove as appealing to women as Viagra has been to men.

More than a dozen compounds are being cooked up in laboratories around the world, and at least half of them are being tested in trials. Researchers are trying to develop drugs that either increase the blood flow to the genitals or increase sexual desire.

The new drugs are often based on the male sex hormone testosterone, the so-called "fuel of love" that triggers desire in both sexes. Testosterone levels are lower in women and fall even lower after menopause. In the past, giving testosterone treatments to women has caused too many incidences of hirsutism, or beard growth, and heart problems. Presently, researchers are looking at ways to combine testosterone with the female hormone estrogen. One such combination drug, called Estratest, has shown promise in test studies with women reporting higher degrees of sexual desire.

In the meantime, doctors can prescribe Viagra for women, although the Food and Drug Administration has not yet approved the drug for women, nor has Pfizer, the drug's manufacturer. In principle, increased blood flow to the genitals is needed just as much in women as in men, which is why Pfizer estimates that several hundred thousand women have received Viagra prescriptions. Anecdotal evidence shows that Viagra has helped enhance vaginal lubrication and produce more arousal and orgasms.

So, as Russian-born comedian Yakov Smirnoff would say, "Do we live in a great country, or what?" Seriously, we have much to be thankful for regarding medical help with ED and sexual desire. Love-enhancing medical advances are something we should not take for granted, and we should be thankful that sex doesn't have to end as it did for generations of couples before us.

Chapter Eight

DON'T DELAY; GO TODAY

Every week for several years, Beverly drove to the local beauty salon to keep her appointment with a hairdresser named Marjorie. My wife can attest to the fact that Marjorie knew how to put a good hairdo together. She even cut my locks on occasion.

You spend a lot of time with your hairdresser, and Bev listened as Marjorie poured out her heart regarding a failed marriage and the absence of children in her life. When Marjorie became the god-mother of two girls, she spoiled them with presents and attention.

Perhaps you've noticed that I'm talking about Marjorie in past tense, and there's a reason for that. After telling Bev and me that she found a lump in her breast one day, eight times I urged Marjorie to see a doctor and ask for a mammogram. She never made the appointment. When I asked her why she failed to see a doctor, she offered a litany of excuses:

- "I don't have good insurance." *Snip, snip.*
- "I don't know who to see." *Snip, snip.*
- "I'm sure it's nothing." *Snip, snip.*

It *wasn't* "nothing." The cancerous cells swirling in her breasts and lungs turned out to be ruthless killers. Marjorie died of breast cancer in 1999; she was only forty-four years old. Death cheated her out of many years and cost Bev and me a budding friendship. The most tragic thing about her situation is that Marjorie didn't have to die. A mammogram or breast exam could have saved her life because early detection measures are among the reasons why breast cancer deaths dipped 5 percent in the 1990s even though the incidence of breast cancer has been increasing 1 percent per year since 1940.[1] Some states have agencies that subsidize mammogram costs. Call the American Cancer Society at (800) 227-2345 to find one near you.

Beverly has submitted herself to annual mammograms for the better part of twenty years, based on her doctor's recommendation. She has received a clean bill of health every year, except for one occasion when a mammogram revealed a small shadow inside one breast. A biopsy proved there was nothing there, but if a malignant tumor had been growing inside her, doctors would have gotten it early. Bev has several good friends who are alive today because of early detection.

Breast cancer is an important topic for *The Act of Marriage After 40* because it is the leading cause of cancer death among women aged forty to fifty-five. For those who survive breast cancer via a mastectomy, the loss of one or both breasts seriously impacts the sexual relationship (I'll have more to say about that later). Early detection *saves* lives.

The National Cancer Institute does not call breast cancer an epidemic, but the illness is common enough that almost every woman has a family member or close friend who has succumbed to breast cancer or is presently fighting the disease. The American Cancer Society estimates that 180,000 women will receive a positive breast cancer diagnosis in the next year; approximately 44,000 women will lose their valiant struggle to remain alive. Those sterile numbers don't reflect the devastation and terrible pain that breast cancer inflicts on families and marriages. I do not begrudge the fact that breast cancer has become a *cause célèbre*, with its pink ribbons and 10k walkathons and special forty-cent "Fund the Cure" U.S. Postal stamps. This is a terrible disease that strikes women—and their families—in their prime.

ALWAYS WORTH A LOOK

Breasts symbolize many things to women: femininity, beauty, attractiveness, nuturance, motherhood, and yes, sexuality. Our culture has exalted women's breasts in an erotic way for decades, so it's no surprise that guys notice a woman's comely figure long before they notice the color of her eyes. Let's not kid ourselves: *both* men and women understand the alluring power of breasts and the way they shape sexuality—and have for thousands of years. King Solomon waxed poetic in the Song of Songs when he described a simple Jewish maiden that he had taken as his wife in these ravishing terms:

> *Your graceful legs are like jewels,*
> *the work of a craftsman's hands.*
> *Your navel is a rounded goblet*
> *that never lacks blended wine.*
> *Your waist is a mound of wheat*
> *encircled by lilies.*
> *Your breasts are like two fawns,*
> *twins of a gazelle.*
>
> *Song of Songs 7:1–3*

At the close of Song of Songs, the young woman knows what she's got. "I am a wall," she says, referring to her stand against sexual temptation, "and my breasts are like towers."

I guess I can see why she attracted King Solomon!

That's one reason why the loss or alteration of a breast through a mastectomy or lumpectomy (the common surgical techniques to fight breast cancer) affects every married couple. The meaning that a woman attributes to her breasts is reflected in her self-esteem and her self-image as a sexual person. The development of breast cancer creates anxiety, depression, and feelings of helplessness as she and her husband implore God for help and a measure of His strength to cope.

The scary thing about breast cancer, beyond the sobering knowledge that one in eight American women will develop the disease during their lifetime, is that the risk for breast cancer increases as women get older. Breast cancer rates spike following menopause; approximately 80 percent of breast cancers occur in women age fifty and older. In addition, white women have a higher risk of developing breast cancer than African-American, Hispanic-American, and Asian-American women. The reasons why are unknown.

If you breastfed your children, your breast cancer risk goes down even further. Helen Smallbone, mother of the sensational Christian singer Rebecca St. James, is an Australian mom of seven who breastfed each child for a year or more. "Australians are very encouraged to breastfeed because our society supports that, not like in the States, where women receive little support to breastfeed their babies," said Helen. "In Australia, the government opens storefront offices where mothers of infants can drop by to talk with 'clinic sisters' about anything: feedings, growth rates, colicky babies, diaper rash, and breastfeeding. We were always told that breastfeeding would reduce the chance of contracting breast cancer, and Australia has one of the lowest breast cancer rates in the world," said Helen.

Research on the link between breastfeeding and breast cancer bears Helen out. An important study by P. A. Newcomb found that mothers who breastfed their children reduced their chances of breast cancer by 11 percent to 24 percent, depending upon how long they breastfed their children.[2]

Researcher Katherine Dettwyler of Texas A&M University was curious whether women who had *been* breastfed also showed a lower risk of developing cancer. The answer is "yes" by 25 percent, prompting this comment from Dr. Dettwyler:

> It is interesting to look at the steady rise in the incidence of breast cancer over the last few decades in light of this new information. Let me use my own mother as an example. She

was born in 1920, when almost all babies were still breastfed for several years, and her mother breastfed her. Thus she got the first type of protection. By the time she started having children in the late 1940s and up to the mid-1950s, many women were not breastfeeding their children any more, although my mother did. That means that there was an entire cohort of women who had been breastfed as infants, but did not breastfeed their own children. Thus they got the first type of protection, but not the second. As they aged, they were at greater risk for breast cancer than their mothers and grandmothers had been. Then you come to my generation, most of whom were born in the 1950s and 1960s and were not breastfed as children, so they missed out on the first type of protection. Then when they started to have kids in the 1970s and 1980s, many still did not breastfeed their own children, thus missing out on the second type of protection. As this cohort ages, those who were neither breastfed nor breastfed their own children are at even greater risk than their mothers had been. Could it be that the steady erosion of these two sources of protection account for the steady rise in breast cancer incidence in the United States over the past four decades?

Now breast cancer strikes about one in eight women over the course of their lifetimes. If one could reduce the chances to one in sixteen, that would be worth doing, I would think. These studies do not promise anyone that they won't get breast cancer if they were breastfed and breastfeed their own children; they merely lower the risk by half. Chances are good that you won't get breast cancer no matter what you do, as seven out of eight women don't. You can play the odds, or you can change the way you live to reduce your risk.[3]

Were you breastfed as an infant? Did you breastfeed your children? Those are good questions to ponder.

TUMORS TRAVEL RAPIDLY

A woman's breasts, designed by God for a purpose, are glands that produce milk after a woman gives birth. The breast itself is made up of milk-secreting glands, ducts, and fatty connective tissues. While doctors have not yet discovered the cause of breast cancer, they do know that cancer cells form a lump or mass in the breast, prompting a tumor to grow. A tumor can either be benign or malignant: benign tumors are not cancerous or life-threatening, nor do they spread like cancerous tumors. A malignant tumor in the breast, however, can travel fairly rapidly to others parts of the body. This spreading process is called metastasis. Interestingly, most kinds of cancer are named after the part of the body where the cancer first begins. Breast cancer begins in the breast tissue, but if it spreads to the lungs, doctors still refer to the disease as "breast cancer."

Doctors believe certain risk factors are linked to breast cancer. A risk factor is something that increases a person's chance of getting a disease. Some risk factors, such as smoking, can be controlled. Others, like a person's age or family history, can't be changed. Since all women are at risk for breast cancer, study the factors listed below so you can understand more about this destructive disease.

RISK FACTORS THAT CANNOT BE CONTROLLED

- *Age.* The chance of getting breast cancer goes up as a woman gets older.
- *Having had breast cancer before.* If a woman has had breast cancer in one breast, she's more likely to be stricken in the other breast as well.
- *Family history.* A woman with close relatives who have had breast cancer is at greater risk. Her risk increases if a relative had breast cancer at an early age or if several of her relatives had the disease. Between 5 percent and 10 percent of breast cancers appear to be linked to changes in certain genes. Studies show that some breast cancer is linked to mutations or changes of the BRCA1 and BRCA2 genes. If a woman

has inherited a mutated gene from either parent, she is more likely to develop breast cancer. About 50 percent to 60 percent of women with these inherited mutations will develop breast cancer by the age of seventy. For them, genetic testing may be a good idea.

- *Undergoing menopause after the age of fifty.* Women who undergo the change of life later rather than sooner have a small increased chance, as do women who began having periods before twelve years of age. The risk is also slightly higher for women who gave birth for the first time after the age of thirty.

RISK FACTORS THAT CAN BE CONTROLLED

- *Weight.* Doctors believe there *may* be a link between being overweight and breast cancer, especially for women over fifty years of age. They stress, however, that the connection between weight and breast cancer risk is complex and could be affected by whether the woman gained weight as an adult or has been overweight since childhood. In addition, having large breasts does not mean a woman is more prone to developing malignant tumors. Women have large breasts mainly because they are overweight.
- *Taking estrogen replacement therapy.* Some studies suggest that long-term use (ten years or more) of estrogen replacement therapy, such as Tamoxifen, for relief of menopausal symptoms may slightly increase the risk of breast cancer. This risk applies to current and recent users. A woman's breast cancer risk returns to that of the general population five years after stopping ERT.
- *Drinking alcohol.* Studies suggest that the use of alcohol is linked to a higher risk of breast cancer.
- *What kinds of food are eaten.* Does a low-fat diet fight the breast cancer risk? Evidence suggests that breast cancer is less common in countries where the typical diet is low in fat. Yet many U.S. studies have not found breast cancer risk to be related to high-fat diets. More studies are needed to clarify this issue.

- *Exercise*. Some studies suggest that exercise may produce a protective effect against cancers, including breast cancer. This makes sense.
- *Smoking*. While a direct link between smoking and breast cancer has not been found, smoking affects overall health and increases the risk for many other cancers, as well as heart disease. All smokers should quit.[4]

EARLY DETECTION MEASURES

With the American Cancer Society sponsoring "Breast Cancer Awareness Month" every October, plus generous press coverage for high-profile breast cancer patients over the years (former First Lady Betty Ford, actress Ann Jillian), nearly every woman over thirty years old has heard about the importance of early detection screening through mammograms, clinic breast exams, and breast self-exams.

• *Mammograms* are an X-ray of the breast produced by a special machine. The test is uncomfortable, but not unduly so I'm told, because the breast is squeezed between two plates while a few pictures are taken. Since mammograms are indispensable in early detection of breast cancer, a debate has sprung up among experts about what age women should begin having annual mammograms. Some lobby for the early forties; others say women can wait until they're fifty. The American Cancer Society, after calling together a special panel to study the issue, renewed its position that women need to start undergoing annual mammograms in their forties. The National Institutes of Health (NIH), however, reached a different conclusion, deciding that mammograms can be optional until age fifty.

My position is, Why wait? Studies indicate that mammograms can reduce breast cancer by nearly one-third, so why not start mammograms in the early forties, especially if you have a family history of cancer? Nearly all health insurance plans cover mammograms under preventive care, so why not have an annual mammogram for peace of mind? The amount of radiation you'll receive from mammography equipment is so low that it's been compared to the amount you'd receive walking down the sidewalk on a sunny afternoon. If a woman had an annual mammogram for fifty years, she would receive only ten rads of radiation compared to several thousand rads a woman receives for radiation treatment.

• *A professional examination.* A doctor, nurse, or other health professional conducts clinic breast exams in which he or she gently touches the breast and examines the area under the armpits for any abnormalities. A clinic breast exam should occur every few years.

• *The breast self-examination* can be done anytime. A woman stands before a mirror and holds one arm high while the other hand touches the breast in search of a lump or a hard knot. Other changes to look for are changes in the nipple, such as an in-drawn or dimpled look. Any difference in the pigmentation or texture of the breast, such as a reddish, pitted surface like the skin of an orange, is another potential breast cancer symptom.

A highly regarded breast self-exam developed by University of Florida researchers is called the MammaCare method. The woman should lie down on a bed, pull her knees up slightly and place her left hand palm up on her forehead. Then she uses her right hand to examine her left breast, first by lying on her right side, and then by lying flat on her back. The side-lying position allows a woman, especially one with large breasts, to perform an effective examination. Once lying on her back, the woman should feel for any lumps from her bra line to the middle of her breastbone.

When men are stroking her breasts during sexual foreplay, they should keep a tactile eye out for any differences in the way the breast feels. That's one more reason to continue making love throughout the midlife years!

IF A LUMP IS FOUND

Helen Tucker and her husband, Irvin, checked into their seaside hotel in Virginia Beach, Virginia, on New Year's Eve, eager to enjoy a long weekend together. Both in their fifties, the Tuckers looked forward to a time of refreshment before the start of the new year.

Before going out for dinner, the Tuckers turned on a college football game—the Sugar Bowl. Helen patted a couple of pillows, then propped herself up on the bed to relax with her husband. She swept her right arm through the air, and that's when she felt the lump on her breast. She definitely felt something hard that wasn't there before.

"Irvin," she said, interrupting the game. "I think I have a lump on my breast."

Her husband's face turned gray, and suddenly the stupid football game seemed very unimportant. He drew himself close to her. She guided his hand to her right breast, and his fingers confirmed Helen's initial assessment. The lump could not be denied.

Upon their return home in Raleigh, North Carolina, Helen underwent tests before submitting to mastectomy surgery that saved her life. Her story underscores the importance of seeing a doctor right away if you suspect a lump on your breast. Tests must be undertaken in due haste to discover if cancer is present.

A doctor will ask you for your medical history and perform a thorough physical exam before suggesting a diagnostic mammogram or breast ultrasound. These imaging tests can sometimes tell if a lump is benign, but the only sure approach is a biopsy of the breast. Cells from the breast are removed, usually by a thin needle, and studied in the lab. If the results return with the dreaded *malignant* diagnosis, you'll experience pain and confusion. You will be thrust into a new world as you study which treatment approach to take. The most common treatments for breast cancer are surgery, radiation therapy, hormone therapy, and chemotherapy.

Most women with breast cancer submit to the surgeon's scalpel: the purpose of surgery being the removal of as much of the cancer as possible. Surgery is often the first line of attack in a one-two punch that's combined with other treatments such as chemotherapy, hormone therapy, or radiation therapy. The following are common types of breast cancer surgery:

- *Lumpectomy.* This is the removal of only cancerous tissues and a rim of normal tissue. A lumpectomy is almost always followed by six to seven weeks of radiation therapy.
- *Partial mastectomy.* This is the removal of up to one-fourth or more of the breast. Radiation usually follows this surgery.
- *Simple or total mastectomy.* This is the removal of the entire breast.
- *Modified radical mastectomy.* This is the removal of the entire breast and lymph nodes under the arm.
- *Radical mastectomy.* This is the extensive removal of the entire breast, lymph nodes, and the chest wall muscles under the breast. Once the surgery of choice, radical mastectomies are rarely performed these days because modified radical mastectomy has proven to be just as effective with less disfigurement and fewer side effects.

The loss of a breast through surgery affects every woman and every sexual relationship. A loss of sensuality comes with the loss of a breast and nipple. A sizable proportion of women describe a mastectomy as a mutilating and disfiguring experience. Women feel no longer whole, no longer sexually attractive. Sex after breast cancer is one of the scariest issues for husbands and wives, and it may be months before they can face the scars together.

Everything's changed because she *looks* different. Gone are the accouterments of her body: her soft, smooth breast and glorious nipple has been replaced by an irreversible red scar line and a flat chest. She's still reeling from the painful mutilation following the surgical excision of a significant portion of her body. She no longer feels whole, no longer feels sexually alluring, no longer feels she can pleasure her loved one as before. She is dealing with wave after wave of psychological pain and perhaps even disappointment with the outcome of the surgery.

Approximately one-fourth of women with mastectomies say that the operation has negatively impacted their sexual relationships, including decreased frequency of intercourse, decreased sexual satisfaction, and more difficulty in achieving orgasm. But here's the good news: a majority of women seem to cope sexually with the stress of surgery and the loss of a breast, with more than 63 percent reporting *no change* in their sexual relationship and 12 percent actually describing increased sexual satisfaction—probably because she's happy to be alive.[5] Some couples find that the intimate bonds forged in battling breast cancer together can actually enhance the sexual relationship. One researcher said that men who "tune out" their partner's missing breast during lovemaking focus on the pleasure of the experience.[6]

No one is discounting the prominent role that the breasts play in sexual foreplay; many men signal their desire to make love by gently stroking the breasts. Since one (or both) of these objects of affection are no longer available, couples need to find other erogenous zones and alternative types of foreplay. Men must express their acceptance of her body and make mental and physical adjustments by reminding her that he's in love with *her*, not her former chest. This is your chance, men, to step up and to love your wife just as Jesus Christ loved the church (Eph. 5:25). This is where you may have to learn that sex is more than intercourse.

If she is reluctant to see herself in the nude or face the scars, that is perfectly fine, says the authors of *Living Beyond Breast Cancer*, Marisa C. Weiss and Ellen Weiss. "Fancy lingerie or night wear may be the immediate solution to avoiding that initial shock," they write. "If you want that protection, that camouflage, go for it. Indulge yourself. Plenty of women keep their clothes on in bed. Beneath clothing, a reconstructed breast or a good prosthesis feels very much like the real thing to your partner; it has the bounce, the weight, and the resilience of a natural breast."

Every couple is different when it comes to intimacy issues. It is perfectly normal to seek counseling following mastectomies. Some have found it helpful to join support groups, such as the American Cancer Society's "Reach to Recovery." Check them out since support groups may be more helpful than you might think. Women can also seek out same-sex support groups. "You draw comfort and encouragement from being with other women surviving breast cancer," said Dr. Weiss. "Women in these groups often share advice that extends to the bedrooms, ways to increase sexual pleasure that are specific for women who've had breast cancer."[7]

RECONSTRUCTION SURGERY

More and more women are opting for reconstructive surgery following a mastectomy, thanks to recent advances in reconstructive surgery. Almost any woman is eligible for breast reconstruction, regardless of her age, the type of surgery first performed, or the number of years since the surgery. What is most miraculous about breast reconstruction is that doctors are often able to perform reconstruction surgery at the same time as the mastectomy. In the early 1990s, about 10 percent of women who were eligible for reconstruction chose this option. Most recent assessments indicate that as many as 30 percent of eligible women opt for reconstruction.[8]

The reconstruction process often involves more than one surgery, but at least it's a start for women desiring to feel whole again. The goal of reconstruction is not to create a "wonder breast" that looks just like the other one during lovemaking, but to provide symmetry of the breasts when the woman is wearing a bra. Husbands will notice the difference between the reconstructed breast and the remaining breast when he sees his wife in the nude. When she's fully dressed, however, the breasts in the bra will hopefully be close enough in size and shape that she will feel good about herself in just about any type of clothing.

Doctors are able to perform wondrous things these days with implants, but the surgical process is still complicated and fraught with peril. For instance, doctors will often take skin grafts from the earlobes to make nipples and grafts from the thighs for breast skin, which are filled with implants.

Men should be aware that some wives will want to defer sexual relations until breast reconstruction is finished. That's fine. Again, this is your chance to serve her as you deal with the overwhelming issues of life and death.

CUTTING THE RISK

Have you ever heard of a drug called Tamoxifen? Based upon a breathtaking study released in 1998, the National Cancer Institute reported that high-risk women who took Tamoxifen decreased their risk of breast cancer by 45 percent.[9] Tamoxifen (and a similar drug called Taloxifene) works by diminishing the effect of estrogen, a hormone involved in the division and growth of cancerous cells. This is an interesting drug. Tamoxifen, on the one hand, is considered an "anti-estrogen" since it blocks the action of estrogen in breast tumors. In other parts of the body, however, the drug acts as a weak estrogen—in other words, as an estrogen replacement therapy for menopausal women. Tamoxifen prevents bone loss, impacts cholesterol levels in a positive way, and improves vaginal dryness. Although Tamoxifen does not make women menopausal, about 20 percent of women on the drug stop having periods.

At-risk women must weigh the potential side effects of using Tamoxifen, which are an increased risk of uterine cancer and blood clots traveling from the legs to lungs. One way of looking at this issue is by noting that most women with cancer of the uterus can be cured with a hysterectomy, whereas breast cancer is a tougher disease to fight. If you think you carry a high risk for breast cancer, discuss Tamoxifen with your ob-gyn or family doctor.

Another consideration is adding soy and soy supplements to your diet. Just as women in Asian cultures do not experience terrible difficulties with menopause, Far Eastern countries have breast cancer rates that are just one-tenth of levels seen in the United States. Out of 100,000 American women, thirty to forty are expected to die from breast cancer. In Thailand and Sri Lanka, that number is an astonishing two to five, respectively![10]

The reason is generally attributed to the generous amounts of soy found in Asian diets. Dr. Bob Arnot, author of *The Breast Cancer*

Prevention Diet, recommends a daily intake of sixty grams of soy found in tofu, tempeh, soy milk, soy flour, etc. To do so, however, may mean eating up to three pounds of these foods each day, says Dr. Arnot, who makes this statement:

> Which brings us to soy shakes. The easiest way to eat the large amount of soy necessary to protect you from breast cancer is a protein powder-based soy shake. Add a banana, water, ice, and some soy protein powder into a blender, then drink it like a milk shake. This is the easiest way to be certain you're getting exactly as much soy as you choose.[11]

Can soy shakes prevent breast cancer? We don't know for sure, but soy products can certainly help you live a healthier life. This I do know: if Marjorie were alive today, Bev would bring her a large jar of soy protein powder to her next hair appointment!

Chapter Nine

NO LAUGHING
MATTER

Whenever any male in my family—including in-laws—turns forty, they receive the same directive from me: "Time to start checking that prostate."

Most aren't ready for what happens next. The scene shifts to the doctor's examination room, where the doctor ominously slips on Safeskin gloves and announces, "Let's have a look at your prostate." (One San Diego physician, displaying poor humor in my mind, was famous for humming Andy Williams's "Moon River" at this point.) Then the commands ring out in succession:

"Turn around and unzip your pants.

"Drop your drawers.

"Bend over.

"Elbows on the table.

"Relax while I spread your cheeks wide."

A description of a gloved finger probing one's rectum is not one I wish to further detail in this book, but suffice it to say, the prostate exam is the male counterpoint to the discomforting "pelvic" that stirrupped women have been enduring since high school. So listen up, guys: you don't you have things too bad. A prostate exam, while unpleasant, is over in a minute.

The doctor's gloved finger is seeking information on the prostate's smoothness, tenderness, or any other abnormalities. While this type of exam sounds thorough, it can only tell the doctor so much. The doctor's digit touches only the back part of the prostate, but the finger can't reach other sections of the gland that could be harboring pockets of malignant growth. A PSA blood test, or prostate-specific antigen test, is commonly rendered at the time of a digital exam because it can detect up to 80 percent of cancers. Although doctors caution that a high reading does not necessarily mean cancer, a PSA test is a good backup to the rectal exam.

Your prostate wasn't always so big. At birth, it resembled a canned pea, but the prostate grew rapidly during puberty and throughout the twenties into a walnut-sized gland about one to one-and-a-half inches wide, weighing between fifteen and twenty grams. Middle age ushered in a second growth spurt due to increased levels of dihydrotestosterone (DHT). The root of DHT is testosterone, which you remember from your high school biology class as the hormone that builds muscles and gives us our sex drive. Unfortunately, increased levels of DHT are responsible for two things that are the bane of middle-age man: male-pattern baldness and prostate growth.

I have an enlarged prostate, and so do nearly all my friends. It's very common. Because an enlarged prostate is as predictable for men as menopause is for women, I want to devote a chapter to this amazing gland.

LIKE A DOUGHNUT

The prostate, located directly below the bladder and just in front of the inner wall to the rectum, has much to do with sexual function.

Made up of muscles, glands, and fibrous tissues, the prostate was designed by God with sex in mind. Among other tasks, this gland brings spermatozoa from the testes and produces fluids necessary for

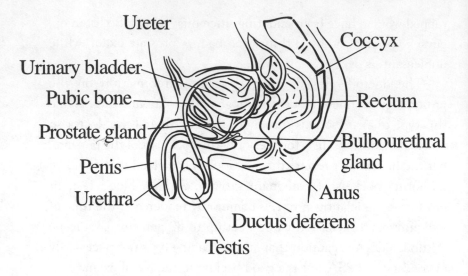

Ureter

Coccyx

Urinary bladder

Pubic bone

Rectum

Prostate gland

Bulbourethral gland

Penis

Urethra

Anus

Ductus deferens

Testis

ejaculation—semen. Prostate fluid is thin and gives ejaculate its characteristic smell. When the male reaches orgasm, the prostate flushes these fluids into the urethra (the tube going from the bladder to the penis), where these fluids are carried out of the penis by spasmodic contractions of the muscles surrounding the urethra. Around 200 million spermatozoa are released into the vagina during an average ejaculation. Only one will make a baby if it reaches a woman's egg.

The urethra passes through the middle of the prostate, much like a tube through the hole of a doughnut. When accelerated prostate growth closes that hole, the urethra is choked off. The result? Interference with normal urinary and sexual functions.

Most men, used to shooting a steady stream into the toilet, find themselves standing closer and closer to the bowl, waiting for the flow to start. When voiding finally presents itself a minute later, the stream force is less than impressive. Another manifestation of looming prostate trouble is nocturia, or the need to roust oneself out of bed one, two, three times a night to urinate.

The aforementioned are symptoms of BPH, or Benign Prostatic Hyperplasia, and they bear watching because left untreated, an enlarged prostate could pinch off all urine flow, resulting in severe sickness or death in rare cases. In a vast majority of men, however, BPH is not life threatening, but it certainly reduces your quality of life.

You're a candidate for BPH if:

- You try to go to the bathroom, but it's several long seconds between "okay, you can pee now" and the start of the urinary stream.
- You notice a definite slowing or decreased strength in your urinary stream.
- You continue to "dribble" after voiding.
- You feel like you could still pee although you're finished.
- You have to go to the bathroom frequently. I've already mentioned nocturia—getting up several times a night—but I'm also referring to several visits an hour during the work day.
- Pain and discomfort brought on by urinary retention, which occurs when you're not able to void.

These symptoms must be discussed with your physician or urologist. Don't be bashful! BPH is not dangerous in 80 percent of the cases, but it can be malignant in 20 percent. By malignancy, we're talking about cancer. Prostate cancer is the second most common cancer diagnosed in men; skin cancer is number one. Prostate cancer is the second most common cause of cancer death in men; lung cancer is number one.

But for now, I want you to know that BPH bothers half of all men by the time they turn sixty. From sixty on up, it's a straight line all the way to your ninety-ninth birthday, where statistics tell us that just about 100 percent of men will develop BPH by their hundredth birthday. In case you're wondering, BPH is *not* caused by having too little—or too much—sex; nor does a man's sexual life have any bearing on the development of prostate cancer. The prostate happens to be a very busy organ, dividing cells frequently. When cells divide, there's a chance that something could go wrong—a mutation. When mutations occur, this starts a process that turns normal cells into cancerous ones.

"Experts believe that cells must be exposed to at least five muta-tions—a process that deregulates normal cell growth—to trigger full-blown cancer," said Rick Chillot in a *Prevention* magazine article.

Unfortunately, the older you get, the greater the odds that you've taken your five "hits." The average age at diagnosis is seventy-two, but the disease is unusual in anyone under fifty. You're at increased risk if you have a father or brother who's had the disease—perhaps because you've inherited one or two mutations already. You're also at an increased risk if you are an African-American, though no one knows exactly why. Scientists are currently looking for a nutritional clue.[1]

Prostate cancer has been called the male counterpart to women's breast cancer. Some grim facts from the American Cancer Society:

- In 1998, 184,500 new cases of prostate cancer were diagnosed.
- In 1998, 39,200 died from prostate cancer.
- Cancer of the prostate is second only to lung cancer as the leading cause of cancer deaths in American men.
- The older you are, the greater chance you have of develop-ing prostate cancer.[2]

The average Joe on the street isn't aware that nearly as many men die of prostate cancer each year as women who succumb to breast cancer. Some men have heard that former senator Bob Dole underwent prostate cancer surgery, but did you know that General Norman Schwarzkopf, New York Yankee manager Joe Torre, former junk-bond king Michael Milken, golfer Arnold Palmer, and singer Harry Belafonte have submitted to the same surgery as well?

The public issues a collective shrug regarding this male scourge because men have been extremely reluctant to talk about it—or pay attention to the health of their prostate. The American Cancer Society recommends that men, when they reach fifty, should submit annually to rectal exams and PSA blood tests. I have been following this advice for years to closely watch my PSA count. I've managed to stay under the 4 range, which is good. Those with numbers between 4 and 5 are counseled to have a PSA test four times a year. If your PSA test comes back with a number 5 or above, it could be a sign of prostate cancer. In case you're wondering, having sex does not increase the PSA level, nor can your wife catch cancer by having sex with you.

Because the success rate of beating prostate cancer is excellent when caught early, I think you should have your first rectal exam and PSA test at age forty, and if everything is normal, then every couple of years. If your family physician is not able to perform the digital exam, then consult a urologist. These specialists conduct dozens each week (or month), so their sensitive fingers should detect any lumps or nodes on the prostate. A urologist may ask you to take a "peak flow" test in which he takes out a stop watch and times how long it takes you to fill a beaker with urine.

Doctors have other methods at their disposal. Ultrasound testing, also known as sonography, is exactly what women go through during their pregnancies. The procedure is painless: the technician slaps a little gel on your lower abdomen, then passes the transducer back and forth. The wand-type instrument transmits sound waves that can be viewed on a monitor. Your bladder must be near the bursting point when taking this test because doctors want a snapshot of a "before and after." After the initial pass, the medical technicians will ask you to urinate, and then they will pass the transducer over the pelvic area a second time. If urine remains in the bladder, that's a sure sign that an enlarged prostate is pinching the urethra.

Sometimes the doctor will conduct a more thorough use of the ultrasound system, but this method is not so user-friendly. A transrectal probe begins when the urologist covers the probe with a rubber device, fills it with water, then inserts it into the rectum. This creates a more complete ultrasonic image of the prostate and bladder area.

If your insurance company will spring for it, I would choose a non-invasive MRI (magnetic resonance imaging). Some people get claustrophobic being rolled into an MRI canister, but I would take an MRI any day over a transrectal probe. Radio waves in a magnetic field produce a three-dimensional cross section of the prostate and are convincing evidence of whether cancer is present in the prostate.

What are your "management options" if tests confirm that you have prostate cancer?

1. *Remove the prostate.* A prostatectomy is your best chance for a long-term cure and is recommended for patients less than seventy years of age whose tumors are confined to the prostate gland. Downside: a shocking 59 percent chance of impotence, according to a study released in 2000 by the *Journal of the American Medical Association*. Although surgical techniques that do not disturb the nerve bundles on either side of the prostate are bind perfected, the fact remains that the prostate lies in a relatively inaccessible place under the pubic bone. These nerves control a man's ability to have an erection and intercourse, and unless they survive the prodecure intact, potency is a thing of the past.

2. *Radiotherapy.* Radiation carries no surgical risks or chance of urinary incontinence, and is recommended for patients seventy years and older. Downside: potentially higher cancer recurrence rate.

3. *Watch the prostate carefully through regular checkups.* This option is for elderly patients with other significant health issues whose prostate cancer may never develop into a life-threatening issue. If cancer progresses, follow your doctor's advice.

BPH TREATMENT PLANS

Let's say you dodge the cancer bullet and are diagnosed with benign prostatic hyperplasia (BPH). Your doctor usually offers two choices for treatment: prescription drugs or surgery. I believe there is a third, which I will get to later.

Proscar, known generically as finasteride, is the prescribed drug of choice for many doctors. The drug succeeds in reducing BPH symptoms in about half of the men who try it. Cost is $700 a year. But Proscar and other drugs such as Leuprolide (lupron) and Flutamide (eulixin) have been known to cause unpleasant side effects. Since these drugs generally block the production of testosterone, the result is a chemical castration. The male sex drive drops off the chart, rendering him impotent. That is a tough side effect, rejected by many men.

Relaxation drugs such as Minipress (prazosin hydrochloride) purportedly relax the smooth muscles around the prostate, the idea being that this will ease the pressure on the urethra. Since BPH has highly subjective symptoms (what bothers one person goes unnoticed by another), it's difficult to demonstrate the efficacy of these drugs. But from my reading, the potential side effects raise too many questions in my mind. Besides decreasing libido and causing problems such as erectile dysfunction, prescription drugs can make prostate cancer harder to detect because they render PSA counts unreliable.

Surgery isn't an attractive option, either. No one wants to get cut *down there*. When surgery is called for, however, the traditional surgical option is a procedure called transurethral resection of the prostate, or TURP. The good news is that there are no incisions, but cutting is done beneath the surface.

Here's how the operation works: The doctor begins with a surgical instrument that he inserts into the penis through the urethra. Yes, this is done under anesthesia. The instrument is a nonflexible hollow tube. Once in place, the urologist inserts a resectoscope, which is a fiber optics microlens system. The surgeon watches a monitor. When he detects abnormal prostate tissue growth, he depresses a foot pedal, which causes the surgical instrument to slice off the offending tissue. The tissue shavings are removed with a glycine wash and sent posthaste to a pathologist, who searches for cancer cells.

Sometimes the surgeon elects to remove all or nearly all of the prostate. Either way, when the surgeon is satisfied that he has done all the necessary cutting, he inserts a catheter, which stays with the patient for several days. Most TURP surgeries involve short hospital stays, but patients won't be playing pickup basketball games for a while. Nor can most people return to office work for several weeks. Sexual activity is verboten for six weeks to allow the canal through the prostate to heal.

TURP surgery is popular: at 400,000 times a year, it ranks behind cataract surgery in procedures covered by Medicare. Yet just because the prostate gets shaved down doesn't mean it stops growing. About 15 percent of all men with TURP surgery notice a return of symptoms within a year, and 20 percent must repeat the procedure within a decade.

TURP has some statistical dangers and side effects that must be pointed out:

• *Retrograde ejaculation*. You're probably wondering, *What's that?* TURP surgery cuts away the bladder neck closure to give the urethra more room for urine flow. Unfortunately, when the bladder neck is open, sperm and fluid—like rush-hour traffic—take the path of least resistance and are propelled into the bladder instead of out of the penis during orgasm.

The upshot, so to speak, is that while it *feels* like you are having an orgasm, nothing is leaving the penis. This may be just fine and dandy with you, especially if you and your wife are beyond the child-bearing years and don't want any more children anyway. For those in their middle-age years still trying to have kids, all hope is not lost. The ejaculate can be gathered up the next time you urinate, and doctors have ways of preserving the semen and using it for artificial insemination.

• *Impotency*. As with any surgery on the prostate, doctors always say that men have a 5 percent risk of impotency. Five percent never sounds like much, but try telling that to the unlucky few. To paint a word picture, a lead surgeon trying to get at the prostate can be compared to trying to find a golf ball at the bottom of a full clothes hamper. If the surgeon ever-so-slightly damages the nerve bundles on either side of the prostate, erections are history, although Viagra has been found to effectively treat erectile dysfunction *if* the operation left certain nerves intact.

Researchers, led by Dr. Craig Zippe of the Cleveland Clinic Foundation in Ohio, tested fifteen men who had nerve-sparing surgery, and 80 percent reported that they had erections sufficient for intercourse after taking one to three doses of Viagra. Those with prostate cancer who had their prostates and nerve endings completely removed (called a prostatectomy), however, did not respond to Viagra.

• *Incontinence*. Not being able to control your urine flow is a terrible side effect of prostate surgery. Incontinence happens to less than 4 percent of all TURP surgeries, usually due to surgical error. The doctor's electric knife strayed too close to the sphincter voluntary muscles that control urine flow. Considering how small a space the doctor works in, it's amazing these type of accidents don't happen more often.

About Those Myths

Now would be a good time to debunk some old wives tales about the prostate gland:

Myth 1. Prostate surgery always causes a man to become impotent. This is simply not true. In the past it was more true than it is today, but now there are newer techniques used in surgery that do not disturb the nerve bundles on either side of the prostate. These nerves control a man's ability to have an erection and intercourse. In cancer surgery, doctors have learned to remove the prostate without damaging the nerve bundles. However, some patients still suffer impotency—generally fixed at 5 percent.

Myth 2. An enlarged prostate, BPH, is a leading cause of prostate cancer. Absolutely not. The enlargement of the prostate is in no way connected to the development of prostatic cancer. The cause of the enlargement is not known, but the cause of the cancer is, and the two are not linked. This myth may have come about because during some surgeries for the relief of BPH, the prostate is found to be cancerous when it had not been diagnosed before. This actually can be one of the hidden benefits of surgery.

Myth 3. Prostate surgery automatically sterilizes you. In one-half to two-thirds of the patients who have prostatic surgery where some or all of the prostate is removed, the normal course of the semen and other fluids usually ejaculated is disrupted. As mentioned before, the fluid takes the course of least resistance and flows upward into the bladder instead of down the urethra and out the penis. To middle-age men, this is usually not important.

Myth 4. Prostate problems turn a man into a wimp. Baloney! There is no physical loss of manhood from prostatic problems. If you turn into a wimp, then you've got a problem in your head.

Myth 5. Prostate problems are embarrassing to talk about because they mean a man is having sex too often. A pure fantasy. Prostate problems are rarely caused by having too much sex (defined as having eight to ten ejaculations over a two-day period, thus overworking the prostate). You shouldn't be embarrassed about your prostate, and an understanding woman should realize that her attitude about prostate testing could save her husband's life.

Myth 6. Orgasm for the man after prostate surgery isn't very satisfying. Again, not true. Whether the ejaculatory fluids go back into the bladder or out the penis, the feeling is exactly the same. That's what men report after surgery.

Myth 7. Your sex life is history after BPH surgery. For at least 95 percent of men, their sex life will be the same after BPH surgery, so whatever your sex life was like *before* surgery, it's going to be the same *after* the procedure as well.

Myth 8. Incontinence is automatic after BPH surgery. Not automatic. With researchers saying that 4 percent of those undergoing BPH surgeries have trouble retaining their urine, those are twenty-five-to-one odds.

Myth 9. Instead of surgery, I can choose from lots of over-the-counter remedies to cure my prostate. Guess again. The FDA and U.S. Postal

Service have shut down dozens of mail-order houses who sold what is nothing more than tonics and potions.

Myth 10. As a gentleman, I should never mention my prostate in mixed company. Yeah, if women can talk nonchalantly about breast exams, we shouldn't be embarrassed discussing the results of our yearly prostate exams.[3]

ANOTHER PATH

I think there is a third option to prescription drugs and surgery, and that's the use of herbs. As you've seen elsewhere in this book, I'm a great believer in vitamins and herbal products, having used them myself for better than three decades. I should point out, however, that if you have health concerns, a visit to you doctor should always be your first line of defense. Herbal solutions are helpful in preventing certain kinds of problems and enhancing medical treatments, but they should never be self-administered for treatment of health problems. When using herbs, always check with your doctor to make sure that they are safe to take in combination with any other medications your might be using.

Whenever I'm talking about health issues with male friends or acquaintances and we start talking about the prostate, I recommend the intake of saw palmetto. This herbal extract is made from the berries of the saw palmetto (*Serenoa repens*) plant, a small palm tree native to the Eastern seaboard.

Saw palmetto works like Proscar, but carries none of the negative side effects mentioned earlier. Julian Whitaker, M.D., editor of the *Health & Healing* newsletter, had this to say about this remarkable natural herb:

> Saw palmetto has been studied in dozens of controlled clinical trials, virtually all of them carried out in Europe, where this herb has been used for decades. In a 1994 Belgian study, 305 men with mild to moderate symptoms of BPH were treated with 160 mg of saw palmetto twice a day for three months. After forty-five days, significant improvements were

noted in urinary flow rates, residual urinary volume, and prostate size. At the study's conclusion, further improvements were observed, and 88 percent of the patents and their physicians rated the treatment as successful.[4]

That's why I've been taking saw palmetto regularly for twenty years, and I thank the Lord that my prostate symptoms are under control. All my sons and sons-in-law are ingesting this herb, and Mike Yorkey, who helped me prepare this manuscript, started gulping saw palmetto after I recommended it to him.

Another herb, pygeum (*Pygeum africanum*) has performed well in studies undertaken in Germany, France, and Austria. More than 250 patients with BPH were divided into two groups and given either 100 mg of pygeum or a placebo. Two months later, two-thirds of the men taking pygeum said they urinated less at night and reported less urinary flow problems. Interestingly, 31 percent of the placebo group noted improvement as well.[5]

What I recommend to family members applies to you as well: sometime in your early forties, you should be taking saw palmetto or pygeum tablets at the usual daily doses of 160 mg and 40 to 50 mg, respectively. You want to get ahead of the curve, so to speak, and keep that prostate from growing and pinching that urethra. These herbs can be found in nutrition and health food stores.

You should consider taking two other vitamin supplements: vitamin E and selenium. Vitamin E researchers from the National Cancer Institute in Finland found that those who took vitamin E reduced their cancer risk by one-third.[6] Selenium, a mineral that is difficult to acquire in today's diets, have been touted as another prostate cancer fighter.

Broad studies have shown that Asian males have fewer cases of BPH and prostate cancer (thirty American men die from prostate cancer for every Asian male that succumbs to the disease), the corollary being that Asians have a low-cholesterol, low red meat diet, as compared to American men. Nutritionists believe soy is the principle reason for the disparate numbers because soy blocks the action of an enzyme called trosine kinase, which has links to cancer.

Asian males take in between thirty and fifty milligrams of soy daily; a traditional soy-based diet contains powerful compounds called isoflavinoids. You can ingest soy in various ways: tofu is a soy-based product; a half-cup a day is enough to match the average Asian diet. As Sandra Aldrich mentioned earlier, add soy to your casseroles, eggs, or whatever you're cooking. You can drink about a cup of soy milk daily as well. You might even look for roasted soy beans as a replacement to snacking on high-fat potato chips.

Chapter Ten

"IN SICKNESS AND IN HEALTH"

I haven't skied in years because the high altitude affects my heart, but when I was a skier, my favorite resort was Mammoth Mountain, nestled high in the Eastern Sierra Nevada mountain range in central California. The best female skier to come out of Mammoth Mountain was a young woman named Jill Kinmont in the mid-1950s. Jill was a tenacious, up-and-coming Olympic hopeful who found herself on the cover of *Sports Illustrated* in 1955.

Then disaster struck. While competing in a big pre-Olympic ski race in Utah, Jill lost her balance and skidded off the course, cartwheeling several times before striking a tree. Within an instant, she was paralyzed from the neck down and would never ski—or walk—again.

Hollywood made a tear-jerker movie about the event called *The Other Side of the Mountain*, which was released in the mid-1970s. I'll never forget a scene in which Jill (played by Marilyn Hassett), committed to a wheelchair for life, falls in love with a wild, impetuous skier named Dick Buek (played by Beau Bridges). They were discussing what it would be like to be married, and Jill mumbles something about not being able to, you know, ah, ah. . . .

"You mean make love?" asks Dick. "Don't worry about that. That's overrated."

Either Dick was uttering the understatement of the century, or he was acting like a gentleman to put his future fiancée at ease. Unfortunately we'll never know if he still feels that way because Dick died in a plane crash several months later.

I tell this story because I believe sex is *not* overrated for couples in which one of the spouses is disabled. Sexual expression and enjoyment remain essential quality-of-life issues for them. What happens is that the act of marriage becomes more about intimacy than about intercourse.

"Intimacy really has much less to do with sexual 'function' than many people assume," writes Gary Karp, author of *Life on Wheels*. "Caring touch is what truly satisfies—giving and receiving it. Love and being loved is ultimately a more powerful human exchange than raw sex and can be expressed in an infinite variety of ways. Subtlety and sensuality between two people who care about each other's happiness can be the sexiest experience available to us in this life. Regardless of any disability, the human need for contact is innate. There is not a person alive who is not nurtured and healed by sincere loving contact."

When Your Lover Is Disabled

The longer you are married, the greater the chance that one of you will be incapacitated by disease, deal with a lingering illness, or be struck by a sudden disability. Under any of these scenarios, every aspect of your relationship changes, including the physical one. Accepting your spouse's disability in the sexual arena will take time. You may have feelings of resentment, flashes of anger, waves of grief, or bouts of depression. Your disabled spouse is experiencing all these emotions times ten.

Couples travel up and down the ladder of health over the span of a marriage. Some illnesses are relatively minor, resulting in a short-term cessation of sexual relations. More serious diseases or a sudden paralysis can permanently change the sexual dynamics of the marriage overnight. Illness can affect sexuality in ways unrelated to specific effects on the sex organs. A wife worried about the possibility of dying from breast cancer can't be expected to jump into bed on a moment's notice, raring to go. Those coping with physical pain can concentrate on nothing else. Disease-related depression saps energy levels and exacerbates fatigue. Chronic illness shuts down emotional responses needed to keep the spark of love burning. One of the first things to be jettisoned when a spouse hunkers down to fight a serious illness is the desire to give pleasure to his or her spouse.

When one of the spouses becomes disabled, the sexual relationship will change forever. Before we go much further, I must state that every serious health condition should be addressed by a physician and that couples will do well to seek counseling if their sex lives are adversely affected.

Counseling is an excellent venue to discuss questions such as: What should I do if my wife cannot make love? What should I do if my husband is physically incapacitated and cannot perform sexually?

This chapter cannot possibly address the complexity of the matter, but I will say that when such an event happens, we must return to the basic principle that we made our marriage vows "for better, for worse, in sickness and in health," and your marriage should never depend solely on whether you can have physical relations.

But Tim, we're talking about sex here.

You're right. I've known couples in your situation in which God's grace became miraculously sufficient in their sexless marriages. Don't ask me how these couples got through it, but when the chips were down, God granted them the necessary grace to persevere.

For most couples with a disability, the sexual relationship can continue, even if intercourse is not possible. When penetration *is* possible, a hurting spouse may experience difficulty reaching orgasm due to the distracting pain. If this event occurs, maintain a positive attitude about staying sexually active. Continue to cuddle, hold each other close, and drift off to sleep holding each other. Your self-confidence will be bolstered, your self-image will improve, and you will feel more feminine or masculine.

Couples can explore dozens of ways to express sexual affection, ranging from snuggling together to finding a new position in which to make love. Consider purchasing a waterbed, which has more "give" than a normal mattress. Keep various-sized pillows on hand to place under aching joints or painful backs. Part of a positive attitude may be viewing this season of disability as a time of experimentation that hasn't happened since your Hawaiian honeymoon. What feels good for both of you? What works and what doesn't? If you're experiencing discomfort, don't grin and bear it. This creates tension. Say something and discuss what can be done about it. If you're not interested in sex, politely say so. Display a willingness to communicate about your sexual future.

This is a time for trial and error, creativity, and patience—not spontaneity. Couples may have to plan their sexual encounters or structure them so that the disabled or ill spouse can take a warm shower or bath to loosen up joints. A walk around the neighborhood may be needed to relieve stiffness.

Let's take a snapshot look at how various ailments affect the sexual relationship:

Chronic back pain. The most common ailment is a bad back. Eight out of every ten persons experience back pain in their lifetime, and an estimated 35 million Americans are hurting at any given time. The reason why so many Americans have bad backs is because they are out of shape. Weak stomach muscles contribute to the possibility of "pulling a back out." A bad back interferes with a healthy sex life and can make the act of marriage a miserable experience.

The partner with the bad back should ice it or take a hot shower to limber up, depending on the recommended medical treatment. Muscle-stretching exercises can also help. A healthy spouse can offer a back massage as part of foreplay. Generally, those with hurting backs will not be able to do much more than lay on their backs during lovemaking. Some could place a small pillow or rolled-up towel under the small of their backs to make themselves more comfortable.

Someone with a back that hurts more to bend backward (extension) but feels better beding forward (flexion) needs to incorporate sexual positions favorable to the forward bending of the back. For a woman, this translates into the missionary position with her legs comfortably bent. For a man, the missionary position may be too painful. He may find it easier to enter her vaginally from the rear with both kneeling on the bed. She can also kneel on the edge of the bed, facing in, while he stands and enters her from behind.

A person with this problem should seek positions that support the arching of the lower back. A man with this type of back pain should aks his wife to bend her knees toward her chest while in the missionary position. She could also straddle him if she is making love on top or sitting in a chair. A woman with an extension problem may feel more comfortable lying on her stomach with a pillow underneath her while her husband enters her vagina from the rear.

Finally, persons with one-sided back pain will have to experiment with various position. Lying side-by-side could work. Couples have to be willing to talk to each other about different positions, which may be something new after twenty or thirty years of marriage. Another intercouse position to consider is one in which the woman lies on her back with her knees bent over her husband's hips, while he is lying on his side. He can enter her without putting any weight on her.

• *Cancer treatment.* Men and women undergoing chemotherapy for cancer will be bowled over by nausea and vomiting, experience chronic fatigue, and endure loss of hair. For cancer patients, there will be times when intercourse is not possible. Libido lowers for women because chemotherapeutic agents interfere with the production of female sex hormones. As described earlier in my chapter on female menopause, the ovaries produce a small but vital amount of testosterone, which is essential for normal sexual functioning. Research by Kapland Owett suggests that chemotherapy virtually shuts down testosterone production by the ovaries, even for premenopausal women. The result is a dramatic loss of sexual desire and a debilitating decrease in the ability to experience orgasm.[1]

Cancer therapy is not the time for a second honeymoon; spouses with cancer have more important things on their minds—staying alive. They can be expected to feel depressed. The emotional stress may cause them to lash out at loved ones. Anxiety and fatigue will sharply reduce their desire for sexual activity. Fill their need for emotional support and physical contact through hugs, kisses, and embraces.

Sexual issues are magnified for women suffering from gynecological cancer. If a woman has her ovaries removed due to cancer, menopause immediately results, usually causing hot flashes and mood swings. Chemotherapy can also trigger menopause and vaginal discomfort (soreness and dryness) associated with intercourse. Application of estrogen cream can relieve inadequate vaginal lubrication, but don't be surprised if your spouse has low sexual interest or feelings of disability.

• *Inflammatory bowel disease.* Patients with Crohn's disease or ulcerative colitis often undergo ostomy surgery. There are various types of ostomy surgery, depending upon the nature of the illness. A common option for ulcerative colitis is the creation of an ileostomy. The entire colon and, in some cases, the rectum are removed. The surgeon creates an opening in the abdominal wall, through which the ileum is rerouted to the outside, creating a stoma. To collect stool as it exits the ileum, a disposable pouch is attached to the skin.

It's natural to be concerned that an ostomy may alter your ability to function sexually, to feel desirable, and to be the recipient of your spouse's love. The same holds true for anyone wearing a urine- or stool-collection device. Keep in mind that your ability to feel attractive and "sexy" comes from feeling good about yourself. If you are wearing an ileostomy bag (also known as an appliance) or a urine-collection device, drape a towel to cover the tubing or appliance. Pretend it isn't there as you make love.

• *Spinal cord injuries.* Depending upon the severity of the injury, all hope may not be lost. You may not have any genital sensations, but your body can compensate in other areas. Your neck, ears, armpits—and your breasts—can prove to be sexually exciting if your husband touches and stimulates them in a loving manner. Look at them as new erogenous zones waiting to be discovered. Women who still have vague, erratic sensations in their vaginas and clitorises need to be lovingly stimulated by their husband's fingers. If you are not able to physically orgasm, do know you can find sexual satisfaction in an emotional or spiritual peak with your husband.

• *Heart disease.* Heart problems are more prominent in men, and a heart attack—even a minor one—can cause older men to give up sex because they fear overexerting themselves or causing a fatal heart attack. The actual risk is low, however. In fact, an active sex life may decrease the risk of future attack, says Saul H. Rosenthal, founder of the Sexual Therapy Clinic in San Antonio, Texas. He further states:

> A quarter of all men who have heart attacks give up sexual relations completely. Another 50 percent decrease the frequency of their sexual relations. Only the remaining quarter continue making love as often as before. This is really a shame. It's not necessary or desirable to give up your sexual life after a heart attack. Resuming sex is good for your confidence, for your feeling of masculinity, for your sense of being a successful person, and for your entire outlook on life. Eighty percent of postcoronary patients can resume their normal sexual activity without any serious risks. The other 20 percent don't have to abstain from sex, but they simply need to adjust their lovemaking style according to their exercise tolerance.
>
> If you have had a heart attack, you may worry: Will sex be too strenuous for me? Will my pulse rate go up too high? Will I get chest pain? Is sex safe for me? You may even worry about dying during intercourse. You may well wonder: Will lovemaking ever be the same again?
>
> The actual facts are reassuring. Dying during sexual activity is actually an extremely rare occurrence. In a recent

study of a large group of men with heart conditions who died suddenly, less than *half of one percent* of them died during sex. Many more died in their sleep.[2]

• *Diabetes*. This chronic disorder is usually caused by a deficient secretion of insulin, a hormonal substance elaborated in the pancreas. The exact cause of pancreatic failure is not yet fully understood, but obesity caused by the excessive consumption of sugar and fat is a large factor. Diabetes affects men and women equally and usually appears in the latter third of life. Diabetic men are at greater risk for impotency than other men; nearly half of all diabetic men suffer impotence for psychological reasons.[3] Woman can experience vaginal dryness and an inability to orgasm. Those in menopause should employ estrogen-replacement therapy since diabetes lowers estrogen levels. Once diabetes is diagnosed and controlled, however, sexual capabilities can be quickly restored.

• *Arthritis*. Since Bev has been afflicted with rheumatoid arthritis for decades, I'm not going to sugarcoat anything here: arthritis can produce pain that limits sexual activity. Surgery and drugs can relieve these problems, but in some cases the medications could decrease sexual activity. Those with arthritis have found that exercise stimulates blood flow. Rest and warm baths help, as do changes in sexual position. Older people who experience arthritis pain in the early morning or late evening hours may want to plan their sexual activity for other times. You should time your pain-relief medication so that its strongest effect peaks during lovemaking.

Take a warm bath or shower before sex to relax and soothe your joints and muscles. Showering or bathing together could help you enjoy pleasant sensations to heighten sexual arousal. Gentle touching feels especially good to a disabled spouse, for whom pain is never very far away.

Severe pain in hips and knees interferes with certain lovemaking positions. Pain in wrists and hands may not allow for stimulation of male genitals to arousal. This may be a time when the healthy partner provides most of the body action. Open communication will take out the guesswork regarding which movements cause pain.

• *Hysterectomy.* A hysterectomy, the surgical removal of the womb, is still the most commonly performed surgery on women, although the numbers have decreased in the last decade. Performed correctly, a hysterectomy theoretically should not change sexual relations because the uterus is not felt by the man's penis during penetration—just the vagina. Some men, however, feel their wives are "less feminine" after a hysterectomy. I won't say it's all in their head, but it is. Men should feel absolutely no difference at all during coitus. Many women report feeling relieved following surgery, which translates to better sex, but others say the hysterectomy caused their sex drive to plummet.

• *Alcohol abuse.* I put this here because alcohol is the most widespread drug-related cause of sexual problems. God knew what He was doing when He commanded us not to succumb to "dissipation." A steady diet of alcohol reduces sexual desire and function; a drunk is often rendered impotent and women experience reduced ability to orgasm. Alcohol abuse decreases the working production of testosterone for men and women and deadens the nervous system. Abstaining from alcohol will improve sexual function and help you live longer.

• *Stroke.* A mild stroke often has little long-term effect on sexual functioning. Severe strokes are a different matter since motor skills are affected; victims can suffer paralysis on one side of the body and loss of speech. If the brain damage sustained has been slight, there is usually complete recovery. Under such circumstances, men and women report a period of low libido following a stroke, usually lasting several months. Chances of urinary incontinence increase, and orgasm often requires more time and attention. It is unlikely that sexual exertion will set off another stroke. Using different positions can help make up for any residual weakness or paralysis that may have occurred from the original stroke.

• *Multiple sclerosis*. This chronic, slowly progressive disease of the central nervous system affects nearly every system of the body. Those with MS experience visual difficulties, emotional disturbances, convulsions, numbness of various regions of the body, and bladder problems. The sex drive decreases during times of extreme fatigue. Orgasm is often difficult because of impaired sensation, and spasms in hips and legs make coitus in certain positions difficult. Its not uncommon for women with multiple sclerosis to lose control of their bladders and wet themselves and their spouses during intercourse. Even if women eschew beverages and empty their bladders just before sexual relations, they can lose bladder control. One suggestion is to place a large piece of plastic on the bed and cover it with several large bath towels.

• *Polio*. Polio, thought to be a childhood disease, also affects older persons. Believed to be extinct following the development of Dr. Jonas Salk's vaccine in 1955, polio has been making a comeback. The illness is marked by fever, headache, stiff neck and back, muscle pain, and tenderness. If there is involvement of the central nervous system, paralysis ensues. Back and hip problems may interfere with certain coitus positions.

• *Cerebral palsy*. Arousal and ability to orgasm are not affected, although spasms in the hips and knees may make some positions difficult.

• *Muscular diseases*. The sexual response is not affected, although deformity of the back and lower extremities may interfere with certain positions.

When Scars Are Left

Strive for good communication with your spouse and with your doctors. If you are too embarrassed to ask your doctor when you can resume your sexual relations, you will never find out. Go ahead and ask. Gather facts. Share books or magazine articles. Good communication discusses what your sexual relationship will look like in the future.

Many cancer surgeries, for instance, leave considerable scars. Besides the scar lines associated with mastectomies, men and women who undergo lifesaving operations for brain tumors, ovarian cysts, and hysterectomies need to be reminded that their beauty is still more than skin-deep, that their beauty is grounded in Christ's love for them and accentuated by kindness, maturity, and humor. If your hair falls out from chemotherapy or some other form of treatment, buy the best wig you can afford. Collect and wear stylish hats and caps. If you feel like wearing a wig or headcovering during lovemaking, go for it.

With nearly every kind of disability (except for paralysis), you will always be able to feel pleasure from touching, which is a form of intimacy. Pleasure and satisfaction are possible, even if some aspects of your love life are misty memories. If possible, don't stop making love in response to your medical situations. Lean on the Lord and not your own understanding. Pray together as never before. The need for touch, affection, and pleasure is strong, and the way you demonstrate Christ's love for your disabled spouse—and each other—will speak volumes to your spouse, your family, and your friends.

Chapter Eleven

THE TEMPTATIONS

For someone in his early fifties, he was still a hunk. Flaming red hair. A lean, muscular body that served him well in war and in peace. Everyone in his country knew of his battlefront exploits and athletic prowess. He was the most famous person in his land, a talented musician, poet, soldier, and king.

He was also married—several times over. God told him not to take more than one wife, but his appetite for sensual indulgence could not be satisfied. At one time he counted eight wives and at least ten mistresses sexually available to his beck and call. He was a virile man who fathered twenty-one sons and one daughter.

When he reached his fifties, he had conquered nearly all his enemies. He gladly turned over his dwindling military responsibilities to a trustworthy lieutenant. Hadn't David earned the right to relax and enjoy his kingdom for a change? He had served his country and his God faithfully; now it was time to relax, smell the roses, and give some up-and-coming warriors a chance to make names for themselves.

One spring afternoon, while his armies were mopping up in the hinterlands, David napped in his palace. He awoke and strolled onto the roof, which

159

offered him a bird's-eye view of most of Jerusalem. As he scanned the horizon, his eyes fell upon a woman of unusual beauty taking a bath in the twilight hour. Her nude body glistened in the orange sunlight, and he began imagining what it would be like to make love to her. He pondered his next move. Wasn't he the most powerful man in the land? Wasn't he deserving of a little pleasure after leading his kingdom to victory in so many battles?

A snap of the fingers, and a trusted aide-de-camp appeared. Yes, he could find out who she was. Yes, he would treat the matter with the utmost discretion.

The answer came back within the hour. "Her name is Bathsheba, the daughter of Eliam and the wife of Uriah," the aide reported.

"Tell her I want to see her."

"Yes, sir."

She was admitted to his drawing room, and the two were left alone. David sensed her apprehension; he realized any subject would feel uncertainty after being summoned to the king's palace at night. Yet he knew that Bathsheba understood she had chosen to bath nude in a place that could be seen from his palace chambers. David turned on his winning charm and engaged her in conversation. Their eyes met and held each other. Then he drew near to Bathsheba and put his arms around her. When he kissed her, she did not resist.

Nor did she resist when he led her to his royal chamber, where they made love. Just as they had both planned it.

The story about David and Bathsheba is one of my favorites in the Bible because it soberly reminds us of sin's consequences. Their one-night stand resulted in her pregnancy and touched off a series of events that spun out of David's control, including the murder of Bathsheba's husband, Uriah. Steve Farrar, author and founder of Men's Leadership Ministries, offered this view:

> When David stood on his roof in the balmy twilight, watching the beautiful Bathsheba step out of her clothes, the only thing on his mind was to enjoy her charms firsthand. That was about as far as he wanted to go. But sin will take you *far-*

ther than you want to travel. David had only planned on a discreet evening of adultery, yet within weeks he was guilty of betrayal, murder, and a heinous cover-up. And that was a winding road he'd never planned to travel.

David was shrewd. Give him that much. When Bathsheba turned up pregnant, David immediately sent a courier to the battlefield for her husband, Uriah. This would cover his bases, and no one would ever be the wiser. David made the classic mistake that men have been making for thousands of years: he thought that he could use deception to cover disobedience. But that's not how it works. Deception *never* covers disobedience. It just makes it worse. Count on it, your sin *will* find you out. And it will take you farther than you wanted to go.[1]

Sin has had consequences ever since Eve took the first bite of the apple. Adultery, forbidden in the seventh commandment, can't remain hidden. Adultery will eventually come out. Adultery will destroy you and your family and cause untold anguish; that's why I recommend couples read Proverbs 5 and 6 once a month as a reminder that roving eyes are the match than can touch off a fiery conflagration that will be impossible to contain.

"Can a man scoop fire into his lap without his clothes being burned?" states Proverbs 6:27–29. "Can a man walk on hot coals without his feet being scorched? So is he who sleeps with another man's wife; no one who touches her will go unpunished."

"No one . . . will go unpunished." Underline those words. Listen to Scripture! A man (or a woman) who violates his marriage vows commits a grievous sin. It's usually the only vow we make with God and another person, for as long as we both shall live. Yet this vow is scorned and treated cavalierly by the world. Another of my pet peeves with the Hollywood entertainment industry is that its films present James Bond-like characters sleeping around with everybody and anybody, but in the final reel, they act morally to save the world from evil. Or the adulterous character plays the role of the white hat

detective, the heart-of-gold lawyer, the salt-of-the-earth doctor, or the respected president. The truth is that sexual immorality reveals a character flaw, and sexual sins are usually followed by other sins: lying, deceit—even murder. They all go together, as we learned in the story of David.

"THE TEMPTING FIFTIES"

David's affair with Bathsheba illustrates a pattern that I've noticed over the years: that the period of greatest opportunity for adultery happens during the "tempting fifties." I can come up with several reasons for this. The decade between fifty and sixty years of age is a time when a couple's most pressing duty—successfully raising their children—comes to an end as the young adult offspring move out to pursue careers and marry and form families of their own. Empty-nest couples have more time on their hands—"We have our life back!" they exclaim. If they were not communicating much before the house emptied, however, the silence around the home can be deafening.

In addition, the swirling hormonal changes wrought by menopause can rock the steadiest of marriages. If a stay-at-home mother re-enters the work force, introducing her to the world of office politics and sexual intrigue, she could be vulnerable to temptation, as could men promoted to powerful positions within the corporation. Since there are no children to come home to, working couples devote longer and longer days at the office, where relationships develop and bonds form. Based on my counseling career, the preponderance of extramarital affairs involves married men with unmarried women.

Another dynamic to consider is that unmarried women in the workplace are far more sexually liberated today ("liberated" being a coined word to justify sexual aggression). Rare is the middle-aged person who can say he or she has not been confronted with an open opportunity to be unfaithful. I remember attending a banquet in a distant city one time when an attractive woman in her mid-forties—

who knew Bev had not accompanied me on this trip—sidled up to me and coyly asked, "Would you like to have some company tonight?"

Frankly, her offer never became a temptation because a happily married man will never trade a Mercedes in the garage for a Volkswagen off the street. Yet we have minister friends who have ruined their ministry by falling to the scarlet sin. True, they were not tempted "beyond what you can bear," but evidently they did not take advantage of the "way out" that God promises to provide (1 Cor. 10:13).

Still, you have to wonder what goes through a man's mind when he throws away years invested in a marital relationship for a weekend, several hours—a few minutes—of sexual pleasure. Was it brain freeze that caused a breakdown in his cognitive thinking when he broke his wedding vows with his executive secretary? Actor Robin Williams, in a flash of brilliance, suggested this explanation regarding men who run off the reservation: "See, the problem is that God gives men a brain and a penis," he said, "and only enough blood to run one at a time."

I once counseled a successful doctor who had an affair with an office secretary who wasn't nearly as good looking as the doctor's wife.

"What did you see in her?" I asked. I really was curious why he was attracted to his plain-looking secretary.

"She made me feel more comfortable," he replied. To hear this respected doctor, highly regarded as a great surgeon, say this was a revelation.

"More comfortable?" I probed.

"Yes. Whenever I went home, my wife would belittle me, talk down to me, tell me what to do."

What he described is a phenomenon that I've witnessed in many middle-age couples who've experienced affairs. In these situations the wife—following the absence of children—begins "mothering" her husband: telling him what to do, complaining about picking up after him, using the exasperated tone of voice that she formerly reserved for rambunctious teenagers. Men mightily resent being mothered, especially by their wives!

The doctor considered his wife's mothering attitude to be an affront, and this direction in their marriage became a sexual demotivator for him. This is not to justify his rationale for adultery, just explain his thinking.

For couples to sail off smoothly into the sunset years, they need to remember three golden expressions that they should communicate throughout the fifties and sixties—and beyond.

1. *"I'm sorry."* Everyone makes mistakes, and by the midlife years, both sides have made enough "unforced errors" to write a book on what *not* to do in a marriage. If you are willing to face your mistakes and apologize for your actions, you should find resistance dissolve and a spirit of forgiveness prevail. If you are unwilling to acknowledge your mistakes, then you have a serious spiritual problem—pride.

One time I counseled with a couple, and the wife tearfully said, "Dr. LaHaye, my husband has never apologized to me in the twenty-three years of marriage."

I turned to the defiant husband. "Is that true?" I asked. "Have you ever done anything wrong?"

"Sure, I have," he quickly replied. "I am only human."

"Why have you never apologized?"

"Because I didn't think it was manly for me to apologize," he replied. "Growing up, I never saw my father apologize to my mother."

"Unfortunately, you grew up under a father who made a terrible decision never to apologize," I said. "For you to do the same would perpetuate that mistake and keep your wife miserable. When you are wrong, face it objectively and honestly admit it—both to yourself and to your wife."

2. *"I love you."* Those three simple words are the second golden expression in a marriage. Your spouse will never tire of you expressing your love. This expression seems to be more meaningful to women than men, but I am inclined to believe women are just more prone to admit their need for it.

The importance of uttering these important words was confirmed when a man came in to see me the day after his wife of fifteen years had left him. He was a brilliant engineer with an IQ of 148 who knocked down $75,000 a year. As he described the shipwreck of his marriage, he acknowledged that he had not told his wife that he loved her for ten years.

"Why is that?" I asked.

"Why should I tell her that I love her? I have demonstrated it faithfully for fifteen years. She didn't like the house we lived in, so I bought her another house. She didn't like her car, so I purchased another for her to run around in. She didn't like the carpeting, so I had the old carpets ripped out and plush carpeting installed. If I didn't love her, would I have given her five children?"

The amazing thing about the whole affair is that his wife had run off with a career sailor making $1,500 a month. "What could that poor sailor possibly give to my wife that I haven't already given her?" he asked with a cry in his throat.

My answer was short: "Just one thing—love."

As brilliant a scientist as he was, this man was ignorant as a husband. Their problem could have been resolved if he had been willing to give of himself and let her know that he loved her and approved of her. He couldn't seem to understand that although saying "I love you" sounded childish to him, it was meaningful to her. Nor did he understand that if he had not been so selfish, he would have been more willing to express in words what she wanted to hear. The more your spouse loves you, the more he or she enjoys hearing you express your love. Say it meaningfully and say it often.

3. *"I forgive you."* Your inability or unwillingness to forgive your spouse will dissolve the band of marriage. I have seen bitter people throw in the towel because they could not forgive. I have seen brokenhearted people give up on a marriage because their spouses would not forgive.

Forgiveness is more difficult for some people than for others, but after years in the counseling room, I am convinced it is a matter of the mind. If you have difficulty forgiving others, consider the following suggestions:

1. Accept the fact that you are commanded to forgive by the Lord Himself.
2. Realize your partnership and happiness with your mate depend on your ability to forgive.
3. Ask God to help you take the steps to forgive. God never demands us to do something that we are unable to do.
4. Tell the Lord that with His help, you do forgive and name the specific sin.
5. Tell your partner you have forgiven him.
6. Never dwell on that sin again. Every time you are reminded of it, thank God that He enabled you to forget it—"Forgetting what is behind and straining toward what is ahead, I press on toward the goal to win the prize for which God has called me heavenward in Christ Jesus" (Phil. 3:13–14).

NOBODY'S MARRIAGE IS PERFECT

It shouldn't come as a great revelation that the person you married is not a perfect person. The Bible reminds us that "all have sinned and come short of the glory of God." Every married couple should realize this; thus, don't be so naïve to think that you can only have sex when your partner is perfect. You will be doomed to a celibate marriage if you think this way.

If you believe our marriage of fifty-three years has been a storybook experience, then you are wrong. Bev and I are two very strong-willed people! When a warm, outgoing, practical, and strong-willed temperament and an analytical, perfectionist, and well-balanced temperament marry (as in our case), you have brought together the "irresistible force and immovable object."

Like every other couple, we have angered each other, treated each other selfishly, and have done things that we have been ashamed of. We have even uttered cruel and unkind things to each other. Although it doesn't happen as often these days, our schedules and priorities occasionally collide; something has to give. I wish I could say we always handled our conflicts "in the Spirit" and "in love," but you know better, so we might as well admit it.

Let me tell you about one of our recent "blowups." When Bev did not communicate her thinking on a subject that was very important to me, I took it more personal that I should have. I lost my cool and said some unkind things that were uncalled for. Yet before nightfall, we had made up, and the reason was FORGIVENESS. We couldn't, of course, take back the things we said, but we found that confessing and forgiving, as modeled in Ephesians 4:29–32, came to our rescue, as it has hundreds of times over the years.

For much of my professional life, I have been a busy pastor and counselor who specialized in marriage relations. It is safe to say that with the Lord's help, many couples are enjoying a good relationship today that were literally on the verge of divorce when they first came to see me. In almost every case, the primary problem was self-induced anger that created conflict and resulted in "unwholesome talk" coming out of their mouths, so I developed the habit of making each couple memorize Ephesians 4:29–32 before they returned for their next interview. The results were often amazing! Note these special words and please memorize them. We believe these are some of the most important verses in the entire Bible for married couples.

Do not let any unwholesome talk come out of your mouths, but only what is helpful for building others up according to their needs, that it may benefit those who listen. And do not grieve the Holy Spirit of God, with whom you were sealed for the day of redemption. Get rid of all bitterness, rage and anger, brawling and slander, along with every form of malice. Be kind and compassionate to one another, forgiving each other, just as in Christ God forgave you.

Ephesians 4:29–32

Please notice what "grieves the Holy Spirit" and in the process, grieves our partner and ruins relationships: "bitterness, rage and anger, brawling and slander, along with every form of malice." A heart filled with malice is a heart mulling insults and injuries from real or imagined affronts over a period of time. This is usually the condition of the heart in one or both mates on the verge of divorce. What they need is not a series of counseling experiences or a marital break-up—they need to forgive "each other, just as in Christ God forgave you." That is not an option. It is a command!

WHEN FORGIVENESS ISN'T DESERVED

A weeping wife once shared in front of her husband some of the mightily selfish things he had done and said to her. When he admitted to God and confessed his wrongs, I told him he should also confess his sins to his wife, as well. What happened next surprised me. She became furious and blurted, "He doesn't deserve my forgiveness!"

"I agree with you," I said, "but that is not the basis on which we forgive. The Bible tells us that we are to forgive as Christ forgave us. We all know that we do not deserve God's forgiveness, but we receive it anyway. I am convinced that there is no lasting love in marriage without lots of forgiveness."

Several times, I have had a spouse say to me, "I can't forgive him" or "I can't forgive her." What this spouse is really saying is, "I won't forgive him" or "I won't forgive her," but if they want to be Spirit-filled Christians and obey the Lord in all things, they will have to seek the Lord's help until they learn to forgive. Admittedly, it is harder for people with certain temperaments to forgive others, but we are all capable of forgiveness if we ask God for His grace in this area. Forgiveness does not always solve friction in a marriage, but a refusal to forgive never does.

Jesus warned, "If you do not forgive men their sins, your Father will not forgive your sins." Not only is this true for your mate, but for others as well. I have known several cases in which the object of a person's bitterness or anger was not their mate but a boss, a parent, a neighbor, or someone living far from them. Their anger not only ruined their relationship with God, but it also ruined their relationship with their married partner and robbed them of a warm, sexually exciting experience before falling sleep. This goes on in millions of households all the time.

Someone wisely said, "Forgive or perish." I agree. I'll never forget reading Dr. S. I. McMillen's book *None of These Diseases*, which listed fifty-one common ailments, including ulcers, heart attacks, and headaches caused by protracted anger. His thesis confirmed my belief that anger kills the sex drive and turns off people who should be turned on by each other.

If you have a problem with forgiveness, admit it to God in prayer and ask for His help, regardless of whether the object of your forgiveness has asked for it or even deserves it. Remember, it's "forgive or perish"—spiritually and sexually!

AVOIDING THE RUINS

One of the reasons I have included this chapter on spouses who break their wedding vows is the seriousness and devastating pain that it causes. Men and women who begin an extramarital relationship act very much like sheep led to slaughter, as Scripture tells us. If you point that out to them, however, you receive a blank look. It's as though you can't talk any sense into them.

I've known too many pastors, elders, and deacons who have fallen to adultery over the years. Their affairs torched their ministries, but more importantly, their sexual dalliances usually destroyed their marriages and seriously wounded innocent family members. I'll never forget receiving a phone call from a woman whose husband was a church deacon. They had been married thirty-five years. Apparently, he became involved with another woman, and they traveled to Las Vegas, where they were married in one of those "quickie" wedding chapels. Like an idiot, he put down his home address when filling out the marriage license form.

When his first wife, sorting through the mail one day, noticed the State of Nevada wedding certificate, she confronted him. Her husband 'fessed up. He and his first wife divorced, he had to be expelled from the church, and in the end, you had a very lonely woman who had given the best years of her life to a man who betrayed her.

Her former husband obviously fantasized about what it would be like to be married to the other woman, and his fantasy gave way to imprudent—and destructive—behavior. I think Christians sometimes have affairs because they can't stop their minds from imagining what it would be like to make love to someone else, a mental exercise that slowly turns them off to their spouses. They dream about undressing her, what it would be like to see her naked, and what it would feel like to be sexually joined to her. They harbor thoughts about acting on that fantasy or at least exploring it further.

In my book *Why Ministers Fall*, I tell a story about meeting a senior pastor in which our conversation turned to the news about another minister who had to resign his pastorate because of his sexual sin. "What was going through that man's mind?" I asked rhetorically.

I never forget the long silence or the tears that started running down my colleague's cheeks. "The same thing happened to me thirty-three years ago," he began slowly. "Then I had to leave my church, and it was two years before I could return to the ministry and start a new church. But you know what was worst? For years after my affair, my wife and I would go to bed, and whenever I moved toward her, she would pound on my chest and scream at me, 'How could you do this to me?'"

I regarded this pastor, a big man at six feet, four inches of height. "What did you do?" I asked.

"I took her hands in mine and told her again how sorry I was. 'Please forgive me,' I begged. It took years and years before she finally got over it. That was a terrible price to pay."

I can assure you that the betrayed women found it very difficult to forgive and forget, but if it can be done, this selfless act can resurrect a dying marriage.

Her Love Had Turned Cold

Let me close this chapter with another story about forgiveness. Years ago, I counseled a couple following her knowledge that the husband had been involved in an affair.

The three of us met for three months, and during that time, I also met individually with the woman for counseling. "Why can't I respond to my husband any more?" she asked one afternoon. "I am absolutely cold to him."

"I feel it's because you haven't forgiven him," I offered. She became irate with me.

"What do you mean, 'Forgive him'? He doesn't deserve forgiveness, and he knows that!"

I waited for her to calm down. "Let me ask you a question," I said. "Do you want to be happy the rest of your life, or do you want to be miserable?"

"Well, we have four kids, so I guess I want to be happy."

"Then you'll have to forgive him. Would you like to do that?"

She considered my request for a long minute. "Yes, I would," she whispered.

We got down on our knees, and that day she forgave her husband for his sexual transgressions. That event happened nearly thirty years ago. Her husband died recently, and at his funeral, she gave me a big hug. "Thank you for what you told us many years ago. Believe it or not, we ended up having a really good marriage."

I believe it.

Chapter Twelve

EXERCISE AND NUTRITION FOR A HEALTHY SEX LIFE

I had just turned forty-one—trim, fit, and carrying the same weight as the day I got married. My eighteen-year-old son, Larry, and a bunch of his friends drafted me to play touch football with them. Larry was playing for the opposing team, and I drew the assignment to cover him against the pass. Midway through the game, Larry huddled up with his buddies.

"Look, I think I can outrun my father, so I'm going to go long on this play," he told the quarterback. "We'll score a touchdown for sure."

When the ball was snapped, Larry sprinted down the sideline. I stayed with him stride for stride, but then he kicked in an afterburner and sped past me as though I was standing still. The quarterback lobbed a long pass downfield, and Larry gathered the ball into his arms for a touchdown.

I doubled over and huffed and puffed while Larry enjoyed hearty congratulations from his teammates. That's when a revelation came over me: there's no way a forty-one-year-old man will physically match an eighteen-year-old, prime-of-his-life young male. I remember telling

Lance Alworth, the NFL Hall of Fame passing receiver who played with the San Diego Chargers, about my touch football story.

"Tim, when I started playing pro football, I was stiff and sore after a Sunday game," said Lance, "but by Tuesday or Wednesday, I was all healed up. When I reached my mid-thirties, however, I was aching until Thursday or Friday. That's when I knew it was time to hang up my cleats."

Getting old is a natural process of life, but it doesn't mean life is over. What matters is the state of your health. Ask anyone who's been hobbled by illness or debilitated by an injury, and they will invariably pat you on the shoulder and say, "Be thankful you're healthy."

I am very thankful to Almighty God for the blessings of good health that He's bestowed upon me, and my appreciation of His bountifulness in this area has not been dimmed with the passage of years. At the same time, however, I understand that I have an important role to play in keeping myself healthy, and that involves ample amounts of exercise and proper nutrition.

This is an important chapter because exercise and nutrition influence sexuality and libido, especially in the later years of life. If you are experiencing a middle-age malaise, then you should examine your fitness level and eating habits to see whether you are destroying your vital energies by not exercising or eating the wrong kinds of foods. This is also the time to investigate lifestyle changes, which reminds me of a couple in their fifties who were tired all the time. They solved this problem by regularly going to bed one hour earlier, and they found they awoke in the morning with zest. And increased sex drive followed this increase in vital energies.

FEWER CALORIES ARE NEEDED

The metabolism slows down as you progress through middle age, meaning that you need fewer calories to maintain your weight. In midlife, it's more than *what* you eat—it's also *when* you eat. You may want to consider eating smaller meals four, five, or six times a day instead of skipping breakfast, grabbing a quick lunch, and feasting on a big dinner. Eating smaller meals more often can stimulate faster metabolism and result in weight loss.

Many health authorities also recommend eating a healthy breakfast, a moderate lunch, and a skimpy dinner without an evening snack as a way to trim unwanted fat. As for my eating schedule, I start off the morning by reaching into my kitchen cupboard and taking out a large plastic container filled with three different cereals: Kellogg's Low Fat Granola, Post Grape-Nuts, and Kellogg's All-Bran, the latter to help keep my digestive system regular. I've also read that eating a decent breakfast allows me to receive the same amount of calories with less stored as fat.

Later in the day, I crave fruit and vegetables for lunch. I believe in keeping fruit around the house, so I eat bananas regularly because they may lower blood pressure. I have high blood pressure, something I inherited in my family genes. So far, two bananas a day and jogging exercises five days a week help me avoid taking prescription drugs for this malady.

For dinnertime, one thing that has been beneficial for keeping my weight down and producing better health has been cutting down on fat grams by eating less beef and more fish or chicken. Substituting fruit for gooey-chocolate desserts is something I try to do, although I admit I am not perfect on this score.

Couples in the midlife years often have the financial resources to eat out more often. Restaurant meals are a regular occurrence for Bev and me these days. Eating healthy is a difficult proposition since restaurants serve steaks the size of hubcaps, baked potatoes dripping in melted butter, and wedges of "mud pie" topped with a flume of whipped cream. We don't have to order artery-clogging beef entrees, which football players eat to bulk up on. Many restaurants offer "lite" meals and low-fat options. I order chicken and fish entrees, along with salads with low-fat or no-fat dressings. I say no to gravies, mayonnaise, and butter-based sauces.

Believe it or not, I have had a weight problem ever since I was a kid, so I try to keep my weight down. These days I weigh 153 pounds, but I could afford to lose five pounds. Restaurants use a lot of grease because it's faster for cooking, but this presents a challenge to eating healthy. My approach is to search the menu for pastas topped with a tomato-based sauce. I've found that a Mediterranean, tomato-based diet contributes to long life, which means Italian food is surprisingly very good for you. The lycopene that gives tomatoes their red hue wards off prostate cancer. I once read a *Newsweek* article about a Harvard study of 48,000 men that found that those who ate the most tomatoes, tomato sauce, and pizza were up to 45 percent less likely to develop prostate cancer. Pass the spaghetti sauce!

EXERCISING NICE AND EASY

Aside from eating healthy, I'm a great believer in exercise. I begin most mornings (about five days a week) by jogging three miles. I have found it important to stretch my legs and hips before and after running. I like jogging for two reasons:

1. *No matter where I am in the world, I can jog.* Running through city streets and parks has been a great way to learn more about God's wonderful creation. One time, I was fortunate to jog in Tianamen Square in Beijing, China. (Don't worry. I know I have to be careful about jogging into certain neighborhoods when I'm on the road.)

2. *I always listen to a tape or CD on my Walkman when I jog.* I usually listen to something related to biblical teaching or prophesy. I call it "redeeming the time." In other words, I'm killing two birds with one stone by exercising and listening to tapes simultaneously.

After cooling down and taking a shower, I walk into my home office, where I have a stand-up desk. I prefer to work and write standing up, and this is how I do some of my most creative writing. At night, while I catch up on the TV news, I perform two sets of fifty push-ups. I can't do as many sit-ups or crunches, but that's okay for someone who's had a pacemaker next to his heart for the last three years. Men my age tend to get flabby in the stomach; even if they are not obese, they begin to sag. I guess I just refuse to give in to the Grim Reaper.

My prevention-type approach and the grace of God have kept me in good health. Actually, an article by Billy Graham in *Reader's Digest* back in 1966 got me started jogging. He found that consistent running kept him in good health, so I began pounding the pavement the next day. More than thirty years later, I have worn out five pairs of jogging shoes, and Beverly figures I have jogged the equivalent of four times across the United States. Jogging has really been fun, kept my weight down, and I've learned a lot listening to taped messages by Dr. Adrian Rogers, Josh McDowell, David Jeremiah, David Hunt, Ravi Zacharias, and many more. Becoming a "tapeworm" has been a great way to get my head into a subject for writing!

I have to admit that I dislike doing push-ups, but I do them to maintain strength because Beverly needs help with her rheumatoid arthritis. She's battled this affliction for thirty-five years and has been under a doctor's care nearly all that time. Bev first noticed her arthritic symptoms while she was in her mid-thirties. She was diagnosed at Scripps Research Clinic in San Diego, where her doctors predicted that it would only be a matter of time before she would be committed to a wheelchair. Like a valiant soldier, Bev has dealt with many physical problems silently and graciously! But she has never given up hope that God would heal her or that some modern medicine would be found to cure this dreaded disease that has caused suffering to her and 30 million Americans. She already had one knee replacement because the pain of bone rubbing on bone became too much for her. We are hoping and praying she can avoid having the other knee replaced. One important thing we have discussed is that someone with rheumatoid arthritis should be under the watchful care of a medical specialist. The good news is that some wonderful new medicines for arthritis are being developed today.

One bone problem that Beverly has avoided has been osteoporosis, a common disease that affects more than 10 million Americans. One in four women develop osteoporosis. Women reach peak bone mass by age thirty, when bone mineral density starts declining. As we discussed in chapter 3, osteoporosis occurs mostly in women following menopause when dwindling estrogen amounts cause the bones to become thin and brittle. I grieve when I see older women walking in a stoop because of their weakened spines. But 20 percent of osteoporosis strikes men, usually starting in their fifties. This bone-loss disease produces noticeable limps and hunched-over walks.

You can reduce your risk of osteoporosis, say some medical experts, by adding 1200 to 1500 milligrams of calcium supplements to your diet. Vitamin D, which promotes bone mineralization, should be taken in conjunction with calcium tablets. The recommended dose is 400–600 IU's daily. Vitamin C helps you absorb calcium and iron to maintain tissues, bones, and teeth. Most health food stores carry calcium and magnesium in the same tablet. This allows your system to absorb the calcium better.

Gym workouts maintain and build bone mass and density, so don't be bashful about pushing plates on Nautilus machines at a local gym. Too many folks shy away from vigorous exercise because of the adage, "No pain, no gain." My philosophy is to exercise with no pain.

Reaching a good sweat is usually good for you. At the minimum, I beg you to start walking, which was the number-one exercise of those who answered our survey. Close to 40 percent of the respondents, however, told us they do little or no exercise. Dr. Laura Schlessinger, host of the "Dr. Laura" radio program, said if she were asked to write a book called *Ten Stupid Things Older People Do*, "not taking care of their health" would rank very high on her list. I should warn you, however, that if you are just starting out on an exercise program, start slowly and work up gradually.

My friend and expert on physical fitness, Dr. Ken Cooper, founder of the Cooper Aerobics Center in Dallas, says that moving from a sedentary lifestyle to an active one starts with a comfortable pair of walking shoes and consistency. Dr. Cooper has had a great influence on my physical fitness, and he is the author of *The Antioxidant Revolution*. (For more information on Dr. Cooper and his Aerobics Center in Dallas, call [800] 444-5764 or visit his Web sites at *cooperaerobics.com* or *cooperwellness.com*.) Here is Dr. Cooper's twelve-week "Walk for Life" program in a nutshell:

- After consulting with your doctor, go slowly at first. Walk five days a week for the first six weeks at a relaxed pace.
- Week 1: Walk one mile in twenty-four minutes five days a week.
- Week 2: Walk one mile in twenty-two minutes five days a week.
- Week 3: Walk one mile in twenty minutes five days a week.
- Week 4: Walk 1.5 miles in thirty minutes five days a week.
- Week 5: Walk 1.5 miles in twenty-nine minutes five days a week.
- Week 6: Walk two miles in less than forty minutes five days a week. If you're feeling good, pick up the pace in weeks 7 through 12.
- Week 7: Walk two miles in thirty-eight minutes four times a week.
- Week 8: Walk two miles in thirty-six minutes four times a week.
- Week 9: This is your goal. Walk two miles in less than thirty-five minutes four times a week. Keep on walking. You will achieve major health and longevity benefits by continuing to walk at the week 6 or week 9 level. If your fitness improves, move on to the third level.
- Week 10: Walk two miles in thirty-four minutes four times a week.
- Week 11: Walk two miles in thirty-two minutes four times a week.
- Week 12: This is your goal. Walk two miles in less than thirty minutes three times a week.

ADDING QUALITY YEARS TO YOUR LIFE

My great desire is that this chapter will serve as a wake-up call to get in better shape. Do the words *it's now or never* mean anything to you? You can add *years* to your life span, enjoy a better sex life, stay around long enough to minister to others, and have a godly influence on your grandchildren by undertaking an exercise program.

Before you take that first walk around the block, however, you should have a medical look-over. Undergoing a stress electrocardiogram is advisable, as is answering questions truthfully regarding family history for heart disease or high blood pressure.

You can't make up ten or twenty years of relative inactivity in a fortnight, so don't expect to go from sans-a-belt slacks to trim trousers right away. Dr. Cooper recommends an age-appropriate balance between aerobic exercise and strength training. "As we age, we lose muscle mass," says Dr. Cooper, "so it's no good if a sixty-year-old man can run three miles in thirty minutes if he can't pick up a sack of groceries without pulling his back out." He counsels midlife men and women to perform aerobic activities (such as brisk walking, swimming, cycling, or jogging) three to five times a week for twenty to thirty minutes each time. Strength training on weight machines a couple of times a week would round out any exercise program. You could also purchase some three-pound and five-pound dumbbells to use at home.

Let's be realistic. Few people have the time or determination to exercise four to five times a week. But can you perform some type of exercise at least twice a week? Perhaps three times?

A person who raises his or her heart rate through consistent exercise is increasing blood circulation and invigorating muscles. If an energetic sex life is valuable to you, this is the time to stop smoking, vastly reduce alcohol intake, change your eating habits, and begin a sustainable exercise program that improves the health of your cardiovascular system. Unless physical exercise has been ingrained in your lifestyle, many people find it difficult to increase their exercise in their middle-age years. Thus, the lack of exercise and continued high caloric intake contributes to weight gain. For women, this weight gathers in the lower body—hips, buttocks, and thighs. The average woman gains one to two pounds a year.

Those of you who are overweight should be aware of the health risks associated with the stresses that extra weight places on the body. In the largest study ever done on obesity and mortality, the American

Cancer Society reported in 1999 that people increase the risk of dying earlier simply because they are overweight.

The researchers, who studied more than one million Americans, calculated each person's body mass index, or BMI, which is a ratio of weight to height. The subjects were then tracked for age and cause of death. The study found a gradually increasing risk of death for people who had a BMI of twenty-five (which translates to a five-foot, five-inch woman weighing 150 pounds or a five-foot, ten-inch man weighing 174 pounds). The heaviest white men, weighing 278 pounds on a five-foot, ten-inch frame and having a BMI of forty or more, were two-and-a-half times more likely to die than their healthy peers, which would be men of the same height weighing between 153 and 170 pounds. (You can find out your BMI by typing out "body mass index" in your favorite Internet search engine. This will take you to several Web sites that can calculate your BMI.)

Obesity also causes a lack of sexual appetite. Psychiatrist C. Don Morgan at the Kansas School of Medicine said that the self-defeating body shame linked to the inability—or unwillingness—to lose weight often results in sexual difficulties. Dr. Morgan discovered a high rate of inhibited sexual desire, sexual aversion, and inability to reach orgasm after evaluating questionnaires completed by obese women. (He also noted the traits in excessively thin women.) Seventy-seven percent of the heavy respondents had negative emotions during sex, compared to 33 percent in the normal weight control group.[1] Severely overweight men are no better off; frequently, they become impotent.

Losing weight is hard work, but I can tell you that staying trim has been well worth the effort spiritually, mentally, physically, and emotionally. Most overweight Christians must realize that their problem is not weighing too much—it's eating too much. The Bible calls this gluttony. Many of us seem more concerned about the penalty for this sin (being overweight) than the sin itself. Such people must come to realize they can never indulge in eating all that the appetite craves. The best exercise of all can be the "push out" from the dining room table and trusting God to give you joy in knowing that you are obeying Him.

The Case for Nutritional Supplements

I once counseled a depressed woman who blithely informed me that she was seeing four different doctors and taking sixteen different drugs all at the same time. You don't have to be a chemist to realize that those drugs could have been working against each other.

As I've marveled elsewhere, we are indeed fortunate to live in an age where modern medicine has so many weapons at its disposal. From lasers to magnetic resonance imaging to cutting-edge surgery techniques, today's medicine bears little resemblance to how doctors practiced health care just twenty-five years ago. The doctor's arsenal includes a dizzying array of new drugs, highly potent and highly publicized. Patients view them as the elixir for longer life, a view promulgated by a medical profession that focuses heavily on prescription drugs before embarking down the surgery route.

My beef with the mainstream medical community is that it should be more forthcoming regarding the debilitating side effects of prescription drugs, such as male impotence for high blood pressure medication. A hard-charging, aggressive male in his late forties, being treated for high blood pressure, might hesitate taking a certain medication if he knew that he had a one-third chance of his penis never becoming erect again. Doctors must impart vital information; otherwise, they solve one medical health issue and create another. Patients should inform themselves by asking questions, talking to friends, and reading up on the latest research.

While many doctors are quick to write prescriptions, they disregard nutritional supplements, either as a form of treatment or as preventative medicine. If you ask why, they'll say vitamins produce expensive urine and that's about it.

I don't share this view, and neither does a growing number of doctors who have expressed to me that nutritional supplements *can* do some good. I believe we are seeing a mini-revolution among doctors alarmed at the various side effects their patients are experiencing. They are more open about promoting nutritional health. One doctor whose work I have been following closely has been Julian Whitaker, who publishes and writes a newsletter called *Health & Healing*. This publication reaches 500,000 homes every month. Whitaker, founder of the American Preventative Health Association, bases his writings on solid medical science and the latest developments in nutritional health and alternative forms of therapy.

Whitaker also publishes books and special magazine issues of importance to me. One is called *Uncensored Secrets to Sizzling Sex at Any Age*, but you won't need oven mitts to handle this one. Whitaker contends that sexual problems in the advancing years, be they rooted in physical or emotional problems, are the result of hormonal changes. Nothing earthshaking there, but he points out that the organs and glands responsive to sexual hormones are vulnerable to "free radical damage." He explains that free radicals are highly reactive particles that attack and damage individual cells in your body. When free radicals roam free, disease and dysfunction can result.

To combat free radicals, Whitaker says we should add nutritional supplements to our diet, particularly antioxidants. Here's what he recommends taking each morning:

- vitamin C (3,000 mg)
- vitamin E (400–800 IU)
- selenium (200 mcg)
- zinc (30 mg)
- beta carotene (5,000 IU)

Antioxidant nutrients are also found in whole grain foods, fresh fruits, and deep green vegetables. Many are best consumed raw. I've long felt that the food we eat has been so overfertilized and stimulated that it doesn't pack the same nutritional wallop as crops grown in generations past or grown naturally. When fruits and vegetables do reach our tables, many families boil their vegetables and cook away the nutritional value. Most people don't realize that when they pour the boiling water off the carrots, they just poured most of the nutrition down the sink.

Nutritionally preventative measures can increase your longevity. If you agree, take these ideas to heart:

• *Eat calcium-rich foods*. Fighting osteoporosis can be accomplished through adding the following foods to your diet. The amount of calcium in an average serving is put in parentheses:

yogurt (450 mg)
milk (300 mg)
orange juice with calcium (300 mg)
Swiss cheese (260 mg)
calcium-enriched cereal (200 mg)
salmon (340 mg per six ounces)
cooked beans (90 mg)
spinach greens (145 mg)
cooked broccoli (70 mg)
orange (55 mg)

• *Load up on pasta smothered in rich tomato sauce*. Mitchell Gaynor is director of medical oncology at Strang Cancer Prevention Center in New York City and co-author of *Dr. Gaynor's Cancer Prevention Program* (Kensington, 1999). Gaynor cites one study showing that men who ate ten or more servings of tomato products a week showed a 45 percent lower chance of developing prostate cancer. Mama mia, that's a lot of spaghetti sauce and pizza. Fortunately, I've always been a pasta lover, and Bev cooks a great tomato-based sauce. The reason tomatoes are singled out for the cancer-fighting ability is because of lycopene, the pigment that gives tomatoes their color.

Most supermarkets stock sorry-looking tomatoes these days. Grown in huge greenhouses and picked green, these light-red hybrids taste like rubber balls. Pay extra for natural, vine-grown tomatoes and other produce.

• *Drink plenty of green tea.* If eating a half-cup of tofu each day sounds daunting, you can drink three cups of green tea each day, which will supply the body with protective, detoxifying enzymes. The main antioxidant in green tea is 200 times more potent than vitamin E and 500 times more potent than Vitamin C.

• *Take nutritional supplements to pick up the slack.* I toss down thirty vitamin supplements after I eat my morning cereal. I know this is a large amount, but I'm a great believer in giving the body all the vitamins and nutrients it needs for the long haul. What's in all those pills? Well, there's magnesium, zinc, calcium, and lecithin. I take antioxidants such as vitamin E, C, and selenium. I ingest a form of natural testosterone and yohimbe to maintain libido.

I buy my vitamins in bulk and keep them in a drawer in my bedroom. Once a month, I fill a thirty-day set of plastic containers with my daily vitamins. That way, when I leave for an eight-day trip, all I have to do is pack eight small plastic containers.

Taking vitamins and herbs have become a new display of flower power for erstwhile Baby Boomers, many whose wariness of conventional medicine has prompted them to be proactive about their health—instead of waiting for something to go wrong with their bodies. It pleases me that more and more Americans are finding herbs and other supplements as appealing as I have, which is why sales of herbal and botanical supplements have more than doubled since 1994. This $12-billion-and-growing industry has 60 million people washing down a handful of vitamins and herbs with their morning OJ each day.

They swallow doses of aloe to fortify their immune systems, echinacea for colds and flu symptoms, valerian and melatonin for fitful nights of sleep, ginkgo bilboba for mental alertness, goldenseal to boost the immune system, and avena sativa to rev up their sex lives.

PASSION POTIONS

Speaking of avena sativa, men have been looking for ways to rev up their sex lives—also known as aphrodisiacs—for centuries. Back in King David's day, raisins were considered helpful because they were seen as "seeds" that could enhance the "seed" of a couple. The Song of Solomon (2:5) says: "Strengthen me with raisins, refresh me with apples, for I am faint with love."

Since David's time, hundreds, if not thousands, of foods and herbs have been viewed as sexually useful. They run the gamut from asparagus, fennel, and garlic to cinnamon, ginkgo bilboba, ginseng, and yohimbe. I once met Dr. Carlon M. Colker, and he gave me a copy of his book *Sex Pills: What Works and What Doesn't* (Advanced Research Press, 1999). In his book, he said:

> For eons man has wanted to make sex better, make it last longer, preserve sexual drive as one ages, reverse sexual dysfunction, restore a waning sex drive, and improve one's sexual prowess. To that end, man has engaged in a seemingly never-ending search for a magic pill or a potent elixir. Some work, some don't. Some are brilliant in design and mechanism of action, while others are simply dangerous and stupid.

If you have low libido, some of these herbs and supplements are worth checking out, but don't be surprised if nothing changes south of your belt line. You need to take a reasoned, sober approach to herbal sexual enhancers. If breathless advertisements tout new breakthroughs, erections galore, and multiple orgasms for the ladies, the old saying—"If it sounds too good to be true, it's probably too good to be true"—can be applied in this arena. For instance, I don't believe that ground-up tiger penises are going to:

- substantially increase energy levels!
- dramatically increase sex drive!
- produce greater pleasure during sex!
- increase genital sensations!
- increase sexual frequency!
- reverse impotency in men!

Instead, investigate some of the more common aphrodisiacs such as: avena sativa (a natural extract from green oats); arginine (an amino acid that is said to stimulate arousal by promoting production of nitric oxide, which produces harder, longer-lasting erections); damiana (an herb with a reputation for sending a woman's libido into the stratosphere); and kava kava root (an herbal muscle relaxant that eases performance anxiety).

Another popular herb is yohimbe bark, an African herb found in the bark of medium-sized evergreen trees in the jungles of West Africa, Cameroon, Congo, and Gabon. Yohimbe has been found to be effective in cases of impotence caused by physical or emotional reasons. A study conducted at Kingston General Hospital in Kingston, Ontario, tested forty-eight men suffering from psychogenic erectile disorder. They divided into two groups and participated in a ten-week, double-blind trial study, with one group receiving yohimbe and the other group a placebo daily.

At the end of the phase, 62 percent of the yohimbe-treated group reported some improvement in sexual function, while only 16 percent of the placebo group reported any improvement. The study concluded, "Although questions about the action of yohimbe in the body and how it improves potency remain to be answered, the extract is a safe treatment for psychogenic impotence and no less effective than current treatment options."

Because of yohimbe's potency, anyone using the herb needs to exercise caution and common sense. It is not advisable for men with high blood pressure; consult your doctor. Indeed, those considering this natural approach should educate themselves, talk to others who have used the herb, seek out medical advice, and realize limitations of herbal products. One final note: the American Urological Association has warned that yohimbe doesn't work.

In closing, please know that I cannot give any medical advice. All I can speak from is personal experience. Herbal supplements have done well by me, and they are worth looking into.

Chapter Thirteen

QUESTIONS AND ANSWERS

Lovemaking in the midlife years is an intricate art that must be practiced by two people for them to enjoy mutual satisfaction. Throughout this book, Bev and I have attempted to address how the physical relationship changes in the forties, fifties, sixties, and beyond. In this chapter, using a question-and-answer format, I will address common inquiries that we've heard regarding sex in the later years.

Q: My wife has a bad back, so she's rarely up for making love. She's basically told me to like it or lump it. Even at my age, I'm not ready to see my sex life sail off into the sunset. What can I do?

A: It may surprise some couples that they experience physical disabilities as they grow older—disabilities that make it unpleasant or even impossible to have sex. I hope you recall that I stated in chapter 10 that we must return to the basic principle that we pledged ourselves to when we made our marriage vows, "for better, for worse, in sickness and in health," and your marriage should never depend on how many time you make love each month.

Have you ever thought about experimenting with "pleasuring" one another by means other than vaginal intercourse? There are other ways to be intimate, you know. I once knew a man in his eighties who was a deacon in our church. He said that when he and his second wife married (a lovely lady, I might add), she was physically too small for them to ever have intercourse. Through thirty years of marriage, however, they had a wonderful, loving relationship— but never any sexual intercourse. So I know that it can be done with God's grace.

Q: After all these years, I'm tired of the missionary position. My wife doesn't like to be on top, and she certainly won't let me enter her vaginally from behind. For once, I'd like to do things a little differently. Do you have any thoughts about what I can do?

A: One of the things about the act of marriage is that it is an expression of love. If it gets to the point where it becomes an expression of sex, then you are looking for something more than what you have. Count your blessings; there are many couples who can't even enjoy the missionary position. If your wife is happy with you making love on top, you should be praising the Lord that you have that kind of relationship.

One of the things about the act of marriage is that it is always best when it's an expression of love; love seeks not its own. If you have talked to your wife and told her you would like to experiment occasionally with something else and she still doesn't want to do that, then enjoy what you have together instead of always seeking something greater.

Q: Is there an age when sex comes to an end?

A: I asked an eighty-one-year-old minister with snow-white hair when sex comes to the end. His reply: "Well, it hasn't happened to me yet!" I've also met people well into their late eighties who occasionally have sex. I always like to point out that Abraham and Sarah fathered their child when they were ninety-nine and ninety, but that was a miracle of God, of course. Generally speaking, sex just seems to gradually fade away, somewhere between eighty-plus years and death. Everyone has their own sexual time clock.

Q: If my husband and lover is impotent, can I use a vibrator to please myself?

A: There's nothing in the Bible that forbids vibrators, if for the simple reason that they didn't exist in those days. Using vibrators is a form of self-manipulation, a topic that the Bible is also silent on. I would say that if using a vibrator is the only means of release and it's something that you don't overindulge or do with impure thoughts, then it's okay.

Q: Since the Bible is silent on masturbation and my wife is unavailable for sex, how often can I avail myself of this type of sexual release? Is there an improper way to masturbate—like looking at *Hustler* magazines?

A: All forms of masturbation have to be evaluated, not in the light of the physical experience, but in the mental attitude at the time. Usually, male masturbation is associated with pornography or fantasies that are pornographic, and that's when it's detrimental. Masturbation can also become self-addicting. I've heard of masturbating addicts who did it several times a day. This drains all energies from academic and vocational pursuits, and the practice can't be good for one's social life.

At the end of the day, I think masturbation is a matter between the individual and God. If you can do it without feeling the need to confess it as a sin, the physical function of bringing oneself to orgasm is not in itself a sinful act—it's the mental thought process that makes it right or wrong. In 2 Corinthians 10:5, Paul says we're to cast out evil imaginations and everything that is contrary to Christ. I would say that as long as you keep your mind clean at the time, it would probably be acceptable, but be careful that it doesn't become an obsession.

Q: My husband came home with some handcuffs and mentioned something about playing "bondage" with me. I recoiled. Now he's mad at me. What was he talking about?

A: That's a form of sadomasochism, and your husband probably learned about it from reading pornographic or sadomasochistic material. He's at a stage in his life where he's reaching out for something that's contrary to what God intended for him. This could be very dangerous. My feeling is that a wife who is willing to have sexual relations with her husband should not be asked to do something that is repulsive to her, like being handcuffed or tied to the bedposts.

You may think this form of behavior is pretty bizarre, but I've heard it before. I once had a sick, sick case in which a registered nurse said her husband had an obsession with feces. He wanted her to put her poop in a plastic bag and keep it until he got home from work because he liked to smell it. When she asked me what she should do about this, I replied that her husband's obsession was unsanitary and obscene, and he needed industrial-strength counseling. This episode only goes to show you some of the bizarre obsessions that people can develop over time. In this case, I also recommended that the couple seek professional therapy.

Q: Why are men drawn to X-rated videos? They are so gross. How could anyone get turned on by watching those things?

A: Watching X-rated videos is a habit, and some men have it more than others. Just as statistics tell us that about 10 percent of the population is vulnerable to alcohol, so is a similar percentage of men vulnerable to watching pornographic material—maybe more. Pornography is contrary to Scripture; it should be shunned at all costs.

Anyone who is hooked on X-rated videos is developing an obsession with sex. Sex is meant to be a natural, loving expression, not something that is a simulation of what was acted out on a TV screen. Besides, many of the actors and models in X-rated movies are just playing a part. They don't even incorporate the same practices in their own personal sex lives!

When men see unnatural positions undertaken in X-rated films, it creates unrealistic expectations, and many women find that not only repulsive but hurtful. I've had wives ask me, "Is it possible to do that?" If so, you'd have to be a contortionist to reproduce some of those sex acts suggested on the screen.

Q: My husband doesn't want to go to bed at night. He stays camped at his computer and surfs the 'Net. Our love life is in the pits. Am I right to be concerned?

A: This creates a challenge to the wife to see whether she can seduce her husband away from the computer. Hour after hour of computer use may indicate that he is addicted to Internet pornography or a chat room filled with "naughty talk." But let's suppose everything is on the up and up, and your husband enjoys clicking his way through cyberspace.

I would think that a normal, healthy man, if his wife came up behind him dressed in a slinky nightie and pressed her body against him, would gladly shut off that computer and go to bed with her. In fact, if she did that drill a time or two and he didn't respond, it shows that he needs counseling to overcome a computer addiction.

Q: After all these years, my husband still has a problem with premature ejaculation. Is it too late to get some help?

A: It's unusual to have premature ejaculation after you hit your forties and fifties since nature takes a toll on our vital energies. My suggestion is that anyone with a long-term premature ejaculation problem needs counseling because there are ways of overcoming it, some of which are well-documented and illustrated in other Christian sex books. When all else fails, self-manipulation an hour or so before lovemaking can also be a means of making it more possible to have a normal sex life. The good news is that premature ejaculation usually passes with age.

Q: Ever since the empty-nest years started, we have been busier than ever, especially with meetings nearly every night at church. We are too tired for sex afterward. How should we handle this?

A: If you're too tired for sex on a permanent basis, you're too busy—even for church activities. I've noticed that many people these days are tired all the time. One of the things that we all have to face—but we don't like to—is that our vital energies begin to wind down and dissipate as we get older. That's why you see very few football players and baseball players in their forties; it's a remarkable person who can compete at a world-class level in his fourth decade and beyond. When pro athletes are said to be "washed up," it's just an indication that they just don't have the rhythm, energy, and vitality that they once did.

You have to learn to cope with it. One of the things you can do is to take a nap. I once read that a twenty-minute nap in mid-afternoon or early evening is the equivalent of four hours of sleep at night. Having said this, I will make a confession about something I like to do to revitalize my energies. I lay down on the floor, put my feet on the bed so that they are high above my head, and fall asleep for fifteen or twenty minutes. The blood travels from my elevated feet to my brain, making my feet tingle, which in turn wakes me up refreshed because of the increased oxygen brought to my brain by my blood.

Let me reveal a little more about this professional secret. When I was in my fifties, I was pastoring a booming church with three morning services and two evening services. I had to preach five times in one day. My Sunday preaching occurred after I arrived home Saturday night following my speaking engagements at a Family Life seminar somewhere in the United States on a Friday evening and all day Saturday.

To cope with this fatiguing schedule, I found it essential on Sunday afternoon to lie down on the floor, put my feet on the bed, and have a quick snooze. I woke up refreshed. These days when I'm on a writing project, there are times when I'll suddenly be overcome with sleepiness. When that happens, I lie down on the floor, put my feet up for twenty minutes, and then I can get right back to work, feeling refreshed and like a new man.

I would think that this concept would carry over for a couple that's too tired for lovemaking. They should rejuvenate their energies by taking naps. In fact, I would suggest that anyone in his or her sixties, seventies, and eighties—looking to maintain maximum efficiency—should take a nap during the day or early evening.

Q: Is it too late to do anything about my wife's frigidity? We're in our fifties.

A: There has to be a serious cause to your wife's frigidity because God naturally made us so that we desire a physical relationship in the act of marriage. You should have gone for counseling years before you reached your fifties, but it's not too late to seek help. For example, a counselor needs to diagnose the causes of her frigidity. Why is she totally turned-off from sex?

In my counseling experience, one of the reasons that I've found for frigidity is that the woman often harbors an angry spirit toward someone. For example, she could have been molested when she was in elementary school. I've had several young women confess that they had this terrible experience. Their spirit of bitterness was such that they never forgot it. Every time their husbands came toward them, they became frigid because what was about to happen reminded them of the times they were molested.

I think one of the reasons that Christians enjoy a physical relationship better than others is because we forgive and forget those things which are behind, as the Bible teaches us. I had an interesting experience one day when I had two women come to see me: one was very loving and affectionate and had a wonderful relationship with her husband; the other was admittedly frigid. They had both been molested in the fourth grade.

Obviously, the one who had no side effects had put those terrible experiences in the back of her mind because she had forgiven that person and moved on. For the other woman, however, her horrible molestations were just as fresh in her mind as if they had occurred yesterday. She would not give them up. That's a choice you make.

Other roots of frigidity are often anger or fear. She might have had some hurtful experience when she was a virgin and then engaged in premarital sex in the back seat of a car. Many women have admitted to me that they didn't enjoy the "back seat" experience, but they gave in because they wanted to please the person they were with. Under those circumstances, those women started their marriages thinking that sex was a bad scene, a duty they did for their husbands. That attitude might have gotten them through the early stages of the marriage and into motherhood, but they never came to grips with the fact that they were mentally frigid—and what you are mentally is what you are.

By the way, if you really love your partner and you know you're the cause of a malfunction, then you're going to go for help to find some solution to rectify the problem.

Q: I am in my early sixties. My first wife died of breast cancer several years ago, and I now I am remarried to a wonderful woman seventeen years my junior. She is, shall we say, more energetic about the physical relationship than I am. How can I keep up with her?

A: It's good that you ask that question because it's not uncommon, especially when there's disparity between the ages of a couple. I once had a doctor friend tell me that one of the questions he was going to ask God was this: "How come You made young men more interested in sex than their young wives, but when they lose that keen interest, their wives became more interested?"

There are some things today that can be done. For example, I highly recommend Korean ginseng, which is helpful and seems to have few, if any, side effects. Yohimbe is another good herb, if you don't have high blood pressure. A summation of my advice on nutritional supplements can be found in the previous chapter.

Q: My husband died of a heart attack at age fifty-two. If I remarry, who should I talk to? What books should I read regarding sexual adjustment? It took us years and years in my first marriage to become fully compatible sexually.

A: You're reading the right book right now! First of all, if your husband died at fifty-two of a heart attack, the chances are high that he was not in good health for some time. Neither of you might have known it, and his condition could have had an effect on every phase of his life, including his lovemaking. Also, and this may come as a shock to some readers, but men are different. You may find a more expressive husband the next time around, maybe a man who had a loving relationship with his wife who passed away. You're wise to go for help because the more good, wholesome information you have on a given subject, the more you're able to cope with the difficulties.

Many who had a good sexual relationship in their first marriage feel a sense of guilt the second time around. That's why I advise a lengthy period of time between relationships—anywhere between one to three years because you will have to learn to love the person you're with and put into the back of your mind the person you were married to before he was removed by death.

You may wonder how that is possible. Well, remember when you gave birth to your first child? You loved that child so much that it didn't seem possible that you could love another child in the same way. Then you had a second child. And a third. Perhaps a fourth. Each child made a place in your heart equal to the first child. We function that way. When you remarry, you're not betraying the love of your first spouse, you're creating a love for a new person.

Q: How can two people who never talk about sex start talking about sex after thirty years of marriage? We have some real issues to bring up.

A: You need to come to grips with this very subject, and talking about it is very important. I'm a great believer in confrontational counseling, meaning that if you sweep something under the rug, it doesn't go away—it just creates a lump under the carpet.

Consequently, if you ignore talking about sex, the problems will fester. The sooner two people talk about something without rancor, the better off they will be. That's why often times a counselor doesn't really counsel the couples. Instead, he serves as a spiritual referee so that the husband and wife can feel more comfortable discussing the subject in the presence of another person.

One of the most difficult subjects in all the world for couples to talk about is sex. The subject has to be approached very gently. When you have a problem, face the fact that you *do* have a problem and then seek a solution, either from outside counseling, talking with a Christian who shares your principles, or through reading some materials. That's why Bev and I write books like this—so that people can look for help in a nonthreatening way and find solutions just between themselves.

Q: Can retirement rob romance? If my husband is suddenly underfoot continually, won't I get sick of him?

A: There's an old saying that familiarity breeds contempt, but it doesn't have to be that way. A sixty-five-year-old man surprised me one time when I asked him how often he and his wife made love, and he replied, "Well, I'm retired now, so we have more time for that sort of thing." But those two people were very loving and very gentle to each other.

If people irritate each other, then they're not talking to each other very lovingly. They are being sarcastic and not kind. A lack of sex in those marriages is usually an indication of a lack of love. A man needs to learn—or be reminded—that his verbal approval and assurances make her feel really loved. The woman who feels sexually used in marriage may go along with it, may even have orgasms, but the act of marriage is not complete to her unless it is an expression of love. Most men don't realize that it is the way they talk and the way they treat their wives between lovemaking experiences that assures her of his love.

Q: You've said that the sexual relationship cements the marital relationship like no other. Then why do so many couples complain about unsatisfactory sex lives?

A: Probably because they don't have a good marriage relationship. Again I come back to the way that a married couple lovingly treats each other. You show me a couple that is gracious, loving, and kind, and as the Bible says, "in honor, preferring one another," and I'll show you a couple that has a good sex life.

Q: My wife does not like to perform oral sex. After all these years of hoping she would change, she never has, and it is starting to bug me. I feel as though she should expand her horizons after all these years. Is it right for her to ignore my needs for thirty long years and never stretch into these areas for my sake?

A: I would be more inclined to think that it's wrong for you to impose your wants on her because oral sex is not a need, it is a want. Our surveys indicated that half of women never use oral sex on their husbands, and 41 percent said "occasionally," but I interpret that to mean that many couples have experimented with it a time or two over the years, but it is not a common practice for them.

Oral sex had never received any endorsement from the church. It seems to be a desire for something more, more, and more. As a rule, I think it's wrong for one person to expect that of another. If she has had an unpleasant experience in that area in her past, or she's been taught that it is taboo, then you may never change her attitude toward it. Why not thank God that she enjoys the act of marriage—which in the long run is far better and far more normal?

Q: I've read in women's magazines that fantasy is a good thing. Somehow, fantasizing about Mel Gibson while making love to my husband doesn't seem kosher. Why is fantasy wrong?

A: It's not only not kosher, it's sinful to entertain evil thoughts. If you want to fantasize about someone, then fantasize about your lover, your married spouse.

Q: My wife and I are in our fifties. She shocked me awhile back and said, "I've never enjoyed sex, and at this age, I'm no longer willing to do the things I don't like. I'm not going to have sex with you anymore." I've really struggled this past year. What am I to do?

A: One of the major purposes of getting married, according to 1 Corinthians 7, is to relieve sexual tension. When she refuses to

participate, she married you under false pretenses. The both of you
have pledged to keep yourselves only unto each other as long as you
both shall live. That expression is talking about the sexual relationship, and you go about this in a way to relieve the tension of your
partner in the normal, God-approved way. If your wife says "I don't
like it, I don't want to do it," I would suggest that the both of you
need counseling, either with a minister or a Christian sex therapist.

**Q: What should I do to romance my husband so that he'll be
more interested in me?**

A: I've yet to meet a man who wasn't excited when he learned
that his wife desired him. The way you dress or the way you conduct yourself can show him that you are interested, and he will usually respond. If he doesn't, then you need to talk to him. For
example, the fear of impotence will make a man less open to receive
those vibrations from his wife. That's why whenever there's an impotency problem, a couple needs to talk and work on it together. But
remember: there is hope for improvement.

**Q: As my wife and I get older, our prayer and devotional life
get stronger, and we spend more time praying before bed. Trouble
is, I'm not in the mood for sex after a long time in prayer. I'm
always feeling I have to choose between sex and prayer. What do
you suggest?**

A: That's the first time I've ever been asked that question.
Usually when people get amorous with each other, their prayer life
goes by the wayside, if they have to make a choice one way or the
other. I would say that if they are physically too tired after a long time
of prayer, they should either (1) shorten the prayer or (2) make love
first and then pray.

Don't forget that you have seven nights a week, and the average couple is probably making love one, two, or three times a week
at your age. That gives you four, five, or six nights just for prayer, if
you are so inclined. I don't think the Lord will hold it against two
lovers who use one or two of those nights for making love.

When I've said what I'm about to say before audiences, people gasp because they think it's a little extreme, but I don't think there's anything wrong with people getting down on their knees and praying together, having their hearts entwined together, and then getting up and making love. Or, I don't think there's anything wrong with making love and then getting down on your knees and praying, if you have the energy. Just be natural. Lovemaking is a God-given act, and there's nothing wrong with it. Remember: married lovemaking was God's idea!

Chapter Fourteen

THE CRITICAL
COMPONENT

Ozne thing that I think you will find interesting is that of the forty
books I have written, *The Act of Marriage* has resulted in more
people coming to personal faith in Jesus Christ than any other book
I've written, except for the *Left Behind* fiction series about the end
times that I coauthored with Jerry Jenkins.

The reason why so many men and women accepted Christ into
their hearts while reading *The Act of Marriage* is because we included
a chapter entitled "The Missing Dimension," in which I presented
the Gospel in very clear terms and showed that Christ in our life
enriches everything we do. I made the point that the human person is really a four-part being: body, emotion, mind, and spirit. I
noted that the present-day humanistic philosophy had reduced man
to body, emotion, and mind and totally blew off the spiritual part
of every person, which is the most significant of the four. This is what
I meant by the "missing dimension" in people's lives.

Following the release of *The Act of Marriage*, I received a letter
from a Christian wife who wrote to say that her unsaved husband had

found her copy of *The Act of Marriage* one night while she was attending a women's meeting at church.

Apparently her husband had settled himself into his recliner to do some serious relaxing when he spied the book in the midst of several magazines.

He picked it up, scanned the title, then began flipping through several pages to understand what *The Act of Marriage* was all about. *I didn't know Christians were interested in such things*, he thought. His interest piqued, the man began reading, and five hours later, when he finished chapter 13, "The Missing Dimension," he got down on his knees and invited Jesus into his life. You can imagine his wife's joy when he greeted her later that evening with the words, "Honey, I received Jesus tonight!"

The couple could now be drawn even closer to each other since the husband had found the "missing dimension." To illustrate its influence, we should examine all four individually.

1. *Physical.* We are all aware of the physical part of our nature. It involves our bodily functions and is of vital importance when considering the art of marital lovemaking.

2. *Emotional.* The motor of a human being is the heart, out of which proceeds "the issues of life" (Prov. 4:23 KJV). The heart is the seat of all emotions, both good and bad—love and hate, joy and bitterness. If our emotions function properly, we will have no problem functioning physically.

3. *Mental.* The mind is the most complex mechanism known to humanity. Some have called it the most complicated computer in the world. The memory bank of the mind registers the lifetime impressions that influence our prejudices, likes, and dislikes, thus indirectly producing our feelings. For example, those who display a continuing distaste for sex are not reflecting a bodily malfunction, but a mental distortion that inhibits their emotional feelings and prohibits normal physical expression. Incompatibility, for instance, hardly ever starts in the body; it almost invariably begins in the mind. For that reason, mental misconceptions replaced by

good mental images usually unstop the flow of good emotions and enable the individual or couple to experience proper physical responses.

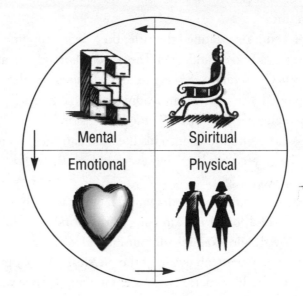

4. *Spiritual.* The least recognized side of a person's nature is the spiritual. The French Renaissance philosopher Blaise Pascal recognized the significance of this aspect when he declared that the "God-shaped vacuum" in the heart of every person can be satisfied by none other than God Himself. Unless that God-shaped vacuum is filled by a personal relationship with God, human beings are condemned throughout their lives to an endless treadmill of activity in an attempt to fill it. Some try to educate it out of existence, others attempt to ignore it, and still others seek a variety of self-gratifying experiences—but all to no avail.

By ignoring the reality of that spiritual side of nature, they compound the problem by violating the laws of God, which activate the conscience and heighten the recognition of futility and emptiness. Interestingly enough, this dilemma increases with age, and I've seen many people in their middle ages and older chase after a host of unproductive activities (starting a new company, being promoted to senior vice president, trying to break ninety on the golf course) in an attempt to escape their own miseries.

Those who neglect the spiritual side of their nature do so at their own peril, for God has implanted this vital part of their nature to stabilize their mind, heart, and body. People who ignore this mighty power station within them are like an eight-cylinder car trying to function on six cylinders. They will be capable of very limited operation and will never be the smooth-running, effective persons God designed them to be.

All human beings want happiness for themselves and those they love, but we believe that they are incapable of complete happiness unless they fill that spiritual void within their lives. Such an endeavor is really not difficult for them if they want it. Let us note five key points that make possible the filling of that void and the resultant happiness everyone desires.

1. God loves you and has designed you with a spiritual side to your nature that has a capacity to enjoy fellowship with Him.

> For God so loved the world that he gave his one and only Son, that whoever believes in him shall not perish but have eternal life.   *John 3:16*

Above all else, people should know that God loves them, regardless of what the circumstances of life seemingly indicate. The gift of His son on Calvary's cross stands as a historical monument that God loves His human creation. It is legitimate to personalize that fact and say that God loves *you!*

God also desires that we enjoy fellowship with Him. "God is spirit, and his worshipers must worship [fellowship with him] in spirit and in truth" (John 4:24).

As we have already seen, we are empty if we do not enjoy that oneness of fellowship with God. The diagrams on the following page illustrate the two views of humanity:

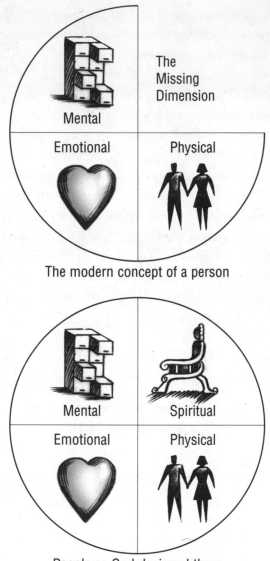

The modern concept of a person

People as God designed them

Mankind's romance with intellectualism based on atheistic humanism pictures secular human beings in three parts as indicated in the diagram. The tragedy of this philosophy is that it limits mankind completely to human resources, producing a futility of life never intended by the Creator.

2. The self-will and sin of human beings have destroyed their spiritual life, separating them from God and making them miserable.

> For all have sinned and fall short of the glory of God.
>
> *Romans 3:23*

In the spiritual quarter of a person's nature we have pictured a throne to clarify that, unlike animals, we humans were given a free will at birth to choose the ruler of our lives. We may wish to enjoy fellowship with God, or we may assert our free will and pride (as most do) and live independent of God. With this decision, consequently, a person's spiritual life dies, thus destroying his or her ability to produce lasting happiness.

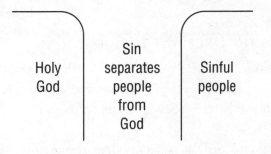

Holy
God

Sin
separates
people
from
God

Sinful
people

HUMAN BEINGS ARE SEPARATED FROM GOD

"For the wages of sin is death" (Rom. 6:23). Since God is holy, the day-to-day sins that people commit when self is in control of their lives separate them from God. The Bible teaches that those who commit sins "will not inherit the kingdom of God" (Gal. 5:21).

People usually try to restore their fellowship with God by good works, religion, philosophy, or church membership. They are helpless to save themselves, however. "He saved us, not because of righteous things we had done, but because of his mercy" (Titus 3:5). The best efforts of people will never restore either their fellowship with God or their happiness.

Although many expressions of sin are described in the Bible, all are caused by self-will in opposition to the will of God.

3. Jesus Christ is God's only provision for your sin, and through Him you can again have fellowship with God and experience the happiness He has for you. The Bible teaches that Christ died in man's place.

> We all, like sheep, have gone astray, each of us has turned to his own way; and the LORD has laid on him the iniquity of us all.   *Isaiah 53:6*

> But God demonstrates his own love for us in this: While we were still sinners, Christ died for us.   *Romans 5:8*

> In him we have redemption through his blood, the forgiveness of sins, in accordance with the riches of God's grace.
> *Ephesians 1:7*

CHRIST IS THE ONLY WAY TO GOD

Jesus said, "I am the way and the truth and the life. No one comes to the Father except through me" (John 14:6). He also said, "I am the gate; whoever enters through me will be saved" (John 10:9).

God has provided the perfect bridge to bring sinful human beings back into fellowship with Himself: the cross on which His own Son was crucified for the sins of the whole world. "Christ died for our sins . . . [and] was raised on the third day according to the Scriptures" (1 Cor. 15:3–4).

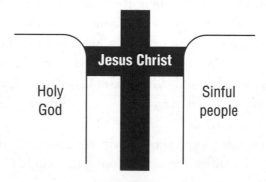

Jesus Christ

Holy
God

Sinful
people

4. You must repent of your self-will and receive Jesus Christ as Lord and Savior by personal invitation to have that fellowship and happiness restored.

THE THREE STEPS TO RECEIVING CHRIST

1. Repent. "Unless you repent [turn from self-will to God's will], you too will all perish" (Luke 13:3). Repentance means a willingness to turn from your own ways, your self-will, and follow God's ways. Some have mistakenly assumed that they must turn from their sins to be converted, but this is impossible until they first look to God. He then will turn you around and cause you to forsake your sins.

2. Believe. "Yet to all who received him, to those who believe in his name, he gave the right to become children of God" (John 1:12). The word *believe* literally means "to rest upon" or "to take completely at His word."

3. Receive. Christ said, "Here I am! I stand at the door [of your life] and knock. If anyone hears my voice and opens the door, I will come in and eat [fellowship] with him, and he with me" (Rev. 3:20).

RECEIVING CHRIST AS LORD AND SAVIOR

Receiving Jesus Christ as Lord and Savior involves turning the control of your life over to Christ, making Him Lord of your life. You may think that at your age, you're too set in your ways to make such a radical change. Not at all! It's never too late to ask Christ to come into your life and cleanse you from past sins and guide your future. No matter how old you are, God has a plan for you, a plan to give you a future and a hope.

These diagrams (at the top of page 208) clearly picture the two kinds of spiritual lives extant. The self life shows self on the throne making the decisions of life, with Christ symbolically pictured outside of life. This individual may be religious, irreligious, atheistic, or profligate; it really makes no difference. In all cases where self is on the throne, God is the missing dimension in that person's life, thus making him or her incapable of experiencing true happiness.

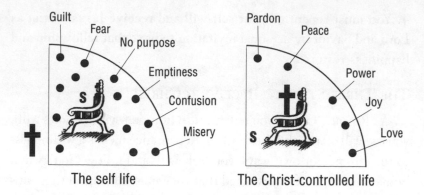

The self life   The Christ-controlled life

Before a person has lived many years, he or she will begin to experience the misery, confusion, emptiness, purposelessness, fear, and guilt with increasing intensity—just as we have pictured it.

As Bev and I have traveled around this country for years, we have been fortunate to meet thousands of people from various walks of life. When some individuals talk to us about how unhappy they are, we ask them about these five keys to happiness. If we have half the chance to demonstrate the empty results of the self-controlled life to people, they almost always agree with us. Indeed, I have never known a person forty years or older deny the fact that this was his or her personal experience.

Perhaps that's because they are becoming more aware of the passage of time. I always take great pains to explain that the Christ-controlled spiritual life is the result of an individual's receiving Jesus Christ as Lord and Savior by personal invitation. Note that we did not say accepting Christ "as Savior." The Bible repeatedly refers to the salvation experience as the result of accepting Christ as *Lord* and Savior. Romans 10:13 says, "Everyone who calls on the name of the Lord will be saved."

Whenever individuals are willing to recognize their self-will and call on Jesus Christ to save them from past sins and become Lord of their future, Christ comes into their lives to take control of the throne of their will. The self-will then becomes a servant to Christ. The S in the diagram no longer represents self; it now stands for *servant*.

Jesus Christ first brings into people's lives abundant pardon for past sins, producing in their hearts a peace that was previously unknown. Believers have the power of God resident within to begin overcoming their sins, bad habits, weaknesses, and hurts. Furthermore, they possess the joy of the Lord and the love of God to extend them abundantly to others. This is the Spirit-controlled spiritual life that produces happiness.

RECEIVING CHRIST PERSONALLY THROUGH PRAYER

Receiving Christ is a very personal experience. No one else can do it for you. As you would invite a guest into your home, so you must invite Jesus Christ into your heart personally. Prayer is simply talking to God, who is more interested in the attitude of your heart than in the words you say. If you need help in forming a prayer, here is a suggested one:

> Dear heavenly Father, realizing I am a sinner and can do nothing to save myself, I desire Your forgiveness and mercy. I believe Jesus Christ died on the cross, shedding His blood as full payment for my sins, and rose bodily from the dead, demonstrating that He is God.
>
> Right now I receive Jesus Christ into my life as personal Lord and Savior. He is my only hope for salvation and eternal life.
>
> Give me understanding and increasing faith as I study Your Word. I surrender my will to Your Holy Spirit to make me the kind of person You want me to be.
>
> I pray this in the name of Jesus Christ. Amen.

Does this prayer express the thoughts of your heart? If so, pray now to the heavenly Father; the Bible guarantees that Christ will answer your prayer and come into your life.

HOW TO KNOW YOU ARE A CHRISTIAN

A Christian is one who has Christ in his or her life. If you sincerely asked Christ through prayer to come into your life, you can be sure He has. God cannot lie, and He promised to come in when invited (Rev. 3:20).

The Bible guarantees to you eternal life. "And this is the testimony: God has given us eternal life, and this life is in his Son. He who has the Son has life; he who does not have the Son of God does not have life. I write these things to you who believe in the name of the Son of God so that you may know that you have eternal life" (1 John 5:11–13).

Thank Him regularly for coming into your life.

HOW TO BECOME A STRONG CHRISTIAN

Although you may have been born many years ago, when you came into this world you needed certain things to grow—food, exercise, and knowledge. So it is spiritually. Here are some helpful suggestions:

1. *Read the Bible daily.* The Bible is God's message to you, but it will meet your needs only if you read it. It is advisable that you concentrate on reading in the New Testament, preferably the gospel of John, the first epistle of John, and the books of Philippians and Ephesians. Then read consecutively through the New Testament. It is impossible for anyone who does not regularly read God's Word to become a strong Christian.

2. *Pray daily.* God is your heavenly Father; He wants you to call on Him regularly (Matt. 26:41).

3. *Go to church regularly.* You will never become a strong Christian unless you consistently attend a Bible-teaching church where you can hear more of God's Word. You have only begun to learn about the many exciting things God has planned for you. You also need to make Christian friends; church is the ideal place to do it (Heb. 10:25).

4. *Identify with Christ.* Make this identification public by following Him in believer's baptism (Matt. 28:18–20). Once you have been baptized, you should officially become a member of the church where you were baptized and seek to serve the Lord with that congregation.

5. *Share your experience with others.* Relating what Christ has done for you will both strengthen you and help your friends to receive Christ (1 Peter 3:15).

6. *Study the Bible*. In addition, take advantage of the excellent Bible study aids available today. Your church no doubt will be able to help you find such aids. If not, the Christian bookstore in your community has an ample supply.

5. Let Jesus Christ direct the daily decisions of your life, and you will enjoy inner happiness regardless of the circumstances around you.

"In all your ways acknowledge him, and he will direct your paths."   *Proverbs 3:6, KJV*

You have to invite Jesus Christ into your life only once, but to let Him control your life requires a daily commitment. He wants to help you make all the decisions of life so that you can experience the maximum happiness He has in store for you.

THE HAPPY LIFE—A CHRIST-CONTROLLED LIFE

The only truly happy Christians are those controlled by Christ. Jesus said, "Now that you know these things [the principles of God found in the Bible], you will be blessed if you do them" (John 13:17).

Happiness is not automatic for a Christian. Each of the diagrams below represents a Christian, but obviously one Christian is miserable, the other happy. The reason is clear. The person with the self-controlled spiritual life reveals that the self is back on the throne and he is living independent of God. This is unfortunately a common

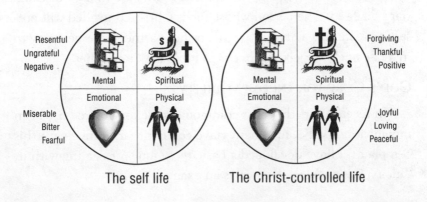

Resentful
Ungrateful
Negative

Miserable
Bitter
Fearful

Forgiving
Thankful
Positive

Joyful
Loving
Peaceful

Mental   Spiritual   Mental   Spiritual
Emotional   Physical   Emotional   Physical

The self life   The Christ-controlled life

state for many Christians, and it always produces unhappiness. In fact, many Christians who live this way are more miserable than non-Christians because, in addition to making a mess of their lives through selfish decisions, they are also increasingly convicted by the indwelling Spirit.

The Christ-controlled spiritual life pictured above shows Christ daily in command of the decision-making processes of life. These individuals, like everyone else, will have to make such decisions as where they will work, how they will treat their families, who will be their friends, and where they will live. However, they will *inquire of the Lord* where they will work, how they will treat their families, who will be their friends, and where they will live. When Christ control's one life, that person seeks to do those things and think those thoughts that please the Lord, who in turn will grant that person an abundance of the love, joy, and peace that guarantees the happiness every person desires.

Christ in control of a person's spiritual life is truly the missing dimension to life. When He directs an individual's spiritual nature, that person's clean thought patterns will produce good feelings and in turn engender the physical responses everyone wants. For this reason we believe that a couple with Christ in control will enjoy the act of love over the long years of marriage more than other people. Good thought patterns and attitudes spark the good actions that all married couples need.

Love is the first of the "fruit of the Spirit" mentioned in Galatians 5:22–23. The person whose life is Christ-controlled will possess a greater capacity to love his or her partner. The best way to increase one's capacity to love is to bestow it on another.

GOD'S CURE FOR INCOMPATIBILITY

In recent years the most common excuse for divorce has been incompatibility. Because many have come into my office with this complaint, I have developed a basic technique for dealing with it. One typical couple will serve as an example.

After the wife had reported her sordid tale of woe, she exclaimed, "There is no hope for our marriage because Sam and I are no longer compatible." This meant that they were no longer together in sexual unity, in this case avoiding intercourse for five months.

I asked Sara, "Has it always been this way?" Naturally she replied no. What couple would ever think of getting married knowing they were incompatible? Some couples who complain of incompatibility were so compatible during their courting days that they could hardly keep their hands off each other. This indicates that they *learned* to be incompatible. Such discord has nothing to do with biology, physiology, or bodily function, but as we shall prove, it has everything to do with mental and spiritual sin.

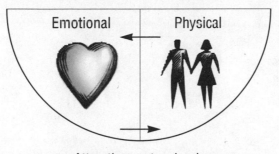

Attraction on two levels

Most couples today were attracted to each other on the emotional and physical levels because they were thrown together in a work or social environment. They noticed that their body chemistry—or as I like to refer to it, biological magnetic attraction—sparked an emotional response. This was always an exciting experience for two red-blooded people as they discovered a lifetime of sex following marriage.

But every couple is destined to discover after marriage that they were not so similar in their likes and dislikes as they had thought before their wedding day. Their backgrounds, intelligence, and education may be different, and they may find themselves strongly disagreeing on such vital issues as money, children, manners, family, business, and social events. If these differences can be faced unselfishly, they will not create incompatibility; but if self reigns on the throne of their will, they are going to indulge in thought patterns of ingratitude, revenge, and animosity. Such thoughts turn love, joy, and peace into bitterness and hatred—the very ingredients that produce incompatibility.

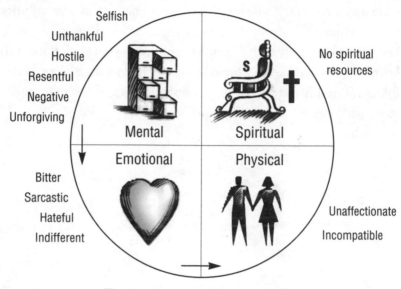

The development of incompatibility

At the time Sara came in, she and Sam shared no spiritual dimension, and thus their individual selfishness had made them incompatible. But when Sara accepted Christ as her Lord and Savior in my office that day, she canceled their divorce proceeding and went home to become a loving, gracious wife.

At my recommendation she did not tell Sam immediately about her new faith in Christ. Instead she waited until he noticed the obvious change in her. It did not take long. At the first spontaneous show of affection he was suspicious that she had been on a spending spree. Before long, however, he was forced to acknowledge her sincerity and candor. Within ten weeks Sam also came to a saving knowledge of Christ, and they have enjoyed a compatible relationship for many years.

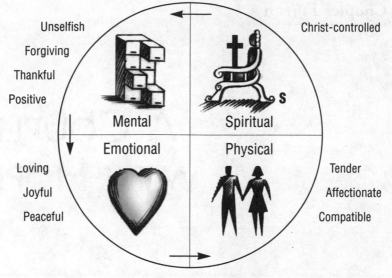

Unselfish			Christ-controlled
Forgiving	Mental	Spiritual	
Thankful			
Positive			
Loving	Emotional	Physical	Tender
Joyful			Affectionate
Peaceful			Compatible

The cure for incompatibility

If this were a rare experience, I would hesitate to cite it. On the contrary, I have found that making Christ the Lord of their life is a couple's best cure for incompatibility, no matter how many years of marriage.

A compatible marriage is a happy, long-lasting marriage, producing the environment for a union that lasts a lifetime. When Jesus Christ warned us that we can do nothing without Him, He knew we were unable to establish a truly happy marriage without His guidance. The first recourse of a couple who are not enjoying the ultimate blessings that God intended for them should be to let Jesus Christ take control of their spirits, minds, and emotions. This can occasion a miraculous improvement in the relationship between two people.

Chapter Fifteen

A Couple
with Hope

Just a few weeks before we decided to write *The Act of Marriage After 40*, Bev and I, along with my daughter, Linda Murphy, sat transfixed in Southwest Community Church in Palm Desert, California. The pleasant Sunday morning was February 14, St. Valentine's Day.

The pastor, David Moore, sat at a table on one side of the platform, while his wife, Sonya, perched herself on the other side at her own desk. "We're going to do something very different this morning," said David, "and I hope you'll enjoy it. If you don't, I've got a sermon ready for the next service," he joked. Then they pretended to write letters to each other.

David explained that he and Sonya—both in their mid-forties— wanted to tell the story of their friendship, how they met, how they fell in love, and how they married. I've chosen to close this book with their charming story because it captures the swirling emotions of midlife couples.

DAVID: Let me take you back to February of 1974. *Dear Diary:* It was just another boring day at the tropical fish store until about four o'clock this afternoon. I was minding my own business, feeding the fish, and ringing up sales, when I noticed a girl sticking her hand into an aquarium. She had long, strawberry blonde hair and wore a great-looking sweater. "Take your hand out of the tank now," I said sternly. It turned out she was a friend of Sharon, my coworker, who gave her permission to stick her hand in the tank. Afterward, Sharon introduced us; her name is Sonya.

SONYA: *Dear Diary:* I met this guy at a fish store today. Can you imagine? I thought anybody that worked at a tropical fish store would be kind of weird. But this guy wasn't too bad; a little rude, though. What's really interesting is that he sells tropical fish, and I sell fish and chips. I wondered what his fish would taste like in our batter?

DAVID: Sharon's been bugging me to call Sonya, so I finally called her today. I was prewarned that she is dating another guy at her high school. I've always liked competition, so I gave her a call. I told her about Light Shine, the Christian rock band that I play in. I invited her to a concert at a Baptist church. I almost told her that if she came she'd have to keep her hands out of the baptistery, but I thought better of it. She surprised me by saying yes. This should be interesting.

SONYA: What kind of name is Light Shine for a rock band? And what kind of rock band plays in a Baptist church? Oh, well, it's only a date, and I've never been inside a Baptist church. This ought to be interesting.

DAVID: It's late Sunday night and I can't sleep, so I might as well write. The concert went well. The band is beginning to sound pretty good. Sonya came to hear us tonight and I think she liked us. I could tell by the look on her face that she was surprised that I could actually carry a tune. So far I can only identify two defects on Sonya. The first is that scar on her chin, and the other is she doesn't know how to eat. She ruined a perfectly good bacon sandwich by putting lettuce and tomato on it. But I think she really likes me.

SONYA: The concert was much better than I expected, and David really can sing. I found out that David's nineteen years old, a junior in college. He told me he might call me on Monday or Tuesday, and I hope he does. I can tell he kind of likes me.

DAVID: Sonya agreed to go out with me tomorrow. I think we'll take a drive up the coast. I'll make a nice lunch, and we'll have a picnic on the beach.

SONYA: David and I went for a ride up the coast. He brought the picnic lunch. I had visions of French bread, cheeses, fruit, pate, perhaps some cheesecake, but he showed up with bologna sandwiches, slapped with mustard and catsup, on white bread. We drove his green 1972 Pinto. The tape deck was under my seat, and he kept changing tapes all day long. Now I know he really likes me.

DAVID: It's clear that if our relationship is to become anything significant, we need to share a common faith. I think I'll ask her over this week to help me study for my theology midterms.

SONYA: I'm really impressed with David's knowledge of the Bible. I went over to his house tonight to help him study. He had me read some questions from flash cards. He seemed to know all the answers to all of them. In my church if we have hard questions about our faith, we're told not to ask questions, just believe. I'm beginning to wonder if our church has the answers to the questions I'm asking. One thing for sure, David is very serious about his faith.

DAVID: Tonight Sonya and I went to my church and then we drove to a youth meeting at her church. I told her, "God loves you and so do I." I wonder if that's the same thing as saying, "I love you"? It just seemed like such a natural thing to say, but I surprised myself by saying it.

SONYA: What an amazing day! I went to church with David tonight. The guest speaker wasn't very good, but he seemed sincere. At the end of the service, he asked that everyone who knew they were going to heaven to come to the front and pray for the ones who didn't know for sure. The whole church went forward except for two ladies and me. I never felt so alone. My church tells us we have to work our way to heaven. You never really know if you've been good enough. David's church talks about the grace of God, and quickly admits that no one will ever be good enough. That's why Christ died for our sins, my sins. I'm beginning to understand. When everyone returned to their seats, a lady turned to me and asked me whether I would like to invite Christ into my life. I nodded, and we prayed. I've never felt so free in my life. God loves me, not just when I'm good, but He loves me unconditionally.

DAVID: It's Wednesday afternoon, the day before Thanksgiving. Sonya and I have been dating for nine months. Tonight's the night I'm going to ask her to marry me. I wonder what I'm going to say to her tonight. I've got to think of something.

SONYA: Guess what? I've got a ring on my finger. That's right, it's the most beautiful diamond ever. It's not the biggest, but I love it. I've got a feeling that life is about to turn into the biggest bowl of cherries ever.

DAVID: Here are some things that I've learned over the years that every woman ought to know before she gets married. Number one: shopping is not fascinating. Number two: common courtesy requires a woman to leave the toilet seat up when she's finished using it. Number three: the man is always in charge of the remote control. Number four: God created man first so he'd get a chance to speak. Number five: any sort of injury involving a man's private parts is not funny. Number six: a Nair bottle looks an awful lot like shampoo when it's left in the shower.

SONYA: I've learned a lot of interesting things about men. It's a medical fact that a man's skull is thicker than a woman's. Men with pierced ears are better prepared for marriage because they've already experienced pain and have purchased fine jewelry. Male menopause is a lot more fun than female menopause. With female menopause you gain weight and you get hot flashes. With male menopause, you get to drive fast cars, purchase motorcycles, and wear gold chains. And finally, I've learned that men forget everything, while women remember everything. That's why men need instant replay in sports.

Nearly twenty-five years of marriage have passed. I now understand that cherries also have pits. Life includes a lot of pits! Thankfully, our marriage has grown stronger because of them. David and I have certainly had some stressful times, but we've learned that faith isn't a bridge over troubled waters, it's a passageway through them.

DAVID: As an example, let me go back to May 3, 1976. Marriage hasn't been quite what I expected. I was hoping for a honeymoon every day. Seems like there are more hassles than honeymoon. This first year has been pretty tough for me. I'm trying to figure out who's in charge of what, and communicating clearly isn't as easy as I thought it would be. I'm learning that I am a task-driven guy. I tend to compartmentalize my life. I've got a time for study. A time for running ministry programs. A time for counseling students. A time for this. A time for that. Including a time for Sonya.

The other day we were driving to my parent's house, and Sonya and I got into a pretty heavy conversation. All of a sudden she pulled out the most powerful weapon in a female arsenal: she started to cry. I didn't know what to say, so I stopped the car and asked her why she was crying. She looked straight at me and said . . .

SONYA: "David, I don't want to be one of your projects."

DAVID: I was stunned. She's absolutely right. I was trying to make her into a Proverbs 31 lady. And suddenly I realized that's not my job. Marriage isn't a workshop for recreating your mate into what you want them to be. God calls us to love one another, not reconstruct one another.

SONYA: May 1976. Wow, what a difference in David. I don't know what got into him, but he's been great.

DAVID: What a difference in Sonya! I don't know what got into her, but she's been great. Ever since I stopped trying to fix her, she hasn't needed fixing.

SONYA: It's May 22, 1982. Today we lost our baby. I'm so glad we've got Jamie and Lindsey. David and I were both stunned as the doctor gave us the news. Our worst fears came true. We will never bring home little Kyle Ashley. After the doctors left the room, David and I prayed. Strangely, that seemed to help. But still the loss is real. As we sat there holding each other David said. . . .

DAVID: "I know the first person I'm looking for when I get to heaven."

SONYA: After we left the hospital, we bought Jamie a balloon, and I explained to her that she wasn't going to be having a little brother just yet. Getting into the car, the balloon slipped out of her little fingers, and she started to cry. Then tonight as Jamie said her prayers, she said, "Lord, please give this little balloon I lost today to Kyle Ashley to play with up there in heaven."

DAVID: What a faith she has: simple, beautiful, healing. Now it's October 1987. I'm only thirty-three years old, but I am tired. Between the pace of high school ministry, traveling to speaking engagements, and trying to be a family man, I'm stretched so thin. The most emotionally exhausting issue I deal with is church politics. It seems like everyone has an agenda for you, so Sonya and I have decided to leave the ministry. It's not because we've lost our love for the Lord but because we're worn out by people who insist they know what God wants for us. I'm tired of explaining to parents why I can't fix their teenage kid. I'm tired of explaining to the elder board why ministry needs to be culturally relevant to reach students today. I'm tired of having to defend the ministry before people who know a whole lot about real estate but not so much about the eternal state.

SONYA: Tonight we had dinner with the director of a television show David wants to work for. He and his wife have become such good friends. They're outside-the-box thinkers; I think that's why David enjoys being with them. David seems more at ease around this couple than many religious people we know. They are authentic, and it doesn't hurt that they both ride motorcycles. Anyway, at dinner our friend said something that really shook both of us. We were talking about the television show when suddenly he said, "This is the second-largest syndicated show in the world, and we have the latest toys and technology. But at the end of our day, nothing we do really matters."

I could tell David was stunned by this comment. God's timing is a funny thing. God was using our friends to redirect us back toward the ministry. I don't know where we're going to end up, but some little church in the California desert called earlier this week. They want to talk to David about becoming the senior pastor. I wonder what that means? The church is in Palm Desert. I hate sand.

DAVID: February 1988. I'm a senior pastor, which I swore I would never be. I'm living in the desert, where I swore I would never live. And our family of five is living in a motor home parked in the sand next to a portable building at the church. Talk about the grapes of wrath. But I figure it's good to live in a motor home—that way we can make a fast getaway if we need to.

SONYA: Did I say I hate sand? When I married David, I knew we'd never be rich, but I never expected to live in the world's largest kitty litter box. I didn't even let our kids have a sandbox when we lived in the city. Today Tyson was sitting outside the motor home on his big wheel when he was attacked by red ants. I hate ants. I hate sand. How long will it be before David can get fired so we can get out of here? It's getting hot!

DAVID: April 1990. I can't believe we've survived. We actually made the transition from a traditional church to a seeker-sensitive church. God has been so faithful. That shouldn't be so surprising. Great things are happening to Southwest Community Church.

SONYA: This church has been great. The people have let me be me. They've let me major on motherhood and haven't put any expectations on me. You know, sand doesn't seem so bad anymore. If the Palm Springs area keeps building golf courses at the current rate, the only sand around will be in the sand traps.

DAVID: July 1993. I don't know what's with Sonya lately; we just aren't connecting anymore. A couple nights ago I caught myself looking at her and wondering, *What happened to us?* I even thought to myself, *This is one love story that's over.* We've had eighteen wonderful years together. Although I'll never leave her, the magic is gone. She seems so distant.

SONYA: David seems so cold.

DAVID: What's wrong with her anyway?

SONYA: I don't know what he expects of me.

DAVID: Touchy, touchy, touchy.

SONYA: Pushy, pushy.

DAVID: Wa, wa, wa.

SONYA: The lights are on but nobody's home.

DAVID: So this is what it's like to have a roommate instead of a mate.

SONYA: David sure seems disappointed with me. He's trying to pretend that everything is okay, but I can see it in his eyes. He's really hurting. I think he's scared. He acts like he's losing his best friend. In many ways, life doesn't get much easier as the years go by. I've learned that being a Christian certainly doesn't exempt us from life's problems and pains. What God does expect of us is to grow through our adversities and to overcome them through Him. I think I'll go see a doctor.

DAVID: She's back! Sonya's back! She's bold, she's beautiful, and she's normal again. Who would have ever thought a little gland could make someone so irritable, and well . . . these have been the toughest two months of our married life, but I'm glad she's back. I've always loved her, but it's nice to like her too.

SONYA: February 1996. I didn't sign up for teenagers; all I wanted was a baby. I thought having small children was tough, but compared to raising teenagers, little children are a piece of cake. Don't get me wrong, my kids are good kids, but these are scary times. The stakes associated with mistakes today can cost a kid for a lifetime.

DAVID: February 1996. I don't know how to describe what I'm feeling. It's like a piece of me is dying. I have a numbness in my heart. This little girl has so much potential. She's so beautiful, so gifted, and she has so much to live for. Why would she want to die? Disbelief and denial meandered through my mind as I read the note that she had left the family. She described the pain of her adolescence. The frustration of feeling like no one really understands. She's a restless spirit looking for release, but she finds it only in her sleep. I don't think she really wants to die; she just wants the pain to stop.

Situations like this are hard enough in the ministry, but when it's your own family, that's a whole different story.

God is really something. He has sustained us and strengthened us through more than either of us could have ever imagined on the day that we said "I do." God isn't a bridge over troubled waters, but He always, always makes a passageway through them.

SONYA: February 1999. *Dear Diary:* The girls are away at the university, and Tyson is in high school. I can't believe how time has passed. I think I now know what love means. I'm hoping that someday David accidentally stumbles upon my journal and reads it. I know that sounds a little silly, but I like to make sure he knows how I feel. I've always told him how I'm feeling and what I'm thinking, but words seem so superficial when describing subjects of the soul. There are so many things I wish we could do over again. Not to change them, but to relive them, relish them, maximize every moment. How thankful I am for what we've learned and how we've loved and lived. I know now what love is. It's exactly what I hoped for.

DAVID: *Dear Diary:* I think I know what love means. I must admit, however, that my understanding of love is much different from when Sonya and I first met. I used to think that love was communicated through words. After all, *I love you* are the most precious words our ears can hear. I know now that love is a decision. Love is choosing to be patient and kind. Love is refusing to be jealous, boastful, or proud. Love doesn't demand its own way. It resists growing irritable, and it refuses to keep a record when it's been wronged. Most important, I used to think that love was something I had to prove. Now I'm understanding that loving acts fuel real love. Love actually begets love. God wasn't kidding when He said we love because He first loved us.

SONYA: David and I have been so blessed. Who could have known twentysomething years ago where we would be today? And who can know today what tomorrow will bring? But today is a good time to reflect on God's goodness and to remember His guidance. As for our future, only God knows. But our future is lit by the light of our past. Since God has been faithful, I must have faith.

DAVID: For today, I have learned this: Life is great, but eternity is better. I want to be ready for both. I've learned that life is what you make of it, and nowhere is that more true than in the arena of love. I've seen so many couples who are just existing. So many live vicariously through the experiences of others; how sad. Jesus said His purpose is to give life in all its fullness. But the fullness of life doesn't just happen. It requires letting go of your fears and allowing God to lead you beyond the horizon of your own vision, into a place that He has prepared just for you. Wow! I think I know now what love really is. . . .

A CLOSING THOUGHT

Wasn't that beautiful? I especially appreciated David's comments regarding the "fullness of life" in his closing statement. When Jesus Christ walked the earth, He said, "Apart from me you can do nothing" (John 15:5). Obviously people can eat, drink, work, make love, and raise children without Christ, but Jesus meant that without Him they cannot enjoy the maximum benefits of life. His presence in individuals during their human existence guarantees enrichment, joy, and fulfillment. He said, "I have come that [you] may have life, and have it to the full" (John 10:10). He beautifies every human experience, particularly interpersonal relationships, and guides us into mental, physical, and emotional satisfaction. No other source can enable us to achieve all the potential for which God created us.

The "abundance of life" was illustrated to me by one of the most wonderful couples I ever knew. Anyone who spent some time with Jerry and Sara knew that these dedicated Christians were crazy about each other and enjoyed a genuine, loving relationship based on years of sacrifice for each other. They were inseparable, constantly holding hands even long past their golden anniversary. In their fifty-ninth year of marriage, however, Jerry suddenly died of cancer. Sara lost him in a heartbeat, it seemed to her.

Sara was not herself after her lifelong friend and partner died. Her health began failing. Then she suffered a stroke, causing her daughter and son-in-law to invite Sara to come live with them. Sara began hallucinating that Jerry was coming back to her, that they would be reunited in marital bliss just as before. There were times when Sara's daughter came into her room and discovered Sara carrying on make-believe conversations with her late husband while she slept—that's how real the hallucinations were to her.

One day, just before her eightieth birthday, Sara asked her daughter to take her shopping. While the two walked the aisles of a nearby drug store, Sara continued to talk about Jerry and how she hoped to see him soon. Sara then asked if she could do some shopping alone. Her daughter, respecting her mother's privacy, said she would wait in the car.

Her mother completed her shopping, but the very next day she died in her sleep. Following the memorial service, her daughter was cleaning Sara's room when she came upon the Longs Drugs bag from her last shopping trip. She opened the bag, and inside was a tube of K-Y Jelly.

Can you believe that? Sara, who delusionally waited to be reunited with her husband, wanted to be ready for his return. She truly loved her husband in all ways possible. This is what I call living the "abundant life." The Lord obviously had many purposes in mind when He deliberately created our sexual capabilities, from reproduction to pleasure to unique union to growing old with each other. Like all things He created, it is all very good and for our good, right up until the time He calls us to live with Him in eternal glory.

It is my sincere hope that you and your lover, the one you pledged to love until the day you die, will remain as close as Jerry and Sara did. To my readers, I finish by saying, "Yes, Virginia, the act of marriage is alive and well after you turn forty, fifty, sixty, seventy, eighty, and beyond because it truly is an expression of love between two lovers."

Appendix:
The "Act of Marriage After 40 Survey" Results

1. Participants

Approximately 800 surveys returned with equal representation between wives and husbands.

2. Your age is:

	Wives	Husbands
40–49	27%	22%
50–59	30	29
60–69	25	21
70 or older	18	28

Comment: We had a well-balanced group respond to our survey but with many more men age seventy than women age seventy and up.

3. How long have you been married to your present spouse?

	Wives	Husbands
0–10 years	7%	7%
11–19 years	12	12
20–29 years	21	21
30–39 years	25	25
40–49 years	21	21
50 or more years	14	14

Comment: 81 percent have been married more than twenty years, signifying that this group comprised couples whose marriages will go the distance.

4. How many times have you been married?

	Wives	Husbands
Once	82%	80%
Twice	16	17
Three	2	3
Four or more	0	0

Comment: Like Old Man River, the vast majority of couples are looking forward to paddling down the river of life with their first spouse. Their marriages have a greater than 50/50 chance of surviving.

5. Which statement fits you?

	Wives	Husbands
I am still married to my first spouse	76%	76%
I am divorced and remarried	14	15
I am widowed and remarried	3	5
My spouse has been married before	7	4

Comment: Not all the surveys were filled out by both spouses, which is why the results are a little different between wives and husbands.

6. How many children do you have?

	Wives	Husbands
None	5%	4%
One	8	7
Two	29	26
Three	29	27
Four	17	19
Five	7	8
Six	3	5
Seven or more	2	4

Comment: Most couples rear two, three, or four children.

7. Ages of your children

	Wives	Husbands
0–11	10%	10%
12–19	23	22
20–29	36	35
30–39	40	38
40 and older	32	32

Comment: These numbers add up to more than 100 percent since couples had children in different age groups. This is a nice cross-section of ages, but a vast majority of their children, around 75 percent, were adults.

8. What is your religious affiliation?

	Wives	Husbands
Protestant	60%	61%
Charismatic	14	14
Reformed	2	2
Mainline denomination	7	8
Roman Catholic	2	3
Agnostic	1	1
Other	14	11

Comment: A majority of those responding to this survey were evangelical Christians.

9. Do you have teenagers or young adults still in the house?

	Wives	Husbands
Yes	34%	27%
No	66	69

Comment: Teenagers in the house! That's the way it is for approximately one-third of our survey respondents.

If so, which statement fits you?

	Wives	Husbands
Having teenagers in the house has definitely put a crimp on our lovemaking	33%	27%
Made no difference	67	73

Comment: I would have thought that more than one-third of couples would have said that have teens around put a crimp in their lovemaking.

10. Years of education

	Wives	Husbands
Did not finish high school	1%	4%
High school graduate	33	20
Attended 1–2 years of college	30	23
College graduate	27	32
Graduate with Masters or advanced degree	9	21

Comment: We have a well-educated group. Two-thirds of women said they said attended or finished college, and more than 50 percent of men earned college degrees or their Master's degrees.

11. Regarding the wife employed outside the home: Which statement comes closest to your situation?

	Wives	Husbands
Wife has never worked outside the home	28%	28%
Wife has generally worked part time outside the home	42	42
Wife has generally worked full time outside the home	20	20
Wife has always worked outside the home	10	10

Comment: Seventy percent stated that the wife did not work full time outside the home.

12. What was your main source of sex education before marriage?

	Wives	Husbands
None	19%	23%
Friends	21	31
Minister	3	2
School	17	12
Reading	41	36
Other (including parents)	16	10

Comment: These numbers add up to more than 100 percent since people chose more than one answer. Twenty percent said they had no help, and around 40 percent learned sex education through reading. A small percentage said their parents taught them the "birds and the bees."

13. What has been your main source of sex education during marriage?

	Wives	Husbands
None	13%	19%
Friends	3	3
Minister	1	2
School	0	1
Reading	75	62
Other (such as spouse)	17	17

Comment: These numbers add up to more than 100 percent since people chose more than one answer. Once married, couples said they mainly relied on books for sex education information. Our counseling experience indicates that one is never too old to learn something new about lovemaking, and no couple should be closed to the possibility that perhaps something they are doing is not in the best interest of one of the partners.

14. What books on marriage have you found most meaningful?

	Wives	Husbands
Love for a Lifetime by Dr. James Dobson	16%	10%
The Act of Marriage by Tim and Beverly LaHaye	45	44%
Sex in Marriage by Cliff and Joyce Penner	4	6%
Others	35	40%

Comment: I was pleased to learn so many read our first book.

15. Do you ever talk to your spouse about your sexual relationship?

	Wives	Husbands
All the time	18%	17%
Sometimes	60	64
Rarely	20	16
Never	2	3

Comment: My gut feeling is that may of those who marked "sometimes" really meant to say "rarely," based upon my counseling experience.

16. Over the last few months, what was the average number of time you had sexual relations?

	Wives	Husbands
Five or more times per week	1%	1%
Three to four times a week	11	9
Twice a week	18	16
Once a week	29	33
Once every two weeks	19	18
Once a month	10	10
Once every few months	6	5
Once in the last year	1	1
Our sex life is nonexistent	5	7

Comment: To those who said "five or more times a week," my goodness! Seriously, 59 percent of couples said they are having intercourse at least once a week or more. I thought it was important, however, to break down the survey results by gender and age.

16. Over the last few months, what was the average number of time you had sexual relations?

Females	40–49	50–59	60–69	70 and over
Five or more times per week	4%	0%	0%	1%
Three to four times a week	13	13	7	4
Twice a week	19	18	17	10

Females (cont.)	40–49	50–59	60–69	70 and over
Once a week	29	34	29	19
Once every two weeks	25	13	17	19
Once a month	6	12	13	16
Once every few months	4	6	7	10
Once in the last year	0	1	0	1
Our sex life is nonexistent	0	3	10	20

16. Over the last few months, what was the average number of time you had sexual relations?

Males	40–49	50–59	60–69	70 and over
Five or more times per week	5%	0%	1%	2%
Three to four times a week	15	12	5	5
Twice a week	16	11	15	10
Once a week	30	43	39	20
Once every two weeks	17	19	18	17
Once a month	11	9	10	15
Once every few months	5	4	4	11
Once in the last year	1	0	0	2
Our sex life is nonexistent	0	2	8	18

17. In relation to your first half of marriage, this frequency is:

	Wives	Husbands
More	11%	10%
About the same	18	18
Less	40	43
A lot less	31	29

Comment: I expect sexual frequency to decrease throughout the course of a marriage, but as you will see in the next question, women are more content than men about this development.

18. Your current frequency of intercourse in your marriage is:

	Wives	Husbands
About right	64%	48%
Too frequent	5	8
Too infrequent	31	44

Comment: This is one of the first questions where we see a significant difference in the responses from wives and husbands. Guess what? Men would like to see frequency increase, as the next question would indicate.

19. How frequently would you like to make love?

	Wives	Husbands
Five or more times a week	2%	5%
Three to four times a week	18	21
Twice a week	20	36
Once a week	38	23
Once every two weeks	14	10
Once a month	3	3
Once every few months	0	1
Once a year	0	0
No desire	5	1

Comment: The 2 percent number for "five times or more a week" matches the number of women who have a lot of sexual desire (see Chapter 4). Isn't it interesting how the men estimated their frequency with consistently higher numbers than the women? And the number of women exhibiting "no desire" was five times that of men.

20. To what extent have you been satisfied with intercourse?

	Wives	Husbands
Very satisfied	45%	56%
Satisfied	35	32
Somewhat satisfied	15	10
Not satisfied	5	2

Comment: People are happy with making love. Despite lower frequency, between 85 and 90 percent of women and men are satisfied. I also had these results broken down by gender and age group.

20. To what extent have you been satisfied with intercourse?

Females	40–49	50–59	60–69	70 and over
Very satisfied	52%	47%	37%	44%
Satisfied	27	29	45	35
Somewhat satisfied	16	18	16	18
Not satisfied	5	6	2	3

Males	40–49	50–59	60–69	70 and over
Very satisfied	62%	54%	62%	45%
Satisfied	27	31	31	35
Somewhat satisfied	8	12	7	18
Not satisfied	3	3	0	2

21. How often do you reach orgasm?

	Wives	Husbands
All the time	20%	67%
Most of the time	46	25
Sometimes	27	3
Never	7	3

Comment: Men still orgasm much more than women, but I found it interesting that 28 percent of men said they reach orgasm "most of the time" or "sometimes."

22. How often does your spouse reach orgasm?

	Wives	Husbands
All the time	62%	22%
Most of the time	30	42
Sometimes	5	28
Never	3	8

Comment: If you cross-check these numbers with the last question, they are very close.

23. How often does the wife attain orgasm during sexual intercourse?

	Wives	Husbands
All the time	13%	12%
Most of the time	34	32
Sometimes	33	32
Never	20	18

Comment: These numbers are very close, so it does show that men are paying attention to their wife's sexual needs. For around half of all women, however, reaching orgasm is a hit-or-miss event.

24. How often does the wife attain orgasm by clitoral manipulation before penile entrance?

	Wives	Husbands
All the time	15%	13%
Most of the time	24	23
Sometimes	33	39
Never	28	25

Comment: Again, the numbers are fairly close, but the fact remains that half of women are fairly non-orgasmic.

25. Does the husband manipulate the wife's clitoris orally?

	Wives	Husbands
All the time	4%	2%
Most of the time	8	9
Sometimes	44	47
Never	44	42

Comment: A majority of respondents have been using cunnilingus in their sexual practices.

26. For the wife: How do you feel about being orally manipulated?

	Wives	Husbands
Enjoy it	48%	40%
Neutral	22	22
Dislike it	30	38

Comment: More women enjoy it than perhaps say to their husband that they enjoy it.

27. How often does the wife reach orgasm before the husband?

	Wives	Husbands
All the time	13%	14%
Most of the time	30	28
Sometimes	39	43
Never	18	15

Comment: If women are going to orgasm at all, they are probably going to reach climax before he will.

28. On the average, about how long must foreplay last for you to become sexually aroused?

	Wives	Husbands
1–5 minutes	26%	63%
6–15 minutes	56	32
16–25 minutes	15	4
25 minutes or longer	3	1

Comment: Guess what? Men are like microwaves and women are like crock-pots. Guys are still ready to go at a moment's notice.

29. Has the husband ever had difficult ejaculating?

	Wives	Husbands
All the time	2%	1%
Most of the time	3	2
Sometimes	41	42
Never	56	55

Comment: Men were honest in answering this question, mirroring what wives said about them. When you look at these numbers closer, you see where 46 percent of men are experiencing some type of erectile dysfunction.

30. How often does the wife use oral stimulation?

	Wives	Husbands
All the time	2%	1%
Most of the time	10	8
Sometimes	41	41
Never	47	51

Comment: Fellatio is not a common practice among Christian couples because their wives do not enjoy this practice. At the same time, however, around half of all couples employ fellatio in their sexual relations.

31. In general, how would you evaluate your sexual relationship?

	Wives	Husbands
Very good	44%	45%
Good	36	35
Fair	12	11
Poor	4	7
Very poor	4	2

Comment: Are we happy campers in the bedroom or what? These results are above national surveys of the entire population, buttressing my argument that guilt-free sex is the best sex.

32. How would you rate your spouse's interest in sex?

	Wives	Husbands
Very interested	75%	41%
Somewhat interested	21	50
Little or not at all interested	4	9

Comment: Well, ladies, the gentlmen don't think you're as interested in sex as they are.

33. Have you ever masturbated since your marriage?

	Wives	Husbands
Often	1%	6%
Occasionally	43	63
Never	56	31

Comment: Men masturbate more than women, which again is not a surprise.

34. Would you describe this as a sexually satisfying experience?

	Wives	Husbands
Yes, always	10%	10%
Yes, sometimes	30	45
No	60	45

Comment: Women clearly are not as satisfied with self-stimulation.

35. If you have masturbated since your marriage, what was the main reason?

	Wives	Husbands
My spouse was unavailable for sex	34%	46%
Coitus was not satisfying	17	2
I used it as a way of relaxing sexual tensions	33	41
Other	16	11

Comment: Very few men are going to tell that intercourse was not satisfying. If they masturbate, it's to release sexual pressure, whether the wife was available for sex or not.

36. Did you have sexual intercourse before you were married the first time?

	Wives	Husbands
Yes	38%	50%
No	62	50

Comment: I appreciate the honesty of the respondents, but this goes to show you how big a job the church has in teaching the biblical injunctions to wait until marriage.

37. Have you ever had an extramarital sexual experience?

	Wives	Husbands
Yes	7%	13%
No	93	87

Comment: I am not shocked by these numbers, based on my years of counseling practice. What these results say is that around 10 percent of Christian couples have succumbed to sexual temptation and strayed from their marriage.

38. What is your self-acceptance of your physical appearance?

	Wives	Husbands
Totally	45%	62%
Minimally	47	30
Reject	4	3
Don't know	4	5

Comment: Guys have always been accepting of their appearance, even if they have a gut hanging over their belt buckles.

39. How does your spouse accept your physical appearance?

	Wives	Husbands
Totally	75%	73
Minimally	15	16
Reject	2	1
Don't know	9	10

Comment: I'm pleased that couples, by a huge margin, accept their spouses for who they are. I hope they are communicating this aspect.

40. Do you still use birth control?

	Wives	Husbands
All the time	11%	11%
Sometimes	1	3
Never	88	86

Comment: Around 25 percent of the survey respondents were under the age of fifty.

41. Have you ever used devices for sexual stimulation in your lovemaking?

	Wives	Husbands
Yes	16%	14
No	84	86

Comment: I'm pleased that Christian couples are not running to sex shops to buy so-called "marital aids." I believe they interfere with lovemaking.

42. If so, what devices have you used?

	Wives	Husbands
Vibrator	40%	43%
Penis-shaped objects	10	10
Oils	30	27
Feathers	10	8
Other	10	12

Comment: I have no problem with couples employing oil as they massage each other, but I'm against indiscriminate use of vibrators and dildoes.

43. Have you ever seen a pornographic movie?

	Wives	Husbands
Yes	25%	53%
No	75	47

Comment: I'm surprised so many couples have availed themselves of porn, which in the last twenty years has become very easy to rent at a local video store.

44. Have you ever used erotic movies, books or pictures as part of your sexual relationship?

	Wives	Husbands
Often	0%	0%
Occasionally	8	9
Once	7	9
Never	85	82

Comment: You can't open a women's magazine these days without reading about how great X-rated videos are in "spicing up" a marriage. Hogwash! All these movies do is create a fantasy image that neither spouse can ever live up to.

45. Check the appropriate statement:

	Wives	Husbands
Pornography in our marriage is a real problem.	1%	1%
At one time we had a problem with pornography, but now we don't.	4	1
We've never had a problem with pornography in our marriage.	95	98

Comment: I'm pleased that couples have steered away from using pornography in marriage, perhaps after "trying it out" and realizing that it was not good for the marriage bed at all.

46. Check the appropriate statement:

	Wives	Husbands
Gambling in our marriage is a real problem.	1%	1%
At one time we had a problem with gambling, but now we don't.	1	1
We've never had a problem with gambling in our marriage.	98	98

Comment: Even though gambling doesn't have anything to do with marital sex, I thought this was an important question to include because gambling can wreak devastation in couples and families.

47. Have you or your spouse ever used Viagra or any other medication to ensure erection?

	Wives	Husbands
Yes, frequently	3%	2%
A few times	6	7
No	91	91

Comment: Viagra has been on the market for just a few years, and I predict its use will increase.

48. If so, how would you rate your satisfaction with Viagra?

	Wives	Husbands
Very happy	31%	25
Okay	45	47
Not at all happy	24	28

Comment: Three-fourths of those using Viagra say they are happy or okay with the results.

49. Have you or your spouse experienced impotence?

	Wives	Husbands
Yes, frequently	20%	16%
A few times	30	28
No	50	56

Comment: If you think impotency can't happen to you, look again.

50. Have you or your spouse sought medical attention for impotence or erectile dysfunction?

	Wives	Husbands
Yes	15%	15%
No	85	85

Comment: Interesting how the sexes agree on this question. This percentage is 50 percent higher than the general population, which an estimated 10 percent allegedly seek medical attention for impotency.

51. How much TV do you watch each day?

Weeknights	Wives	Husbands
None	18%	11%
1–2 hours	44	49
2–4 hours	29	32
4–6 hours	8	7
more than 6 hours	1	1

Comment: Research studies show the TV is on about seven hours a day, so these numbers are significantly lower.

Weekends	Wives	Husbands
None	13%	10%
1–2 hours	29	22
2–4 hours	24	28
4–6 hours	30	35
more than 6 hours	4	5

Comment: Couch potatoes unite! TV viewing (and video watching) jumps dramatically on weekends with 34 percent watching four or more hours a day, compared to 9 percent during the week.

52. Which statement best describes your reading habits?

	Wives	Husbands
I'm an avid reader who enjoys reading in my spare time	71%	48%
I enjoy reading, but I never have time to read a book	27	43
I am not a reader and do not read at all	8	9

Comment: Reading is a wonderful pastime. I hope it doesn't become a lost art with the next generation.

53. Which statement best describes your marital situation?

	Wives	Husbands
We still continue to court each other by having a regular date time or participating in activities and hobbies we enjoy.	61%	60%
We have fallen out of doing any romantic activities together, although we occasionally go out to dinner together or take in a movie.	37	38
We never do anything together.	2	2

Comment: These are distressing numbers. You mean 40 percent of couples are doing practically nothing to keep the romantic fires burning?!

54. How long have you been a Christian?

	Wives	Husbands
0–10 years	2%	3%
11–19 years	6	10
20–29 years	2	21
30–39 years	20	16
40–49 years	20	17
50 or more years	32	33

Comment: Our respondents have been Christians for a long time, which I'm happy to see.

55. Were you a Christian before you got married?

	Wives	Husbands
Yes	79%	78%
No	21	22

56. Was your spouse a Christian before you got married?

	Wives	Husbands
Yes	79%	83%
No	21	17

Comment: I'm pleased that so many couples were "equally yoked" in Christ when they married.

57. Which statement best describes your spiritual life?

	Wives	Husbands
Mature, spirit-filled Christian	56%	46%
Maturing Christian	43	48
New Christian	0	0
Not sure	1	5
Not a Christian	0	1

Comment: I have a gut feeling that many mature Christians marked the "maturing" category out of a humble attitude. But five percent of the men weren't sure they were Christians? Please read my chapter called "The Critical Component"!

58. Are you involved in a couple's Bible study?

	Wives	Husbands
Yes	21%	20%
No, but we have been in one in the past	44	46
No	35	34

Comment: This is a good percentage since many men and women choose to also attend men's or women's Bible studies.

59. Are you involved in a Bible study?

	Wives	Husbands
Yes	53%	43%
No, but I have been in one in the past	42	46
No	5	11

Comment: On the other hand, I think these numbers should be higher.

60. How often do you and your spouse go to church?

	Wives	Husbands
Every Sunday	78%	75%
Most Sundays	14	18
One Sunday a month	1	1
Seldom or never	7	6

Comment: Church attendance is very high, as it should be.

61. How often do you and your spouse pray together?

	Wives	Husbands
Every day	37%	40%
Several times a week	23	25
Seldom or never	40	35

Comment: I'm surprised so many said they seldom or never pray with their spouse since couples experience so many difficulties together.

62. Do you drink alcohol?

	Wives	Husbands
Yes	21%	28%
No	79	72

Comment: I'll raise a glass and toast those figures.

63. If so, how much?

	Wives	Husbands
Several times a week	19%	24%
Once a week	25	38
Once a month	30	17
Once every few months	26	21

Comment: Around one-fourth drink regularly of those who said they drink alcohol.

64. Do you smoke?

	Wives	Husbands
Yes	2%	6%
No	98	94

Comment: I'm happy that so many people are not smoking.

65. Does your spouse smoke?

	Wives	Husbands
Yes	5%	2%
No	95	98

Comment: These numbers match up for what the spouses said in question 64.

66. How many times a week do you exercise or participate in sports?

	Wives	Husbands
None	23%	21%
Once a week	19	17
2–3 times a week	34	36
4 or more times a week	24	26

Comment: Although these are good numbers, I'd like to see them higher.

67. What sports do you participate in? (Check all that apply)

	Wives	Husbands
Golf	6%	21%
Tennis	3	6
Basketball	1	3
Softball	1	3
Skiing or snowboarding	6	7
Running	2	17
Bicycling	13	19
Aerobics	13	6
Gym workouts	13	12
Walking	72	55
Other	23	20

Comment: Couples could check off more than one physical activity, which is why the numbers add up to more than 100 percent. Walking, by far, is the top category. But golf for men, as expected, is a popular activity.

68. Do you belong to a health, golf, or tennis club?

	Wives	Husbands
Yes	15%	14%
No	85	86

Comment: The country club set did not answer this survey.

69. Are you retired?

	Wives	Husbands
Yes	33%	40%
No	67	60

Comment: More are retirees than I thought.

70. If so, do you work part time?

	Wives	Husbands
Yes	33%	42%
No	67	58

Comment: Many find a part-time job to give themselves something to do.

Why?

	Wives	Husbands
To supplement our retirement income	33%	30%
To give me something to do	6	20
Because I enjoy it	61	50

71. How many vacation days have you taken in the last year?

	Wives	Husbands
None	6%	5%
One week	11	12
Two weeks	20	18
Three weeks	17	16
Four weeks	10	12
Five or more weeks	14	12
I am retired	22	25

Comment: Couples in the midlife years should have plenty of time to do things together!

NOTES

Introduction

1. Stuart D. Perlman and Paul R. Abramson, "Sexual Satisfaction Among Married and Cohabiting Individuals," *Journal of Consulting and Clinical Psychology*, Vol. 50, No. 3, 1982, 458–460.

Chapter One: Love for a Long, Long Lifetime

1. Bernard D. Starr and Marcella Bakur Weiner, *On Sex & Sexuality in the Mature Years* (New York: Stein and Day), 15.

2. Starr and Weiner, *On Sex & Sexuality*, 15.

3. Joel D. Block, *Sex Over 50* (West Nyack, N.Y.: Parker, 1999), 5.

4. Ibid.

5. Richard H. Davis, *Sexuality and Aging* (Los Angeles: University of Southern California, 1974), 187.

6. David Reuben, *Everything You Always Wanted to Know About Sex But Were Afraid to Ask* (New York: HarperCollins, 1999), 342–43.

7. G. D. Smith, et al., "Sex and Death: Are They Related?" *British Medical Journal*, 315 (Dec. 20–27, 1997): 1614.

8. Marianne K. Hering, "Believe Well, Live Well," *Focus on the Family* (September 1994): 2.

9. Hering, "Believe Well, Live Well," 4.

Chapter Two: The Change of Life

1. David Reuben, *Everything You Always Wanted to Know About Sex, But Were Afraid to Ask* (New York: HarperCollins, 1999), 312.

2. Stephanie DeGraff Bender, *The Power of Perimenopause* (New York: Three Rivers, 1998), 5.

3. Ivor Felstein, *Sex and the Longer Life* (London: Penguin, 1970), 56.

4. Morton Walker, *Sexual Nutrition* (New York: Instant Improvement, Inc., 1994), 128.

5. Winnifred B. Cutler, *Love Cycles: The Science of Intimacy* (New York: Villard, 1991), 70–71.

6. Reuben, *Everything You Always Wanted to Know About Sex*, 318.

7. The American Heart Association can provide you with much more information on the risk of heart disease and stroke. Contact the Women's Health line toll-free at (888) MY-HEART, or you can find this organization at *www.americanheart.org*.

8. The National Osteoporosis Foundation has information on the causes, prevention, detection, and treatment of osteoporosis. Call the national office at (202) 223-2226, or you can find more information on the Internet at *www.nof.org*.

9. *Consumer Reports*, published by Consumer Union, (January 1999): 53.

10. Ibid., 52.

11. Walker, *Sexual Nutrition*,131.

Chapter Three: The Male Menopause

1. Joel D. Block, *Sex Over 50* (West Nyack, N.Y.: Parker, 1999), 180.

Chapter Four: A Streetcar Named Desire

1. James C. Dobson, *What Wives Wish Their Husbands Knew About Women* (Wheaton: Tyndale House, 1975), 121.

2. Archibald D. Hart, Catherine Hart Weber, and Debra L. Taylor, *Secrets of Eve: Understanding the Mystery of Female Sexuality* (Nashville: Word, 1998), 66.

3. Hart, et al., *Secrets of Eve*, 69.

4. Winnifred B. Cutler, *Love Cycles: The Science of Intimacy* (New York: Villard, 1991), 42.

Chapter Five: A Refresher Course

1. Tommy Nelson, *The Book of Romance* (Nashville: Thomas Nelson, 1998), 121–22.

2. Clifford L. Penner, and Joyce J. Penner, *Getting Your Sex Life Off to a Great Start* (Nashville: Word, 1994), 79.

3. Penner and Penner, *Getting Your Sex Life Off to a Great Start*, 180.

Chapter Seven: When You're Dealing with ED

1. Morton Walker, *Sexual Nutrition* (New York: Instant Improvement, 1994), 12.

2. Bernie Zilbergeld, *The New Male Sexuality* (New York: Bantam Doubleday, 1992).

3. Julian Whitaker, *Healthy & Healing* newsletter (July 1998): 7.

4. *The Healthy Cell News* (April 1999): 4.

5. Joel D. Block, *Sex Over 50* (West Nyack, N.Y.: Parker, 1999), 200–201.

Chapter Eight: Don't Delay; Go Today

1. Bob Arnot, *The Breast Cancer Prevention Diet* (New York: Little, Brown, 1998), 12.

2. P. A. Newcomb, et. al., "Lactations and a Reduced Risk of Premenopausal Breast Cancer," *The New England Journal of Medicine* 330, no. 2 (1994): 81–87.

3. Katherine Dettwyler, "Breastfeeding and Breast Cancer," *Prairienet Web site*.

4. This information comes from the American Cancer Society's *Cancer Resource Center Web site* at *www.cancer.org*.

5. T. Greer Morris and P. White, "The Psychological and Social Adjustment to Mastectomy: a Two-Year Follow-Up Study." *Cancer* 40 (1977): 2381–87.

6. H. S. Kaplan, "A Neglected Issue: The Sexual Side Effects of Current Treatments of Breast Cancer." *J Sex Marital Therapy* 18 (1992): 3–19.

7. Marisa C. Weiss and Ellen Weiss, *Living Beyond Breast Cancer: A Survivor's Guide for When Treatment Ends and the Rest of Your Life Begins* (New York: Times, 1997), 146.

8. J. E. Woos, "Breast Reconstruction After Mastectomy," *Surgical Gynecol Obstet* 150 (1980): 869–74 and National Cancer Institute, Cancer Statistics Review 1973–89, Bethesda, Md.: National Cancer Institute; 1992. Publication No. NIH 92–2789.

9. Arnot, *The Breast Cancer Prevention Diet*, 10.

10. Ibid., 13.

11. Ibid., 52–53.

Chapter Nine: No Laughing Matter

1. Rick Chillot with Paula Rasich, "Guard Against Your Secret Fear," *Prevention* (July 1999): 121.

2. A. Von Eschenbach, R. Ho, G. P. Murphy, M. Cunningham, N. Lins, American Cancer Society guideline for the early detection of prostate cancer: update 1997.

3. Chet Cunningham, *Your Prostate* (Encinitas, Calif.: United Research, 1990), 7–10.

4. Julian Whitaker, *Health & Healing* (June 1999), 6.

5. Ibid.

6. Chillot with Rasich, "Guard Against Your Secret Fear," 124.

Chapter Ten: "In Sickness and in Health"

1. Owett Kaplan, "The Female Androgen Deficiency Syndrome," *J Sex Marital Therapy* 19 (1993): 3–24.

2. Saul H. Rosenthal, *Sex Over 40* (New York: Tarcher/Putnam, 1987), 154–55.

3. Joel D. Block, *Sex Over 50* (West Nyack, N.Y.: Parker, 1999), 228.

Chapter Eleven: The Temptations

1. Steve Farrar, *Finishing Strong: Finding the Power to Go the Distance* (Sisters, Oregon: Multnomah, 1995), 79.

Chapter Twelve: Exercise and Nutrition for a Healthy Sex Life

1. C. Don Morgan, et al., "Sexual Functioning and Attitudes of Eating-Disordered Women: A Follow-Up Study," *Journal of Sex & Marital Therapy* 21, no. 2 (1995): 67–77.

INDEX

Vibrators, 189
Vitamins, 181–84

Walking, 97–98, 177–79
Weight gain: and breast cancer, 125; and exercise, 179–80;
    midlife, 173–75; and sexual desire, 76–77
Widows and widowers, 194–95, 225–26. See also couples;
    relationships
Women: and alcohol, 125; attitude toward sex in, 28, 64–72; and
    breast cancer, 119–33; and breast cancer treatments, 128–30;
    and breast reconstruction, 131–32; and breast-feeding, 122–
    23; and breasts, 121–23; and children, 77; and clitoral
    stimulation, 87–90, 88–89; and detection of breast cancer,
    126–28; and diet, 125; and diminished sexual desire, 64–72,
    193–94; and emotions during menopause, 44–45; and
    estrogen, 48–52; and hysterectomy, 156; increasing sexual
    desire in, 72–80; and Kegel exercises, 46–47; and
    mammograms, 126; and menopause, 27, 38–53; and
    perimenopause, 42–43; and prevention of breast cancer, 132–
    33; and sexual desire, 64–80, 67, 117–18; sexual peak in, 23;
    and sexual phases, 83–85; and sexual response, 85; and
    smoking, 126; and symptoms of menopause, 43–47; and
    Tamoxifen, 132–33; and vaginal changes during menopause,
    45–46; and weight gain, 76–77; as widows, 225–26. See also
    breast; breast cancer

Yohimbe bark, 186

Revelation Unveiled

Tim LaHaye

IN THE TWINKLING of an eye, millions of people across the world vanish, resulting in highway catastrophes, plane crashes, utility breakdowns, and more. Chaos reigns. With the stage set, a dictator emerges who persecutes Christians horribly. But tribulation is about to give way to incredible joy—for the return of the King of Kings is at hand.

In *Revelation Unveiled*, Dr. Tim LaHaye explains such critical topics as:

The Rapture	The Return of Christ
The Great Tribulation	The Final Battle Against Satan and His Host
The Seven Seals	The Millennial Reign
The Seven Trumpets	The Great White Throne
The Seven Bowls of Wrath	Judgment
The Destruction of Babylon	The New Heavens and Earth

Previously titled *Revelation Illustrated and Made Plain*, this revised and updated commentary includes numerous charts. With simple and accessible language, *Revelation Unveiled* will help you better understand this mysterious, final book of the Bible and its implications for our times.

Softcover 0-310-23005-5

Pick up a copy today at your local bookstore!

ZondervanPublishingHouse
Grand Rapids, Michigan 49530
http://www.zondervan.com

A Division of HarperCollinsPublishers

Anger Is a Choice

TIM LaHaye and Bob Phillips

ANGER IS EVERYBODY'S PROBLEM—but it need not be yours! It becomes a problem when we fail to realize where it comes from, how it shows—or doesn't show—and what we can do about it. Either it will control us or we can control it—because anger is a choice.

Best-selling authors Tim LaHaye and Bob Phillips tell us what we need to know to control the emotion of anger. They not only examine it from beginning (its origins) to end (its effects), but they help us to evaluate our own "Irritability Quotient" through the Anger Inventory and other exercises throughout this book.

In learning how to handle conflicts and anger, we are enabled to heal damaged relationships, and help others deal with their anger as well. We can make our lives more peaceful, rewarding, and meaningful.

Learning to control anger is the best choice you can make today.

Softcover 0-310-27071-5

Pick up a copy today at your local bookstore!

ZondervanPublishingHouse
Grand Rapids, Michigan 49530
http://www.zondervan.com
A Division of HarperCollinsPublishers

We want to hear from you. Please send your comments about this book to us in care of the address below. Thank you.

ZondervanPublishingHouse
Grand Rapids, Michigan 49530
http://www.zondervan.com